Congress and the People's Contest

Perspectives on the History of Congress, 1801–1877

Donald R. Kennon, Series Editor

Congress and the Emergence of Sectionalism: From the Missouri Compromise to the Age of Jackson, edited by Paul Finkelman and Donald R. Kennon

In the Shadow of Freedom: The Politics of Slavery in the National Capital, edited by Paul Finkelman and Donald R. Kennon

Congress and the Crisis of the 1850s, edited by Paul Finkelman and Donald R. Kennon

Lincoln, Congress, and Emancipation, edited by Paul Finkelman and Donald R. Kennon

Congress and the People's Contest: The Conduct of the Civil War, edited by Paul Finkelman and Donald R. Kennon

Congress and the People's Contest

The Conduct of the Civil War

Edited by Paul Finkelman and Donald R. Kennon

PUBLISHED FOR THE
UNITED STATES CAPITOL HISTORICAL SOCIETY
BY OHIO UNIVERSITY PRESS • ATHENS

Ohio University Press, Athens, Ohio 45701
ohioswallow.com

Printed in the United States of America
Ohio University Press books are printed on acid-free ♾ paper ™

28 27 26 25 24 23 22 21 20 19 18 5 4 3 2 1

Library of Congress Cataloging-in publication data available upon request.

Names: Finkelman, Paul, 1949- editor. | Kennon, Donald R., 1948- editor.
Title: Congress and the people's contest : the conduct of the Civil War / edited by Paul Finkelman and Donald R. Kennon.
Description: Athens, Ohio : published for the United States Capitol Historical Society by Ohio University Press, 2017. | Series: Perspectives on the history of Congress, 1801-1877 | Includes bibliographical references and index.
Identifiers: LCCN 2017043708| ISBN 9780821423042 (hc : alk. paper) | ISBN 9780821423059 (pb : alk. paper) | ISBN 9780821446164 (pdf)
Subjects: LCSH: United States–Politics and government–1861-1865. | United States. Congress–History–19th century.
Classification: LCC E459 .C755 2017 | DDC 973.7–dc23
LC record available at https://lccn.loc.gov/2017043708

Contents

Paul Finkelman

Introduction: Freedom and Democracy in "The People's Contest"

A Complicated Role for Congress in a Complicated War

IT BEGAN LIKE no other war in American history. The forms of government, the rules of the Constitution, the role of Congress did not exactly work. The Constitution requires that Congress vote to declare war before the United States can actually fight a war. Congress had done that in 1812 against Great Britain and in 1846 against Mexico. (Congress would also do this in 1898, 1917, and 1941.) In the wars with Great Britain and Mexico, Congress had appropriated funds for soldiers, weapons, uniforms, and supplies. Congress had even created new slots for officers needed during the wars, with the understanding that these positions might be eliminated after the war. Since the creation of the government under the Constitution in 1789, Congress had also appropriated funds for excursions against Indian tribes, allowing the president, as commander in chief, to send small armies to the frontier to battle Indians, negotiate treaties, and then, starting with the Madison administration, remove them to lands west of the Mississippi River. Although often called "wars," they were really something less than wars—short-lived military encounters, often consisting of only a few battles,[1] more like police actions. But as a result of these scattered military adventures, relatively

[1] One exception was the "Seminole War," which lasted, on and off, for almost four decades. But even this was not a "war" in the traditional sense, but rather a series of episodic and inconclusive conflicts.

small appropriations, and piecemeal laws and programs, by 1860 the vast majority of eastern Indians were no longer in the East.[2]

In the experience of the nation, wars—even major wars—were short, involving few men, leading to relatively few casualties, and fought against distant enemies—Great Britain, Mexico, and Indians living on the edge of American society. Only about 2,200 Americans were killed in the War of 1812 (although another 13,000 or so died of disease and other causes). The war with Mexico lasted less than two years and had similar human costs: there were about 2,000 combat-related deaths, although more than 11,000 died of disease. Historically, the involvement of Congress had been minimal: declaring war, appropriating funds, and ratifying the peace.

But the Civil War was different in so many ways. Unlike the second war with Britain and the recent war with Mexico, there was no deliberative consideration of whether or not to go to war. In 1812 and 1846 the president had sent a war message to Congress, the Congress had debated the message, and then it declared war. In April 1861 there was a crisis, but almost no one seemed to believe it would lead to war.

Congress was not even in session as the nation moved toward war. The Thirty-Seventh Congress, elected in November 1860, was not scheduled to start its first session until December 1861. The old Congress, elected in November 1858, had expired on March 4, 1861, the day Lincoln became president. By the time Lincoln entered the White House, seven states had seceded, declaring that they had left the United States to form a new nation, the Confederate States of America. Trying not to antagonize these rebellious states, in hopes that they would voluntarily return to their normal status within the Union, the president did not call Congress into special session. He believed—or at least hoped—that if he acted with patience and did nothing to initiate conflict, the crisis would evaporate. His plan was to give Southerners time to cool off and reconsider their dangerous (indeed suicidal) course. He assumed Southerners would then return to their rightful place in the Union.

---

[2]See Tim Alan Garrison, "United States Indian Policy in Sectional Crisis: Georgia's Exploitation of the Compact of 1802" and "The Devil and Andrew Jackson: Historians and Jackson's Role in the Indian Removal Crisis," in Paul Finkelman and Donald R. Kennon, eds., *Congress and the Emergence of Sectionalism* (Athens, Ohio, 2008), pp. 97–124, 221–57.

Optimistic that his strategy would work, he promised Southerners that his administration would not threaten slavery, reiterating from his previous speeches, "I have no purpose, directly or indirectly, to interfere with the institution of slavery in the States where it exists. I believe I have no lawful right to do so, and I have no inclination to do so." He pledged to preserve the Union, but only in the most peaceful ways possible:

> In doing this there needs to be no bloodshed or violence, and there shall be none unless it be forced upon the national authority. The power confided to me will be used to hold, occupy, and possess the property and places belonging to the Government and to collect the duties and imposts; but beyond what may be necessary for these objects, there will be no invasion, no using of force against or among the people anywhere. Where hostility to the United States in any interior locality shall be so great and universal as to prevent competent resident citizens from holding the Federal offices, there will be no attempt to force obnoxious strangers among the people for that object. While the strict legal right may exist in the Government to enforce the exercise of these offices, the attempt to do so would be so irritating and so nearly impracticable withal that I deem it better to forego for the time the uses of such offices.

With these peaceful and nonthreatening promises set out, he ended his first inaugural address on a hopeful and conciliatory note: "Though passion may have strained it must not break our bonds of affection. The mystic chords of memory, stretching from every battlefield and patriot grave to every living heart and hearthstone all over this broad land, will yet swell the chorus of the Union, when again touched, as surely they will be, by the better angels of our nature."[3]

Southern leaders were far less patient than Lincoln. Perhaps they understood, as Lincoln hoped, that if "nothing" happened for a long enough time, the states would soon resume normal communication, trade, and political discussions. Moreover, as long as nothing happened, the largest and most important slave states—Tennessee, Kentucky, and most of all Virginia—were unlikely to join the Confederacy. Thus, Confederate officials pushed for some sort of military action to prove they had an independent nation.

---

[3]Abraham Lincoln, "First Inaugural Address, March 4, 1861," in Roy P. Basler, ed., *The Collected Works of Abraham Lincoln*, 9 vols. (New Brunswick, N.J., 1953–55), 4:263, 266, 271 (hereafter *Collected Works*).

Lincoln refused to cooperate and continued to bide his time. Finally, on April 12, Confederate troops in South Carolina opened fire on the U.S. Army detachment stationed at Fort Sumter, in Charleston harbor. The fort, built to protect the harbor against an invasion from the ocean, was not well suited to withstand an attack from the mainland. On the 14th, Fort Sumter surrendered.

Four years later, Lincoln recalled in his second inaugural address, "Both parties deprecated war, but one of them would make war rather than let the nation survive, and the other would accept war rather than let it perish, and the war came."[4]

Raising an Army without Congress

The day after the fall of Fort Sumter, the president took charge. Lincoln noted that "the laws of the United States" were being "opposed" and "obstructed" by "combinations too powerful to be suppressed by the ordinary course of judicial proceedings or by the powers vested in the Marshals by law." He asked the states to provide 75,000 militia troops to quell the rebellion "and to cause the laws to be duly executed."[5]

Significantly for the role of Congress in the war, Lincoln initially acted under existing federal legislation passed in 1795 to quell the Whiskey Rebellion. While Lincoln did not mention the 1795 law in his proclamation, Secretary of War Simon Cameron cited it in a letter sent to loyal governors the same day.[6] Even as this monumental war began, the president did not

---

[4]Abraham Lincoln, "Second Inaugural Address, March 4, 1865," in *Collected Works*, 8:331–33.

[5]Abraham Lincoln, "Proclamation Calling Militia and Convening Congress (Apr. 15, 1861)," ibid., 4:331.

[6]"An Act to Provide for Calling Forth the Militia to Execute the Laws of the Union, Suppress Insurrections, and Repel Invasions; and to Repeal the Act Now in Force for Those Purposes," Act of Feb. 28, 1795, ch. 36, 1 Stat. 424 (1845). Simon Cameron, Secretary of War to the Governors of 24 States, Apr. 15, 1861, in U.S. War Department, *The War of the Rebellion: The Official Records of the Union and Confederate Armies* (Washington, D.C., 1880), ser. 3, vol. 1, p. 68 (hereafter *O.R.*). This letter asked for volunteers for three months and contained a list of how many regiments each state was being asked to send. The letter was sent by telegraph to the governors of Maine, New Hampshire, Vermont, Massachusetts, Rhode Island, Connecticut, New York, Pennsylvania, New Jersey, Delaware, Maryland, Virginia, North Carolina, Tennessee, Arkansas, Kentucky, Missouri, Illinois, Indiana, Ohio, Michigan, Wisconsin, Iowa, and Minnesota. The

need new legislation to act. Existing statutes provided the powers he thought he needed for the emergency.

However, Lincoln did see the need for congressional action at some point in the future, and in the April 15 proclamation the president also called for a special session of Congress:

> Deeming that the present condition of public affairs presents an extraordinary occasion, I do hereby, in virtue of the power in me vested by the constitution, convene both Houses of Congress. Senators and Representatives are therefore summoned to assemble at their respective chambers, at 12 o'clock, noon, on Thursday, the fourth day of July, next, then and there to consider and determine, such measures, as, in their wisdom, the public safety, and interest may seem to demand.[7]

Significantly, Lincoln was not in any particular hurry to bring Congress back to Washington. He was willing to wait two and a half months before turning to Congress for help in suppressing the rebellion. Equally important, he chose to convene Congress on the Fourth of July. Always aware of the importance of symbolism, Lincoln wanted Congress to begin on the eighty-fifth anniversary of the signing of the Declaration of Independence.

In the meantime, Lincoln would prosecute the war for the Union on his own. Lincoln's call for troops went to the governors of twenty-four states, with a follow-up letter from Secretary of War Cameron specifying how many regiments each state should provide.[8] Most governors responded quickly,

---

administration asked for a total of seventeen regiments (13,260 men) from the slave states still in the Union, but these soldiers would not be mustered by the slave state governors. However, other states sent more soldiers than were requested. Cameron could not send a telegram to California and Oregon, so any troops from those states would have to wait. It is not clear why Cameron did not send the telegram to the governor of Kansas, which had become a state on January 29, 1861. Perhaps it was an oversight, or perhaps based on the belief that this new state could not yet muster a militia regiment. By this time Kansas had been connected to the rest of the nation by telegraph for a few years. See John E. Sunder, "Telegraph Beginnings in Kansas," *Kansas Historical Quarterly* 25 (1959):32. This failure to include Kansas is particularly odd, because on April 14 Senator James Lane of Kansas had organized 120 men from his state (who were in Washington at the time) to form a "Frontier Guard," which was billeted at the White House to serve as security for the new president (http://www.kshs.org/kansapedia/frontier-guard/16898). Eventually about 20,000 men from Kansas, approximately two-thirds of the military-age men in the state, served the Union cause (http://www.kshs.org/kansapedia/civil-war/14565).

[7]Lincoln, "Proclamation Calling Militia and Convening Congress," in *Collected Works*, 4:332.

[8]Simon Cameron, Secretary of War to the Governors of 24 States, cited in n. 6.

often the same day they received the telegram. Some responded with enormous enthusiasm. Governor Alexander Ramsey of Minnesota actually telegraphed Secretary Cameron on April 14, the day *before* Lincoln asked for troops, offering 1,000 men to protect the nation.[9] Within days of issuing his proclamation, Lincoln knew that troops were on their way to protect the Nation's capital.

Cameron's telegram went out on the 15th, and Governor Israel Washburn of Maine replied that day, saying that, in his state, the people "of all parties will rally with alacrity to the maintenance of the Government and of the Union." In Massachusetts, Governor John A. Andrew did not bother with flowery language or patriotic blather. The hard-nosed abolitionist governor of the Bay State cut right to the point, simply asking, "By what route shall we send?" Two days later, he told Secretary Cameron that two regiments had left the state, one headed to Washington and another to Fortress Monroe, in Virginia, and that a third regiment was leaving the next day. Governor William Denison of Ohio, who would later serve in Lincoln's cabinet as postmaster general, said there was "great rejoicing" in the Buckeye State over the proclamation and that Ohio would "furnish the largest number" of troops the government would "receive." Governor Oliver P. Morton of Indiana promised six regiments in three days. Iowa's governor wanted to know if he could send more than the one regiment the secretary of war had requested. Senator Zachariah Chandler of Michigan wrote that his state would provide 50,000 troops if requested.[10] This might have seemed like braggadocio on Chandler's part, but by the end of the war about 90,000 men from Michigan—nearly 25 percent of the adult male population—would serve in the army, with nearly 15,000 dying.

Lincoln hoped to contain secession and avoid a military conflict that would lead to a full-blown civil war. He initially believed, incorrectly as it turned out, that Southerners would quickly come to their senses and return to the Union. He now assumed (again incorrectly) that the conflict would be short, and thus 75,000 militia troops would be able to finish the job

[9]Letters from various Northern governors (Apr. 1861), in *O.R.*, ser. 3, vol. 1, pp. 70–90; Alex Ramsey, governor of Minnesota to Simon Cameron, secretary of war (Apr. 14, 1861), in *O.R.*, ser. 3, vol. 1, p. 67.

[10]This correspondence is found in *O.R.*, ser. 3, vol. 1, pp. 71, 73, 75, 78, 79, 87. For a fuller account of the war governors and mobilization, see Stephen D. Engle, *Gathering to Save a Nation: Lincoln and the Union's War Governors* (Chapel Hill, N.C., 2016).

quickly, and that the huge size of this army would intimidate the South. While 75,000 militia troops seems small compared to the more than 2.2 million men who would eventually serve in the U.S. Army and Navy in the Civil War, this was the largest military call-up in the history of the nation, and, combined with the 15,000 or so troops in the regular army, created the largest military force in the history of the nation. It was more than the total number of troops used in the Mexican War of 1846–48. Similarly, when the War of 1812 began the U.S. Army had only about 12,000 troops, and there was never any mass mobilization of the state militias, although many militia units fought in the war at various times. When George Washington took command of the Patriot Army in July 1775, he was expecting 20,000 troops, but in fact only had 14,000.[11] Thus, by historic American standards, 75,000 troops constituted a very large army. Lincoln assumed that the unprecedented size of this army would be sufficient to show the Confederates that they should avoid war, or if necessary, this large force could quickly crush the insurrection.

Lincoln was, of course, wrong about the impact of mobilization, and the war quickly evolved. Events moved faster than Lincoln could have imagined, and without Congress in session the president governed the nation alone. This had always been done in an era when Congress was not continuously in session, but this was the first time a war had started when it was not in session. In addition to mobilizing the army, Lincoln, acting without the help of Congress, faced two major issues that set the tone for the war and would later lead to shared responsibility during the war. The first involved internal security and domestic terrorism; the second involved slavery and emancipation.

---

[11]As of June 30, 1860, the regular army had just over 16,000 men: "1,080 officers and 14,926 enlisted men" consisting of "10 regiments of infantry, 4 of artillery, 2 of cavalry, 2 of dragoons, and 1 of mounted riflemen." Richard W. Stewart ed., *American Military History*, vol. 1: *The United States Army and the Forging of a Nation, 1775–1917* (Washington, D.C, 2009), p. 204 (http://www.history.army.mil/books/AMH-V1/ch09.htm). By April 1861 the army was smaller because of the defection of some Southern soldiers and most Southern officers. When the War of 1812 began, there were fewer than 12,000 soldiers in the regular army. There were about 450,000 militiamen in the country, but most never saw action in the war. Ibid., p. 133 (http://www.history.army.mil/books/AMH-V1/PDF/Chapter06.pdf). The United States had used only 78,700 soldiers in the entire Mexican War, which lasted nearly two years. Susan B. Carter et al., eds., *Historical Statistics of the United States: Earliest Times to the Present*, 5 vols. (New York, 2006), 5:350–51. On Washington's troops, see Henry Wiencek, *An Imperfect God: George Washington, His Slaves, and the Creation of America* (New York, 2003), p. 196.

National Security, Terrorism, and the Suspension of Habeas Corpus

While Northern militiamen poured into Washington, D.C., to protect the city from Confederate attack, Lincoln faced a series of other decisions, over and above mobilizing his (in retrospect) small volunteer army. Three interrelated issues were (1) national security and the problem of domestic terrorism and sabotage; (2) the status of U.S. Army officers who were defecting to the Confederacy, taking up arms against their former comrades, and making war on the nation they had sworn to serve; and (3) the political status of Maryland.

All three of these issues were tied to the suspension of habeas corpus. The writ of habeas corpus—the "great writ"—is the legal process used to bring an incarcerated individual before a judge to determine if the incarceration is legal. The writ is a key component of the rule of law, because it protects people from arbitrary arrest and incarceration. Without the writ, police officials can arrest and hold people indefinitely without charges.

The Constitution provides that "The Privilege of the Writ of Habeas Corpus shall not be suspended, unless when in Cases of Rebellion or Invasion the public Safety may require it."[12] This Suspension Clause is located in Article I, Section 9 of the Constitution, which delineates limitations on the power of Congress. The language of the clause makes it clear that it can only be implemented if two things simultaneously occur: there is a "Rebellion" or an "Invasion," and "the public Safety" requires the suspension.

The location of the clause in Article I has led some scholars (and anti-Lincoln politicians) to argue that *only* Congress can suspend habeas corpus. However, this argument raises a number of problems. Unlike some other provisions of Article I, Section 9, this clause does not explicitly or implicitly contain any specific delegation of power to Congress or state which branch of the government can actually suspend the writ. Furthermore, there are other provisions in Section 9 that lack a specific delegation of power to Congress, precisely because the limitation could also apply to the executive branch. For example, Article I, Section 9 also prohibits the granting of any title of nobility by "the United States," which would prevent the president from granting such a title on his own. Similarly, the ban on giving any

---

[12]U.S. Constitution, Art. I, Sec. 9, cl. 2.

"preference" by "any Regulation of Commerce" to the "Ports of one State over those of another" limits the actions of the executive branch as well as the Congress. Moreover, the requirement of the publication of "a regular Statement and Account" of "Expenditures of all public Money" seems to imply an expectation that the executive branch will give the accounting and possibly do the publishing. Similarly, in the years between the adoption of the Constitution and the Civil War, the courts had found that Congress had legislative powers that were not in Article I and that were not explicitly granted to Congress. For example, in 1842 the Supreme Court ruled that Congress had sole power to regulate the return of fugitive slaves, even though the Fugitive Slave Clause is in Article IV, which deals with interstate relations, and the provision does not even mention Congress.[13] Thus, placement of a clause may not fully determine where the power lies.

The very nature of the Suspension Clause plausibly implies that a suspension could be imposed by the executive branch. There are two reasons for this. First, the clause allows suspension *only* during an emergency, an invasion, or a rebellion when the "public Safety" is endangered. In the eighteenth and nineteenth centuries, Congress was often not in session, and even today Congress is often in recess. In a real emergency, where lives are at stake and the future of the nation might be in the balance, there might not be time to wait for Congress to gather. Second, an invading army or a rebellious force could prevent Congress from even meeting and might thus prevent the suspension, even though the existing conditions might "require it." The War of 1812 offers an example of this. During the war the British had invaded Washington and burned part of the capital. President Madison did not have time to suspend habeas corpus in the city, because he was too busy trying to escape. But had he remained and defended the city, he might very well have wanted to declare martial law. There was, of course, no Congress in town to suspend habeas corpus, but it seems likely that the Father of the Constitution would have made the call—and the suspension—on his own if he thought it was necessary.

Though not witnessing an invasion of the national capital, Lincoln faced an enormously complicated situation in the weeks after he became president. Congress was not in session, and calling Congress back into session would have been cumbersome. Furthermore, it might have been impossible

[13] *Prigg v. Pennsylvania*, 41 U.S. (16 Pet.) 539 (1842).

for members of Congress to reach Washington, because of pro-Confederate terrorists and mobs in Baltimore and other parts of Maryland who threatened the public safety, particularly at the train stations that members of Congress had to use to get to Washington. Even more ominous, Confederate sympathizers in Maryland were blowing up bridges and destroying railroad tracks, as well as raising military forces, in order to isolate Washington, D.C., from the rest of the nation. This situation, along with the Confederate attack on Fort Sumter, constituted a "rebellion" as set out in the Suspension Clause. This was also a situation that deeply threatened "the public Safety."

At the time there were no federal laws to prevent some of these activities and no national police forces to stop them. It was a state crime to destroy a railroad bridge or railroad tracks, but not a federal crime. Public safety, in 1861, was almost entirely in the hands of state and local officials. In Maryland many officials, including the governor, sympathized with the Confederacy and were unwilling to prevent sabotage, terrorism, or the organizing of troops to fight against the United States. At the same time, the Maryland legislature was meeting in special session to debate secession. In addition to activities in Maryland, there were former U.S. military officers (some who had just resigned their commissions) who were trying to reach the Confederacy to make war on the United States, and in parts of the Confederacy (such as Florida and Virginia) there was a U.S. presence that was threatened by Confederate civilians and military forces.

The only tool Lincoln had at hand to protect railroad tracks, bridges, telegraph lines, and the nation itself, was the army. Under federal law, the military had no power to arrest civilians or in any other way keep the peace. However, by suspending habeas corpus, Lincoln could use the military as a police force to arrest and incarcerate people who were actively in rebellion. These would be preventive arrests, since the army could not try them for any crimes. But such arrests would thwart terrorists and saboteurs.

In a series of orders from April to June, Lincoln, acting unilaterally (since Congress was still not in session), ordered the army to arrest Confederate activists and terrorists and to secure the railroad lines from Washington to Philadelphia, and later all the way to New York. In October he would extend this order to the entire East Coast.[14] At the same time, respectful of

---

[14]Lincoln to Winfield Scott, Apr. 27, 1861, in *Collected Works*, 4:347 (suspending habeas corpus from Washington, D.C., to Philadelphia); Lincoln to Winfield Scott, July 2, 1861,

the political process in the loyal slave states (and working very hard not to push them into the arms of the Confederacy), Lincoln specifically ordered the military *not* to interfere with the Maryland legislature's scheduled meeting to vote on secession.[15] During this period Lincoln also suspended habeas corpus in Florida and specifically directed General Winfield Scott to arrest a former U.S. Army officer who was trying to reach the Confederacy.[16]

The suspension was controversial. Confederate sympathizers and some Northern Democrats considered it an act of tyranny. None of these critics ever suggested an alternative—which modern constitutional law scholars might call a "least restrictive means"—to protect the nation from sabotage and terrorism. Illustrative of the need for the suspension was the arrest of John Merryman, a wealthy Marylander and militia lieutenant, who was trying to recruit Confederate soldiers in Maryland and was also destroying railroad bridges, railroad tracks, and telegraph wires with the avowed purpose of preventing Northern militia troops from reaching Washington to protect the nation's capital.[17] At the end of May the army arrested Merryman and locked him up in Fort McHenry. Oddly, even though Merryman was arrested under the suspension of habeas corpus, military authorities allowed him access to an attorney, who immediately applied to Chief Justice Roger B. Taney for a writ of habeas corpus. It is not clear whether Taney acted as chief justice or in his role as circuit justice for Maryland, but the distinction is not really important. Taney ordered that Merryman be brought to his court under a writ of habeas corpus. Major General George Cadwalader refused to comply with the writ, explaining to Taney that the president had suspended the writ. Cadwalader was a lawyer in civilian life and fully understood the legal issues. Taney's long and angry response, published

ibid., 4:419 (extending the suspension to New York City); Lincoln to Lieutenant General Winfield Scott, Oct. 14, 1861, ibid., 4:554 (extending the suspension to Bangor, Maine).

[15]Lincoln to Lieutenant General Scott, Apr. 25, 1861, ibid., 4:344.

[16]Abraham Lincoln, "Proclamation Suspending Writ of Habeas Corpus in Florida," May 10, 1861, ibid., 3:364–65; Lincoln to Winfield Scott, Lieutenant-General, June 20, 1861, ibid., 4:414 (ordering the arrest of "Major Chase, lately of the Engineer Corps of the Army of the United States, now alleged to be guilty of treasonable practices against this government").

[17]Brian McGinty, *The Body of John Merryman: Abraham Lincoln and the Suspension of Habeas Corpus* (Cambridge, Mass., 2011), pp. 154–55. Jonathan W. White, *Abraham Lincoln and Treason in the Civil War: The Trials of John Merryman* (Baton Rouge, 2011), pp. 19–21.

as *Ex parte Merryman*,[18] excoriated Cadwalader, and by implication President Lincoln, for suspending the writ and arresting Merryman. But the military and the administration ignored Taney, who by this time was correctly seen as a Confederate sympathizer who would do anything in his power to impede the war effort and aid the cause of the slaveholders' rebellion. Merryman remained in custody until July, when the emergency was over, and he was allowed to post bail while awaiting trial for treason, which would never take place.

In July, when Congress met, Lincoln explained why he had suspended habeas corpus. At this point Congress might have acted, either to support the president or to express its opposition to the suspension. Instead, Congress did nothing. Two years later Congress passed the "Habeas Corpus Suspension Act," which ratified Lincoln's actions.[19]

Facing the Real Cause of the War

Slavery and racism were the root causes of secession and the war. Those slave states that published an explanation for their secession put bondage and the suppression of black people front and center.

In its Declaration of the Causes of Secession, South Carolina noted that eight years earlier the state had asserted its right to secede, but, "in deference to the opinions and wishes of the other slaveholding States, she forbore at that time to exercise this right." Significantly, this forbearance was not connected to the wishes of the free states or the national government. For South Carolina the decision to remain in the Union or leave it was based entirely on the needs of the slave states and the protection of slavery. Among the state's grievances was the failure of Northern states to vigorously assist in the recapture of fugitive slaves, the "increasing hostility on the part of the non-slaveholding States to the institution of slavery," the refusal of free states to allow Southerners to bring their slaves into those states, and "the election of a man to the high office of President of the United States, whose opinions and purposes are hostile to slavery. He is to be entrusted

---

[18]17 F. Cas. 144 (C.C.D. Md. 1861) (No. 9487).

[19]An Act Relating to Habeas Corpus and Regulating Judicial Proceedings in Certain Cases, Act of March 3, 1863, 12 Stat. 755 (1863).

with the administration of the common Government, because he has declared that that 'Government cannot endure permanently half slave, half free,' and that the public mind must rest in the belief that slavery is in the course of ultimate extinction."[20]

The second sentence of the Georgia declaration addressed the same concerns: "For the last ten years we have had numerous and serious causes of complaint against our nonslaveholding confederate States with reference to the subject of African slavery." The Georgia secessionists went on to note that:

> The party of Lincoln, called the Republican party, under its present name and organization, is of recent origin. It is admitted to be an anti-slavery party. While it attracts to itself by its creed the scattered advocates of exploded political heresies, of condemned theories in political economy, the advocates of commercial restrictions, of protection, of special privileges, of waste and corruption in the administration of Government, anti-slavery is its mission and its purpose. By anti-slavery it is made a power in the state.[21]

Mississippi noted that "Our position is thoroughly identified with the institution of slavery—the greatest material interest of the world. Its labor supplies the product which constitutes by far the largest and most important portions of commerce of the earth." The state tied its economic well-being to both slavery and racism, noting that the products it produced "are peculiar to the climate verging on the tropical regions, and by an imperious law of nature, none but the black race can bear exposure to the tropical sun. These products have become necessities of the world, and a blow at slavery is a blow at commerce and civilization."[22] Texas recounted that it had joined the Union "holding, maintaining and protecting the institution known as negro slavery—the servitude of the African to the white race within her limits—a relation that had existed from the first settlement of her wilderness by the white race, and which her people intended should exist in all future

[20] *Declaration of the Immediate Causes Which Induce and Justify the Secession of South Carolina from the Federal Union,* adopted Dec. 24, 1860 (http://www.civilwar.org/education/history/primarysources/declarationofcauses.html).

[21] Georgia explanation for secession, "Approved, Tuesday, January 29, 1861" (http://www.civilwar.org/education/history/primarysources/declarationofcauses.html).

[22] *A Declaration of the Immediate Causes Which Induce and Justify the Secession of the State of Mississippi from the Federal Union* (http://www.civilwar.org/education/history/primarysources/declarationofcauses.html).

time." Texas was committed to slavery and white supremacy, and this justified secession:

> That in this free government *all white men are and of right ought to be entitled to equal civil and political rights*; that the servitude of the African race, as existing in these States, is mutually beneficial to both bond and free, and is abundantly authorized and justified by the experience of mankind, and the revealed will of the Almighty Creator, as recognized by all Christian nations; while the destruction of the existing relations between the two races, as advocated by our sectional enemies, would bring inevitable calamities upon both and desolation upon the fifteen slave-holding states.[23]

Shortly after Lincoln's inauguration, the vice president of the Confederacy, Alexander Stephens, summed up the relationship between slavery and secession. He began with a weird and historically inaccurate claim that when the United States had been created, "the prevailing ideas entertained by [Thomas Jefferson] and most of the leading statesmen at the time" was "that the enslavement of the African was in violation of the laws of nature; that it was wrong in principle, socially, morally, and politically. It was an evil they knew not well how to deal with, but the general opinion of the men of that day was that, somehow or other in the order of Providence, the institution would be evanescent and pass away."[24]

There is no evidence that Jefferson believed this, and support for any of these principles among the Founders was surely mixed. But Stephens was not concerned with historical accuracy. He was interested in asserting that the purpose of the Confederacy was to establish white supremacy and to protect slavery. Thus he continued: "Those ideas, however, were fundamentally wrong. They rested upon the assumption of the equality of races. This was an error. It was a sandy foundation, and the government built upon it fell when the 'storm came and the wind blew.'" He then asserted the racist and proslavery basis of the Confederacy:

---

[23]*A Declaration of the Causes Which Impel the State of Texas to Secede from the Federal Union*, "Adopted in Convention on the 2nd day of Feby, in the year of our Lord one thousand eight hundred and sixty-one and of the independence of Texas the twenty-fifth" (http://www.civilwar.org/education/history/primarysources/declarationofcauses.html).

[24]Alexander Stephens, "The Cornerstone Speech," Mar. 21, 1861, in Henry Cleveland, *Alexander H. Stephens, in Public and Private: With Letters and Speeches, before, during, and since the War* (Philadelphia, 1886), pp. 717–29 (http://www.TeachingAmericanHistory.org/library/index.asp?documentprint=76).

> Our new government is founded upon exactly the opposite idea; its foundations are laid, its corner-stone rests, upon the great truth that the negro is not equal to the white man; that slavery—subordination to the superior race—is his natural and normal condition. This, our new government, is the first, in the history of the world, based upon this great physical, philosophical, and moral truth.

This led Stephens to denounce Northerners who he claimed almost universally believed in racial equality. Their arguments, he concluded, were:

> a species of insanity. One of the most striking characteristics of insanity, in many instances, is forming correct conclusions from fancied or erroneous premises; so with the anti-slavery fanatics. Their conclusions are right if their premises were. They assume that the negro is equal, and hence conclude that he is entitled to equal privileges and rights with the white man. If their premises were correct, their conclusions would be logical and just but their premise being wrong, their whole argument fails.

For Stephens, the Confederacy answered all these questions:

> With us, all of the white race, however high or low, rich or poor, are equal in the eye of the law. Not so with the negro. Subordination is his place. He, by nature, or by the curse against Canaan, is fitted for that condition which he occupies in our system. The architect, in the construction of buildings, lays the foundation with the proper material—the granite; then comes the brick or the marble. The substratum of our society is made of the material fitted by nature for it, and by experience we know that it is best, not only for the superior, but for the inferior race, that it should be so. It is, indeed, in conformity with the ordinance of the Creator.[25]

Despite the clear connection to slavery and secession, Lincoln promised in his first inaugural address not to touch slavery in the states where it existed. Furthermore, when the war began, he refused to make it about slavery and similarly resisted demands to allow blacks to serve in the army.[26] While Lincoln personally hated slavery—he would later say, "If slavery is not wrong, nothing is wrong"[27]—he had neither the constitutional authority

---

[25]Ibid.

[26]See Paul Finkelman, "Lincoln's Long Road to Freedom: How a Railroad Lawyer Became the Great Emancipator," in Paul Finkelman and Donald R. Kennon, eds., *Lincoln, Congress, and Emancipation* (Athens, Ohio, 2016), pp. 162–210.

[27]Lincoln to Albert G. Hodges, Apr. 4, 1864, in *Collected Works*, 7:281.

to touch it nor the political flexibility to do so. Any overt move against slavery would likely drive Maryland, Missouri, and most importantly Kentucky, into the Confederacy. With more than 225,000 slaves in the state, Kentucky was vulnerable to Confederate entreaties. Lincoln believed that losing Kentucky to the Confederacy would be a disaster for the Union cause. Due to both its geography and its size, Kentucky was the most crucial of the loyal slave states. A Confederate army on the southern bank of the Ohio River would interrupt east–west commerce and troop movements; threaten the vast agricultural heartland of Ohio, Indiana, and Illinois; and endanger key manufacturing, commercial, and politically significant cities, such as Cincinnati, Columbus, Indianapolis, and Pittsburgh. As Lincoln told Senator Orville Browning: "[T]o lose Kentucky is nearly . . . to lose the whole game." Early in the war, a group of ministers urged Lincoln to free the slaves because, they said, God would be on his side. He allegedly responded, "I hope to have God on my side, but I must have Kentucky."[28]

But while Lincoln did not move against slavery, the slaves themselves recognized that the war was about *them*, and that this was their moment to seek freedom. Most slaves had no opportunity to do this, since they were trapped in the Confederacy or the loyal slave states where slavery was protected by all social, political, and legal institutions. But where the war created chaos, social dislocation, and legal and political uncertainties, slaves moved away from their masters, running to U.S. Army lines. In Virginia, General Benjamin F. Butler famously declared that slaves who escaped to Fortress Monroe, where he was encamped, were "contrabands" of war, and could not be returned to their owners. By the end of July there were about 850 slaves in the fort, working as civilian employees of the army and being paid for their labor. The end of slavery had begun, whether the president had a policy or not. By August the president had endorsed Butler's solution and humorously called it "Butler's Fugitive Slave Law." The endorsement went from Lincoln to the secretary of war to Butler and then to all U.S. Army generals and other commanding officers. Secretary of War Cameron told General Butler that President Lincoln understood that "in States wholly or partially under insurrectionary control," the laws could not be enforced, and it was "equally obvious that rights dependent on the laws of the States within which military operations are conducted must be necessarily

[28]Lincoln to Orville H. Browning, Sept. 22, 1861, ibid., 4:531–32.

subordinated to the military exigencies created by the insurrection if not wholly forfeited by the treasonable conduct of the parties claiming them." Most importantly, "rights to services" could "form no exception" to "this general rule." Two days before Cameron sent this letter, Congress passed the First Confiscation Act, which allowed for the emancipation of some slaves owned by Confederates.[29]

This law, and other acts passed that summer, signaled the emergence of Congress as a full partner in the war effort. In the next year and a half—from July 4, 1861, when Congress first came into session during the war, until January 1, 1863, when Lincoln issued the final Emancipation Proclamation—Congress would reshape the nation's legal and political landscape. During this period Congress would end slavery in Washington D.C., prohibit slavery in all federal territories, reverse seven decades of public policy by allowing blacks to serve in the state militias and the U.S. Army, approve the appointment of black commissioned and noncommissioned officers, and create public schools for the now free black population of Washington. Meanwhile, the Homestead Act, the Land-Grant College Act, and the Pacific Railroad Act (all enacted in 1862) would point the way to a newly activist government that would promote western settlement, higher education, and transcontinental communication and transportation.

As the essays in this book show, congressional involvement was essential to the war. The articles on Congress in 1860 and 1861 by Jonathan Earle and Eric Walther show how Congress was involved in the events that led to session and the war. The fight over the speakership in the House and the maneuverings of the fire-eaters for decades leading up to 1860 can be seen as political "prewar" battles. These battles are important for understanding the tense politics *before* Lincoln's election. Thus, before secession Congress was already rehearsing for the Civil War. But, as noted in this introduction, when the war began Lincoln was on his own, relying on the 1795 militia statute and his own powers as commander in chief.

After July 4, 1861, and until the end of the conflict Congress actively supported the war effort while considering how to deal with its consequences. The interaction took a variety of forms. Recruiting troops and getting them

[29]Simon Cameron to Benjamin F. Butler, Aug. 8, 1861, *O.R.*, ser. 2, vol. 1, pp. 761–62. An Act to Confiscate Property Used for Insurrectionary Purposes (First Confiscation Act), Act of Aug. 6, 1861, ch. 60, 12 Stat. 319 (1863).

ready for battle was complicated and not always successful, as the chapters by Lesley Gordon and Mischa Honeck demonstrate. The role of black troops was even more complicated, requiring executive initiative and congressional action. Diane Barnes, Chandra Manning, and Nikki Taylor explore this issue in their chapters. All of this cost money, as the economic historian Jenny Bourne demonstrates in her chapter on how Congress paid for the war. Allowing black troops was part of a larger congressional expansion of black rights that I explore in my own chapter. That chapter also notes that secession and the war allowed for other significant statutory changes. For Congress, the war became part of a giant reform and modernization movement in the nation.

In the end, what was the war about? Freedom and ending slavery were often at the center of congressional debates over military and domestic policy and the remaking of the nation when the war would finally be over. Fergus Bordewich explores how the key congressional committee overseeing the war effort grappled with demands to make this "an Abolition War," as Diane Barnes notes in the title of her chapter. Beyond these issues, as my chapter demonstrates, Congress moved to create equality and took large steps toward remaking and modernizing the nation. Emancipation, racial equality on Washington's street railroads, and building a railroad that connected the West Coast to the East Coast all merged in the war, especially in the dramatic and far-reaching legislation of the spring and summer of 1862, which culminated with Lincoln issuing the Preliminary Emancipation Proclamation.

Freedom and an end to slavery were connected to the larger problem of democracy. All of the chapters in this book connect to this. Mischa Honek's newly arrived German immigrants were fighting to preserve a nation they had just moved to, but they were also fighting for the right to be part of the nation, just as were the black soldiers discussed in the chapters by Nikki Taylor, Diane Barnes, and Chandra Manning. The white, native-born American kids from Connecticut in Lesley Gordon's chapter were similarly fighting for their place in the new nation that the Congress and the president were shaping. Congress, which had to pay for all this, had to think of new and creative ways to fund this mammoth enterprise, and Jenny Bourne teaches us how they did it. The losers in all this would be the slave owners, the Southern fire-eaters, and, to some extent, many of the political players of the previous decade, whose relevance disappeared in the smoke of battle and the fog of war.

In his message to Congress on July 4, 1861, Lincoln described the war in the context of democratic theory:

> This is essentially a People's contest. On the side of the Union, it is a struggle for maintaining in the world, that form, and substance of government, whose leading object is, to elevate the condition of men—to lift artificial weights from all shoulders—to clear the paths of laudable pursuit for all—to afford all, an unfettered start, and a fair chance, in the race of life. Yielding to partial, and temporary departures, from necessity, this is the leading object of the government for whose existence we contend.[30]

The "People's contest" could be fought only with the support of the people and their representatives in Congress. In the end, all the chapters in this volume circle back to the problem of democracy and the meaning of "the People" during the Civil War era.

[30]Abraham Lincoln, "Message to Congress in Special Session," July 4, 1861, in *Collected Works*, 4:438.

Jonathan Earle

A Martyr, a Speaker, and *Impending Crisis*

A Prologue to the Election of 1860

Elections have often been fractious in our rough-and-tumble American democracy, and the pivotal presidential election of 1860 was no exception. That year no fewer than four major candidates vied for the nation's highest office, and the winner—Abraham Lincoln of the six-year-old Republican Party—claimed less than 40 percent of the popular vote. Lincoln's election was the immediate spark for the secession crisis of 1860–61, as states from the Deep South quit the republic rather than remain in a union governed by a "Black Republican." Confederates fired the first shots of the Civil War just five weeks after Lincoln's inauguration.[1]

The particular fractiousness of the 1860 canvass neither began nor ended on election day, however. Even the normally humdrum selection of a Speaker of the United States House of Representatives almost tore that institution apart, and the agonizing inability to organize the lower house of Congress threw the once hazy specter of disunion into full relief. Between December 5, 1859, and February 1, 1860, a bitter leadership battle hijacked the Thirty-Sixth Congress and nearly tore the Union asunder more than a year before the attack on Fort Sumter, as Republicans who made up a large plurality of the body doggedly attempted to install their choice, John Sherman

[1]The author wishes to thank Don Kennon and Paul Finkelman for the invitation to appear not once, but twice, at the United States Capitol Historical Society's annual symposium.

FIG. 1. John Sherman in a photograph taken between 1855 and 1865. *(Brady-Handy Collection, Prints and Photographs Division, Library of Congress)*

of Ohio (fig. 1), in the Speaker's chair. Democrats and their allies, however, were equally intent on depriving Sherman of the honor. The nasty, brutish, and not-at-all-short contest over the speakership is one of three interrelated events that frame the beginning of the presidential election of 1860, an election that, ultimately, proved the death knell of the Union.

A great many of the events described in this essay took place not in 1860 but in 1859, a year in which there was considerable maneuvering, speechmaking, legislating, and pontificating about an event long planned to take place the Tuesday following the first Monday the following November. Just as during our own recent presidential election cycles in which there were countless candidate profiles, endless C-SPAN debates between crowds of presidential contenders, and reports about the "money primary," so too in 1859 some politically attuned Americans began to think seriously about the next canvass. And then, as now, there was a distinct sense that (to borrow the term of the modern pollster that called to mind a very nineteenth-century metaphor) the country was "on the wrong track." The run-up to the 1860 election represented an extremely fluid time in the nation's politics, and each of several issues discussed here could have resulted in any number of different electoral contingencies.

Each of the three events in this chapter—John Brown's raid on Harpers Ferry (including his trial and execution), the somewhat surprising emergence of Hinton Rowan Helper's *The Impending Crisis of the South: How to Meet It* as a major campaign issue, and the disastrous tug-of-war over the speakership in the House of Representatives, which threatened briefly to force a clash between the sections a year and a half before the start of the Civil War—had a number of serious consequences for the fateful election already under way. First, each involved the American public in ways the early stages of campaigns rarely do. Second, they forced politicians and parties to commit themselves firmly to positions in a compressed period of time (between December 1859 and the beginning of the nominating conventions in March 1860)—positions they could not gracefully or easily retreat from. Finally, they dealt a blow that turned out to be fatal to the advancement of the wing of the Republican Party associated with William Seward and Salmon Chase, while aiding other Republicans considered more "moderate" on the slavery issue—like Abraham Lincoln or Edward Bates. Centrists and "Douglas" Democrats also limped out of the crises of late 1859 with far gloomier political futures, while disunionists and "fire-eaters"

Table 1 Makeup of the Thirty-Sixth Congress (by party and percentage)

Republican Party	116	+26	48.7%
Democratic Party	83	−49	34.9%
Opposition Party (Whig)	19	+19	8.0%
Anti-Lecompton Democrats	8	+8	3.3%
Independent Democrats	7	+6	2.9%
American Party (Know-Nothing)	5	−9	2.1%
Totals	238	+1	100%

could hardly have asked for more fruitful opportunities to strengthen their political hands.

For the first eight months of 1859, the campaign for the White House, already in full swing, had proceeded fairly routinely. The Republicans gained twenty-six seats in the elections of 1858 by capitalizing on the Democratic crack-up over the Lecompton Constitution in Kansas and the steady weakening of the Know-Nothing movement, which earlier in the decade had shown itself to be a potential rival for anti-Democratic votes. Because of the vagaries of the political calendar, the Thirty-Sixth Congress (table 1) would not be seated until December 1859—more than a year after most votes were cast. But with 116 seats out of 238 (in other words, 3 short of a majority) and 19 more won by members of the overwhelmingly Whig (and decidedly anti-administration) opposition party, Republicans were confident, even cocky, that they would win control of the lower chamber. The Democrats, on the other hand, had been mauled at the polls, losing 49 seats, leaving them with just 83, less than 35 percent of the total. The American Party had also lost nine of its thirteen seats in the elections, leaving them only five in the entire House.

Ever the optimist, Stephen Douglas—still fresh from his 1858 senatorial victory over challenger Abraham Lincoln—saw the election results as an opportunity for his party and . . . for himself. He reasoned that the best hope for his party in 1860 was if Democrats of both sections coalesced in a national centrist coalition behind popular sovereignty, his plan to defuse the issue of slavery expansion, and a presidential candidate with the initials "S.D." Remaining in Washington with his young wife, Douglas teamed up with fellow Democrat and historian George Bancroft to compose an article on popular sovereignty for *Harper's Monthly Magazine* to be the centerpiece of his presidential campaign. The article offered no concessions to either Congress's right to halt slavery in the territories or a federal slave code; it even drew a harsh official rebuttal from the Buchanan administration.[2]

After the article's publication, Douglas toured Ohio to assist Democrats in state elections. In an effort to exploit the growing rift in the party of Jackson, Ohio Republicans invited Douglas's old nemesis to follow him on the campaign trail. In a memorable duo of speeches—one at the state house at Columbus and another before a rally in Cincinnati—Abraham Lincoln engaged Douglas's popular sovereignty arguments while also making a pitch for his own party to leave unchanged its own policy on slavery's expansion into new territories: a moratorium on any new slave soil. He also warned against watering down the Republican brand in an attempt to gather more "recruits": "What gave the party its authority," he told his audience, "was its guaranteed hostility to slavery's spread. Weaken that, to attract southern opponents of 'the rotten democracy,' and you gain nothing in the South and lose everything in the North."[3]

Lincoln had famously promised to devote the year 1859 to replenishing his personal finances, but the early part of the year had been good enough to him that he spent the closing months traveling four thousand miles to make twenty-three speeches. In these he attempted to tamp down demands from more militant antislavery voices who wanted to overturn the Fugitive Slave Law. "Why manufacture slang to be used against us by our enemies?" Lincoln asked when a conservative downstater called more radical Republicans "ultras" and "nigger stealers." He implored fellow Republicans to "*help* . . . instead of trying to *hurt* one another."[4]

This was the comparatively humdrum state of the presidential election "BJB": before John Brown. Brown's spectacular and astonishing attack on

---

[2]Stephen Douglas, "The Dividing Line between Federal and Local Authority: Popular Sovereignty in the Territories," *Harper's Monthly Magazine*, Sept. 1859. Douglas copyrighted the article, an unusual move for a politician in the nineteenth century. At that time an article could suffice in the place of today's obligatory "campaign autobiography."

[3]Roy P. Basler, ed., *The Collected Works of Abraham Lincoln*, 9 vols. (New Brunswick, N.J., 1953–55), 3:387–88. Conservative Republican spokesmen, including Henry J. Raymond of the *New York Times*, advocated broadening the GOP tent by replacing nonextension with popular sovereignty, to draw Southern Whigs and Know-Nothings into a broad opposition party.

[4]Ibid., 3:389–91; Richard J. Carwardine, *Lincoln* (Harlow, U.K., 2003), pp. 94–95.

the arsenal at Harpers Ferry made Lincoln's task of reconciliation considerably harder, and—more importantly—had the very real potential to damage the new party at the polls. Think about how unwelcome this event was for those who had so recently seen themselves in a kind of inevitable ascendancy. For the year since its victory in the 1858 elections, Republicans had been working hard to burnish their unionist credentials and unite opposition to the Democracy in places like Missouri and other border states. (Horace Greeley had recently embarked on a platform-diluting strategy to win mildly antislavery votes in border states and had even advanced the candidacy of the barely Republican Edward Bates.) But the potentially untamable forces unleashed by the raid—slave insurrection, disunion, race war—quickly overwhelmed unionist efforts on both sides. Putting aside the numerous instances where Southerners demonized all antislavery Northerners as potential John Browns and Northerners often slipped into hagiographic language to describe Brown's actions, commentators at the time tended to focus more on the topic of how the events at Harpers Ferry might affect the election.

The *Baltimore Sun*, heretofore the voice of border state moderation, sounded more like the *Charleston Mercury* after the raid, announcing that the South could not afford to "live under a government, the majority of whose subjects or citizens regard John Brown as a martyr and a Christian hero, rather than a murderer and a robber."[5] Editorials and public comments circled back again and again to New York Senator William Seward, who rapidly became the face of the party defending John Brown. "Mr. Seward and his followers . . . have declared war on us," said one Mississippi legislator, leading the senator to more forcefully repudiate Brown's actions and offer the comment that his execution was "necessary and just," although pitiable. Even the Seward-friendly *Albany Evening Journal* bent over backward to speak against Brown and reassure the South: "Though we 'would that all men' were Free, we should as readily go to Virginia to run off their Horses and Cattle, as their Slaves. By the Constitution and Laws, Slavery is recognized and tolerated. It was a compact made by our Fathers, and one that binds their heirs. We will oppose both its extension and its encroachments."[6]

---

[5]Oswald Garrison Villard, *John Brown, 1800–1859: A Biography Fifty Years After* (Boston, 1910), p. 568.

[6]David M. Potter, *The Impending Crisis, 1848–1861* (New York, 1976), p. 383; *Albany Evening Journal*, Nov. 30, 1859, quoted in Jonathan Earle, *John Brown's Raid: A Brief History with Documents* (Boston, 2008), p. 108.

The *Petersburg* (Virginia) *Express* called out Northerners by name to denounce not only Brown's actions, but what he stood for: "What Seward teaches from New York State, Wilson and Sumner from Massachusetts, Fessenden from Maine, Chase from Ohio, Collamer from Vermont, Grow from Pennsylvania . . . all lead inevitably to collision as bitter as the late affair. . . . Unless a change—a speedy and effectual change—sweep over Northern society, the great conflict must come." Thus, even before Brown's execution it was becoming clear that the more antislavery Seward wing of the Republican Party and Douglas's centrist Democrats were in line to pay the steepest political price for John Brown's actions.[7]

The same would hold true in a strange legislative battle mentioned only in passing by most historians of the period. The Thirty-Sixth Congress convened on December 5, just seventy-two hours after John Brown's body was brought down from the gallows. Again, due to the strange lag in time between the 1858 midterm elections and the meeting of the Congress, the new House was convening for the very first time, despite the Buchanan administration being more than half over (and already plumb out of political steam). But to borrow a much-overused political cliché from our own century, the world had changed since those 1858 elections thirteen months earlier—or rather (to avoid a passive construction), John Brown had changed the world.

The first thing that happens in every new Congress, of course, is that the body organizes itself, chooses its leaders, swears in its members, and begins conducting the nation's legislative business. The atmosphere in 1859 was tense but subdued as the first ballots to organize the chamber were cast in the speakership selection. Thomas S. Babcock of Virginia, a Democrat, led the first round with eighty-six votes, followed by two Republicans: John Sherman of Ohio with sixty-six votes and Galusha Grow of Pennsylvania with forty-three. A fourth candidate for Speaker represented the choice of the roughly two dozen Southerners who had until recently been Whigs and Know-Nothings. (They were sometimes called "South Americans.")[8] Thus far in the speakership

[7]*Petersburg* (Virginia) *Express*, Oct. 25, 1859, quoted in Earle, *John Brown's Raid*, p. 109. Sean Wilentz called Seward's paying the political price for Brown's raid "an encouragement of restraint that Brown did not foresee and would have detested" (Wilentz, *The Rise of American Democracy* (Boston, 2005), p. 752.

[8]*Congressional Globe*, 36th Cong., 1st sess., p. 2. The best source on the speakership controversy remains Ollinger Crenshaw, "The Speakership Contest of 1859–1860: John Sherman's Election a Cause of Disruption?" *Mississippi Valley Historical Review* 29 (1942): 323–38.

election there was nothing unusual except the lack of a true majority (by eleven votes if you add together the two Republican candidates).

It was the very next action in the House that started things on an unusual and potentially treacherous path. John B. Clark of Missouri took the floor and offered a resolution bitterly condemning, of all things, a book: Hinton Rowan Helper's *Impending Crisis of the South.* With this resolution, Clark leveled an implicit attack on his Republican colleague Sherman, as well. Since the "doctrines and sentiments" of Helper's book were "insurrectionary and hostile to the peace and tranquility of the country," the resolution stated, "no member of this House, who has indorsed and recommended it, is fit to be speaker." The next day Clark produced direct evidence against the Ohioan: a letter recommending that a "copious commend" (a kind of *Reader's Digest* version) of Helper's book be printed and that 100,000 copies be distributed in Pennsylvania, New York, New Jersey, and Illinois—in other words, that it become a Republican campaign manifesto. The letter, dated March 9, 1859, was signed by a committee that included more than sixty members of Congress—one of them the would-be Speaker, John Sherman.[9]

In some ways it should not have been surprising that the inflammatory book—published by a twenty-seven-year-old white North Carolinian (fig. 2) two years earlier—would be front and center in the nation's politics in the immediate aftermath of John Brown's execution. The book attracted relatively little notice when it appeared, self-published, in 1857, but it was recycled as a potential campaign document of sorts in mid-1859 by some Republicans. Horace Greeley published large extracts of the book in the *New York Tribune* during the week leading up to John Brown's hanging, hoping to lend additional arguments—southern-accented ones, to boot—to the Republicans' anti-restrictionist message. (Greeley left out Helper's more stridently anti-black statements—as much as he hated slavery as a cause of the wretchedness of poor Southern whites, Helper avidly called for the deportation of blacks from the United States and later became a virulently white supremacist author.)

---

[9] *Congressional Globe*, 36th Cong., 1st sess., p. 16. Grow also signed the motion, but withdrew after the first ballot. The *Compendium* also included some intentionally offensive captions, including "The Stupid Masses of the South" and "Revolution—peacefully if we can, Violently if we must." Hinton R. Helper, *Compendium of the Impending Crisis of the South* (New York, 1860).

Fig. 2. Engraving by A. H. Richie of Hinton Rowan Helper, frontispiece of 1860 edition of *The Impending Crisis. (North Carolina Collection, University of North Carolina at Chapel Hill Library)*

Democrats, meanwhile, saw something else entirely in the book. Like John Brown's raid, they believed, *The Impending Crisis* provided an opening to reclaim some of the political ground lost during their 1858 drubbing. The remaining administration backers in the House thus began to store their powder for a long, drawn-out struggle over the organization of their chamber.

But what, precisely, was so incendiary about Helper's book? What about it threatened the "peace and tranquility" of the nation? It certainly wasn't its narrative structure or readability. The book is a cavalcade of facts, numbers, empirical observations, and statistics. But those statistics painted a politically poignant tale of the numerical, financial, and moral superiority the North had gained over the South, and slavery's central role in creating, perpetuating, and widening this chasm between the sections. The victims of Helper's tale were not the region's slaves, but the nonslaveholding whites (like those in North Carolina's Piedmont region, where Helper was raised), people he believed continued to suffer under the boot of a small aristocracy of wealthy slave owners.

Helper was a master at using the U.S. census to buttress his scathing critique of the world the slaveholders had made. When the first enumeration was made in 1790, Virginia had twice the population of New York State (747,610 to 340,120). By 1850 New York had more than twice the number of people as the Old Dominion. In terms of real and personal property, New York City was worth more than the entire state of Virginia. Charleston, which had imported $2.6 million worth of articles in 1760, imported just $1.75 million worth in 1855, while Philadelphia had imported $21 million the year before. To make the comparison even more stark, Pennsylvanians spent more than $1.3 million on their schools, possessed 393 public libraries, and provided a readership for 310 newspapers circulating more than 84 million copies. The Palmetto State could not come close to these numbers. Its school budget was $200,000, the state had just twenty-six libraries, and forty-six newspapers produced just 7.1 million copies for circulation. Helper's words weren't anything like John Brown's pikes and threats of insurrection—but his attack during this most competitive and commercial era was powerful nonetheless. Something was extremely amiss in the South economically, politically, and (by extension) racially and morally. How else to explain the widening gulf between the sections?[10]

[10]Hinton Rowan Helper, *The Impending Crisis of the South: How to Meet It* (New York, 1857), chap. 1. On the making of the book, see David Brown, "Attacking Slavery from Within: The Making of *The Impending Crisis of the South*," *Journal of Southern History* 70 (2004):541–76. George M. Fredrickson, "Antislavery Racist: Hinton Rowan Helper," in George M. Fredrickson, *The Arrogance of Race: Historical Perspectives on Slavery, Racism, and Social Inequality* (Middletown, Conn., 1988), pp. 28–53.

Southerners in Congress initially responded to Helper's claims with the usual agricultural boasts about "King Cotton." Yet Helper presented agricultural records showing that one Northern hay crop was worth more than the cotton, tobacco, rice, hay, *and* hemp crop of all the Southern states. The balance of the value of all agricultural products tilted north by $44 million. Worse still for Southern nationalists was where the profits from their crops often ended up: in the counting houses of Northern shippers, factory owners, insurers, and bankers.

What was to blame? For Helper, it was slavery. Here, finally, is where Helper earned his reputation as a figure every bit as dangerous to the Old South as John Brown: his clear enumeration of the deficits of slavery, complete with a ten-point plan to abolish the institution in the South (these went from organizing nonslaveholding whites to organizing boycotts against proslavery merchants to a system of taxation to discourage human bondage). If this program were enacted, according to Helper, "fifteen years will not elapse before every foot of territory, from the mouth of the Delaware to the emboguing of the Rio Grande, will glitter with jewels of freedom."[11]

To many of the slaveholders in Congress, a book delivering this advice was as much an assault on the South as John Brown's abortive raid. Men like John Sherman who endorsed it were thus potentially as dangerous as the "Secret Six," who had bankrolled Old Osawatomie Brown. What is sure is that the *Compendium* was enough to turn enough border state representatives and "South Americans" against Sherman. Thus it was that for eight tumultuous weeks, the House of Representatives remained unorganized, the members unsworn, and comity unraveled.

John Sherman's first line of defense was one all too common in politics: that he hadn't even read the book he had endorsed, or the *Compendium* derived from it. Instead, he suggested, he had merely offered his good name to help the Republican Party in its work. In the type of "nondenial" denial common to twenty-first-century politicians, he said, "I do not recollect signing the paper referred to; but I presume, from my name appearing in the printed list, that I did sign it." I should mention here that Sherman, beginning his third term in the House, was in every measurable way a moderate on the slavery issue, and a fairly thoughtful person in a body in which these were in short supply. Sherman continued his defense by pledging fairness

[11]Helper, *Impending Crisis*, p. 76.

to all parties and reiterating the Republican Party line (perfected by Lincoln and others) as the basis for his candidacy as Speaker: "Allow me to say, once and for all . . . that I am opposed to any interference whatever by the people of the free States with the relations of master and slave in the slave States."[12]

For the next two months, congressional Republicans stuck together behind Sherman. Despite several different candidates and a rotating coalition of anti-Republican representatives, no one else could muster more than 112 votes for Speaker, either. The closest rival contender for the post was John A. McClernand of Illinois, a man wholly identified with Stephen Douglas. If the tiniest number of Lower South Democrats had defected to vote for McClernand, Sherman would have been denied and the minority party would have pulled off a surprising political coup; but (in a pattern that would prevail throughout the election year) both Seward Republicans and Douglas Democrats were fatally weakened by the impact of John Brown's raid and the speakership battle.

Democrats won one major victory in the House, however. The original Clark resolution, though never passed, successfully placed the Republicans on the political defensive during the entire crisis—the "frame," as twenty-first-century political linguist George Lakoff would say, was firmly set in place, with Republicans forced to "explain" their endorsement of a dangerous and potentially explosive piece of literature. Instead of making the case that they were relying on the sound arguments of a son of the South to explain the present gap between the slave and free states, they were forced to defend their signatures endorsing the *Compendium* and protest that they had no quarrel with slavery where it already existed. It was a perilous time for the new party as it headed into the election year.

Slaveholders, for their part, explicitly suggested the speakership contest was a proxy for the upcoming presidential election. And, once again, the choicest attacks were reserved for the Seward wing of the party. To freshman Representative Roger A. Pryor of Virginia, the elevation of Sherman would be "a dismal vaticination of the ultimate catastrophe in the election of William H. Seward." J. L. M. Curry of Alabama concurred: "I am not ashamed or afraid publicly to avow that the election of William H. Seward or Salmon P. Chase, or any other representative of the Republican party,

---

[12] *Congressional Globe*, 36th Cong., 1st sess., pp. 21, 427, 547–48.

upon a sectional platform, ought to be resisted to the disruption of every tie that binds this confederation together." Martin J. Crawford of Georgia also used presidential reasoning and threats of disunion to buttress his speakership vote: "In regard to the election of a Black Republican President, I have this to say, and I speak for the sentiment of every Democrat on this floor from the state of Georgia, we will never submit to the inauguration of a Black Republican President (*Applause from the Democratic benches and hisses from the Republicans*)."[13]

There were several times when the rhetorical vitriol threatened to explode into actual violence. North Carolina Representative Lawrence Branch challenged the mild-mannered Pennsylvanian Galusha Grow to a duel, and a pistol fell from the pocket of one New York member onto the floor during a melee. In another incident, John A. Logan of Illinois was shouted down during a debate and actually pulled a pistol on his opponent, threatening that "By God, if I can't talk, I can do something else."[14]

Things were getting dire in other ways as well. Since they hadn't been formally sworn in and there was no Speaker to sign salary warrants, the members of the Thirty-Sixth Congress continued to serve without pay. Luckily for many of the less wealthy representatives, the outgoing House sergeant at arms was actively pursuing another term and privately borrowed money to advance to the members in the form of no-cost loans. Alas, this small chapter in the history of American public graft amounted to nothing for the self-interested office seeker: the post went to someone else.[15]

When they don't have the votes in Congress, parties often try to change the rules. An attempt by the Republicans to select the Speaker on a plurality vote (as had been done twice before, with the election of Howell Cobb as Speaker in 1849 on the sixty-second ballot and Nathaniel Banks in 1856 on the 133rd) failed to persuade the South Americans. Finally, the Republicans—mindful of the success of the opposition in exploiting Brown, Helper, and Sherman—completely and utterly caved. On the forty-fourth ballot they abandoned Sherman in favor of first-term Representative William Pennington of New Jersey (fig. 3), a member of the oppositionist People's Party who had backed Sherman but, conveniently, had not signed the Helper

[13]Emerson David Fite, *The Presidential Election of 1860* (New York, 1911), p. 42.

[14]Ibid., p. 43.

[15]Ibid., p. 44, n. 1.

FIG. 3. William Pennington in an engraving from a photograph taken by Mathew Brady. *(Prints and Photographs Division, Library of Congress)*

Compendium—he couldn't have since he wasn't even in Congress when the endorsement came before the House. Pennington won the bare minimum number of votes necessary, a few of them from South Americans who noted that while governor of New Jersey Pennington had supported the Fugitive Slave Law.

One lasting effect of the prolonged speakership contest was an increase in Congress-watching among the general public. Papers in every section carried the episode in detail: "every phase of the two month's battle, every excoriation of Helperism, every bit of Southern bluster, every Northern argument and expostulation, every physical clash, was eagerly read about the next morning by hundreds of thousands," wrote one early twentieth-century historian. Helper's *Crisis* became a runaway best seller in the North, topping 150,000 copies, and was suppressed both legally and extralegally in the South. In Maryland, state legislators regulating the police commissioners of Baltimore insisted that "no Black Republican or indorser [*sic*] or supporter of the Helper book" could serve as a policeman or in any other type of law enforcement.[16]

By far the worst case of suffering over Helper's book, however, was borne by a hapless missionary named Daniel Worth. Worth was arrested in Greensboro, North Carolina, for selling the book and—failing to possess anywhere near the $15,000 in assessed bail—he languished for three months in a tiny, dirty jail cell. When the case finally came to trial, it was proved that Worth had, in fact, sold four copies of the book: one buyer had buried his copy, another hid his in a hollow log, and another testified Worth had told him to be careful who he showed the book to. He was convicted and sentenced to another year in prison, but was freed on bail. The story had a happy ending, though, as Worth jumped bail and escaped to New York, where he joined Helper on the lecture circuit, owing to his status as a cause célèbre in the Northern press.[17]

As Pennington took his oath of office as Speaker on February 1, 1860, much had changed since the night John Brown led his men across the Potomac into Harpers Ferry fourteen weeks earlier. Robert Toombs of Georgia, who in early January had seemed resigned to a Sherman victory in the House and a Seward victory in November, was jubilant.[18] So was his fellow senator from Georgia, Alfred Iverson, who declared that if Sherman had prevailed he would have led his fellow Southerners out of Congress until his constituents sent him back with new orders: "[but] I would go further than that," he said. "I would counsel my constituents instantly to

[16]Ibid., p. 46.

[17]Ibid.

[18]Crenshaw, "The Speakership Contest of 1859–1860," p. 328: "They have broke the back of Helferism [*sic*]."

dissolve all political ties with a party and a people who thus trample on our rights." It seems hard to believe, but in the wake of John Brown's raid a hardening group of Southern congressmen equated John Sherman's potential elevation to Speaker with "incitement of servile insurrection."[19]

Some Republicans mocked this notion. "Can it be possible that gentlemen of the South would be willing to encounter the fatal consequences of a disruption of the constitutional Confederacy, merely because a particular individual shall be elected Speaker of this House?"[20] But others were not so sure. The *New York Courier and Enquirer* on January 18, 1860, interpreted speeches by Southern radicals like Laurence M. Keitt (South Carolina) and Lucius Gartrell (Georgia)—and even those of Independent Democrats like Shelton Leake—as implying that Sherman's election as Speaker *or* Seward's election as president would be cause for secession.[21]

How serious was the threat by Southern radicals in Congress to disrupt the workings of government—or the Union itself—over the speakership of the House? Historian Ollinger Crenshaw noted that previous historians had ignored the "extreme gravity" of the situation and the narrow escape of Congress from what he called an "indescribable holocaust" (Crenshaw wrote this during World War II, before that term assumed a more precise meaning). But there were some comments by Southern nationalists that went beyond the usual sectional squabbles, a full year before South Carolina voted to secede. R. Barnwell Rhett Jr., editor of the *Charleston Mercury*, wrote an ally about what he called his "proposition"—"that Southern Representatives should withdraw from Congress in the election of a Black Republican speaker"—and not wait for the elevation of the hated Seward to the White House.[22] Some of Rhett's fellow South Carolinians went even further, threatening physical violence *in Congress* if the Republicans prevailed. In a letter to the Charleston Congressman William Porcher Miles, South Carolina Governor William H. Gist alluded to another's plan—he didn't specify whose—for Sherman, should he be elected Speaker, to be ejected by force and the federal government dissolved. "If that plan was adopted a bloody revolution would be inevitable," Gist wrote, "and although I am prepared

[19]Ibid., p. 331.

[20]*Congressional Globe*, 36th Cong., 1st sess., p. 72.

[21]Ibid., pp. 526–27; Crenshaw, "The Speakership Contest of 1859–1860," p. 331.

[22]Rhett to W. P. Miles, Jan. 29, 1860, quoted in Crenshaw, "The Speakership Contest of 1859–1860," p. 334.

to wade in blood rather than submit to inequality & degradation . . . [a bloodless revolution] would be preferable." He continued: "If however, you upon consultation decide to make the issue of force in Washington, write or telegraph me, & I will have a regiment in or near Washington in the shortest possible time."[23]

The election of Pennington quelled the "revolution" for the time being. But the swift combination of Brown's raid, trial, and execution and the speakership fight significantly deepened the threat of very real sectional violence. David Potter noted as "ominous" the fact that "many Southern members did not really want to organize the House," but I'm willing to go even farther than that. A dazzling number were willing to gum up the gears of the legislative branch by engaging in disorderly and derisive debate and paralyzing a supposedly deliberative body during a deepening sectional crisis. Disunion was brought out of the shadows and into open discussion in letters, newspaper editorials, and speeches. The struggle on the floor of the House evocatively illustrated the depths of sectional division, and set the tone for a congressional session that witnessed a Northern bloc ready to enact a new economic program to win votes across the region and saw Southern members resort to measures designed to shore up the slave system by forcing their territorial ambitions on the Northern wing of a weakening Democratic Party.

Politically, the events of the winter of 1859–60 had devastating (if still mostly invisible) effects on the presidential campaigns of strongly antislavery Republicans like Seward and Chase and "centrist" Democrats like Douglas. Much of the literature (and contemporary commentary) on the early phase of the campaign is about how the more "moderate" Lincoln "came out of nowhere" to secure the Republican nomination in Chicago. And, sure enough, most of the delegates arriving for the convention in May believed Seward would coast to the nomination. But party insiders, especially those who dealt day in and day out with Southerners, knew how damaged Seward's candidacy was. Lincoln and his strategists did not necessarily know this themselves, but they knew enough to continue making moderate statements, heal the rifts in the Illinois Republican Party first, and then shoot to be the delegates' second choice should the front-runner falter.

---

[23] William H. Gist to W. P. Miles, Dec. 20, 1859, ibid., pp. 334–35.

Similarly, historians have tended to believe Stephen Douglas's own press that the national Democrats was ready to endorse popular sovereignty and his candidacy before the fire-eaters torpedoed the party. But the damage was already done. Rifts large enough to be perceived had opened up new possibilities for both Southern nationalist radicals and Republicans not yet tarred with the "radical on slavery" label. The crisis, by the time of the spring thaw in 1860, was no longer impending.

Eric Walther

"Shatter This Accursed Union"

The Fire-Eaters in Congress in 1860

IN 1860 THE most important leaders of disunion—called the fire-eaters since 1850 because of their inflammatory rhetoric—did *not* serve in Congress. The three most important, Edmund Ruffin of Virginia (fig. 1), Robert Barnwell Rhett of South Carolina (fig. 2), and William Lowndes Yancey of Alabama (fig. 3), were able to achieve their influence precisely because they did not occupy elective office; they had no electorates to placate, were beholden to no party organizations, and therefore were free to let loose their extremism unfettered, untempered, and unrestrained.[1]

Within Congress, the three most conspicuous fire-eaters were men far less known to the general public: Louis Trezevant Wigfall, senator from Texas, and two South Carolina congressmen, William Porcher Miles of Charleston and Laurence Massilon Keitt of Orangeburg.[2] Yet to conclude that office seeking, office holding, and the compromises necessary in order

[1]See Eric H. Walther, *The Fire-Eaters* (Baton Rouge, 1992). The most current biographies of the three most important secessionists are William C. Davis, *Rhett: The Turbulent Life and Times of a Fire-Eater* (Columbia, S.C., 2001); Eric H. Walther, *William Lowndes Yancey and the Coming of the Civil War* (Chapel Hill, N.C., 2006); Betty L. Mitchell, *Edmund Ruffin: A Biography* (Bloomington, Ind., 1981).

[2]Alvy T. King, *Louis T. Wigfall: Southern Fire-Eater* (Baton Rouge, 1970). There are no book-length studies of either Keitt or Miles. The best studies remain John Holt Merchant Jr., "Laurence M. Keitt: South Carolina Fire-Eater," Ph.D. dissertation, University of Virginia, 1976; Ruth McCaskill Daniel, "William Porcher Miles: Champion of Southern Interests," M.A. thesis, University of North Carolina, Chapel Hill, 1943. For these three and other secessionists, see Walther, *Fire-Eaters.*

Fig. 1. Edmund Ruffin. *(Prints and Photographs Division, Library of Congress)*

Fig. 2. Robert Barnwell Rhett. *(Prints and Photographs Division, Library of Congress)*

to function within national political parties and the flexibility to craft legislation on national issues constrained their words or actions is inaccurate, because these three men found unflinching support from their respective constituencies, voters as radical as they. Therefore only in contrast, only by

Fig. 3. William Lowndes Yancey. *(Prints and Photographs Division, Library of Congress)*

degrees, were these three men distinct from their more vocal and independent brother disunionists.

Wigfall, Miles, and Keitt all had much in common. All were born in South Carolina. Wigfall was born in 1816 on a plantation near Edgefield in the upcountry, Miles was born in 1822 in Walterboro in Colleton District in the low country, and Keitt was born in 1824 in St. Matthews, Orangeburg District, closer to the middle of the state. Typical of boys from well-to-do Southern families, each attended a private academy. Wigfall went to the Rice Creek Springs School, a military academy near Columbia. Keitt attended the local St. Matthews Academy. Miles attended the renowned Willington Academy, where a generation before the future congressman and senator John C. Calhoun began his education. Miles graduated from the College of Charleston in 1842. Wigfall completed his education at South Carolina College (now the University of South Carolina) in 1837, the same school that Keitt attended a little later.[3] South Carolina College had a well-deserved reputation for political radicalism. One of its first presidents, Thomas Cooper, advised Carolinians in 1827 to seriously consider whether there was still value in remaining in the Union. The college provided the bulk of politicians for this singular, well-unified, and problematic state for the entire antebellum era.[4]

But more important for each of these three was the extracurricular education received by their entire generation in South Carolina. Wigfall, Miles, and Keitt were twelve, six, and four years old, respectively, when the Nullification Crisis began in 1828, when John C. Calhoun rallied Carolinians to defy enforcement of a federal tariff by citing state sovereignty, and his able but even more radical lieutenant, Barnwell Rhett, beseeched Carolinians to go even further and secede from the Union.[5] Believing with Calhoun that protective tariffs were unconstitutional, Rhett explained that

---

[3]King, *Louis T. Wigfall*, pp. 8–12; Merchant, "Laurence M. Keitt," pp. 11–16; Daniel, "William Porcher Miles," pp. 1–2.

[4]See Daniel W. Hollis, *University of South Carolina*, 2 vols. (Columbia, S.C., 1951), vol. 1; Lacy K. Ford, *Origins of Southern Radicalism: The South Carolina Upcountry* (New York, 1988), pp. 113–19; James M. Banner, "The Problem of South Carolina," in Stanley Elkins and Eric McKitrick, eds., *The Hofstadter Aegis: A Memorial* (New York, 1974); Rachel Klein, *Unification of a Slave State: The Rise of the Planter Class in the South Carolina Upcountry, 1760–1808* (Chapel Hill, N.C., 1990). See also Lorri Glover, *Southern Sons: Becoming Men in the New Nation* (Baltimore, 2007).

[5]Davis, *Rhett*, pp. 45–107; William W. Freehling, *Prelude to Civil War: The Nullification Movement in South Carolina, 1816–1836* (New York, 1966) and *The Road to Disunion: Secessionists at Bay, 1776–1854* (New York, 1990), pp. 253–86; Richard E. Ellis, *The Union at Risk: Jacksonian Democracy, States' Rights, and the Nullification Crisis* (New York, 1987); Merrill D. Peterson, *The Olive Branch and the Sword: The Compromise of 1833* (Baton Rouge, 1982); Elizabeth R. Varon, *Disunion! The Coming of the American Civil War, 1789–1859* (Chapel Hill, N.C., 2008), pp. 87–96.

if the federal government could do one thing that was unconstitutional, then it could do anything else it decided to do, including abolishing slavery.[6] With the concurrent rise of abolitionism in the North, and given the fact that slaves greatly outnumbered whites in the state, Rhett rightly declared, "A people, owning slaves, are mad, or worse than mad, who do not hold their destinies in their own hands."[7] As early as 1828, Rhett tried in vain to rally Carolinians for war against the federal government in order to secure their rights and liberties. Through speeches and editorials in the *Charleston Mercury*, Rhett played to Carolinians' fevered sense of honor and manhood: "If you love life better than honor,—prefer ease to perilous liberty and glory; awake not! stir not!—impotent resistance will add vengeance to your ruin. Live in smiling peace with your insatiable Oppressors, and die with the noble consolation, that your submissive patience will survive your beggary and despair."[8] In 1830 Rhett projected but two choices for the people of his state: resistance to the federal government at all costs, or submission. If Carolinians chose the latter, Rhett declared, "yo[u] are vassals and slaves of a consolidated empire." Of course, Rhett advocated resistance: "Ay—disunion into a thousand fragments." He told others not to fear being branded with treason, and concluded proudly, "If to think, to speak, to feel such sentiments as these, constitutes me as a disunionist and a traitor . . . then, gentlemen, I am a Disunionist!—I am a Traitor!"[9] As the Nullification Crisis grew more ominous in July 1832, Rhett announced that rather than becoming political slaves of the North, Carolinians should "let our free spirits wing the glorious way in the death of freemen."[10] Like all youths of their generation, Wigfall, Miles, and Keitt could not recall a time when the relationship between their state and the federal government had not been seriously questioned.

---

[6] *Charleston Mercury*, June 18, 1828.

[7] *Charleston Mercury*, Mar. 26, 1833.

[8] *Charleston Mercury*, June 18, 1828. On Southern honor, see Bertram Wyatt-Brown, *Southern Honor: Ethics and Behavior in the Old South* (New York, 1982), *Yankee Saints and Southern Sinners* (Baton Rouge, 1985), and "God and Honor in the Old South," *Southern Review* 25 (1989): 283–96; Kenneth Greenberg, *Honor and Slavery: Lies, Duels, Noses, Masks, Dressing as a Woman, Gifts, Strangers, Humanitarianism, Death, Slave Rebellion, the Proslavery Argument, Baseball, Hunting, and Gambling in the Old South* (Princeton, N.J., 1996). For the confluence of honor and the political defense of slavery, see William J. Cooper Jr., *The South and the Politics of Slavery, 1828–1856* (Baton Rouge, 1976) and *Liberty and Slavery: Southern Politics to 1860* (New York, 1983).

[9] *Charleston Mercury*, Oct. 19, 1830.

[10] *Charleston Mercury*, July 14, 1832.

In 1844, when Wigfall, Miles, and Keitt were twenty-eight, twenty-two, and twenty years old, Barnwell Rhett launched another disunion effort, and did so in outright defiance of John C. Calhoun. In the town of Bluffton in St. Luke's Parish, on July 31 Rhett announced that three new developments necessitated nullification, secession, "or anything else" except "base and cowardly submission." The failure of Congress to admit into the Union the vast slaveholding Republic of Texas, the end of the eight-year-old Gag Rule that had stifled congressional debate over slavery, and a new tariff combined to alarm Rhett and others. The Bluffton Movement had begun, and hundreds of young men, already schooled in disunion, proudly proclaimed themselves the Bluffton Boys.[11] One of these was Louis Wigfall (fig. 4). In Edgefield, Wigfall explained that his state should not "be hindered by our supposed allegiance to the Federal Government," and that Texas annexation was "the paramount issue of the times." He called for South Carolina to call a special convention to address these three issues. "I confess my decided preference of Secession over Nullification," he told his hometown crowd. But not long after Rhett began his crusade, the heavy hand of Calhoun crushed his efforts by pressuring the fire-eater's associates to abandon the cause.[12]

As Louis Wigfall cut his teeth as a secessionist in 1844, Laurence Keitt (fig. 5) passed his bar exam that year, and politics almost immediately captured his attention. He traveled to Washington to observe Congress firsthand in 1846. He was "astonished" to find "the fat and cumbrous errors of hoary headed and renowned Politicians, upon certain points which appeared to me lucid and obvious," particularly the expansion of slavery into western

[11]Barnwell Rhett to Robert M. T. Hunter, Aug. 30, 1844, in Charles Ambler, ed., *Annual Report of the American Historical Association for the Year 1916: Correspondence of Robert M. T. Hunter, 1824–1876* (Washington, D.C., 1918), pp. 70–71; *Charleston Mercury*, July 27, Aug. 8, 1844.

[12]*Charleston Mercury*, Aug. 8, 10, 12, 16, 22, 28, Sept. 3, 5, 10, 19, 1844; Rhett to R. M. T. Hunter, Aug. 30, 1844, in Ambler, ed. *Correspondence of Robert M. Hunter*, p. 70; Rhett to Armistead Burt, Sept. 9, 1844, Armistead Burt Papers, William Perkins Library, Duke University, Durham, N.C. (hereafter WPL); Chauncey S. Boucher, "The Annexation of Texas and the Bluffton Movement in South Carolina," *Mississippi Valley Historical Review* 6 (1919):3–33; John Stanford Coussons, "Thirty Years with Calhoun, Rhett, and the Charleston Mercury: A Chapter in South Carolina Politics," Ph.D. dissertation, Louisiana State University, 1970, pp. 168, 173–74, 182–83; Davis, *Rhett*, pp. 194–213; Ford, *Origins of Southern Radicalism*, pp. 191, 200; Varon, *Disunion!*, pp. 169–72. For the Gag Rule, see William Lee Miller, *Arguing about Slavery: John Quincy Adams and the Great Battle in the United States Congress* (New York, 1996).

Fig. 4. Louis T. Wigfall. *(Prints and Photographs Division, Library of Congress)*

territories. He returned to South Carolina and won election to the state assembly in 1848.[13] Two years later he called for disunion. In 1850, when Senator Henry Clay proposed a massive legislative package intended to end all sectional antagonisms in the country, across the South calls rang out for secession and even for civil war. Eventually called the Compromise of 1850, Clay's proposal included provisions to end the slave trade in the District of Columbia and to prohibit slavery in California. That March in Orangeburg, Keitt insisted that the South must have its way or secede. Rhett pronounced Keitt's speech "brilliant and powerful." By 1851 Keitt took to the stump with Rhett and insisted, "Loyalty to the Union is treason to liberty." This disunion movement unraveled quickly in 1851 as unconditional secessionists such as Rhett and Keitt lost to a group called Cooperationists, who believed that grounds existed for secession but who also wanted other slave states to secede first, sparing Carolina a repeat of its alienation during the Nullification Crisis. Keitt was beside himself, but his grateful constituents rewarded his efforts by sending him to Washington in 1853 to assume Rhett's old seat in the House of Representatives. He had just turned twenty-nine. He would serve there until his state seceded in 1860.[14]

William Porcher Miles (fig. 6) experienced quite a different journey to political radicalism and to his seat in Congress. Like the others, Miles studied law, but decided on an academic career instead at the College of Charleston. Politics did not seem to interest him at all, until 1846 when New York Congressman David Wilmot proposed that any and all lands the United States might take as it began its invasion of Mexico that year would be closed to slave expansion. That proposal challenged Miles's concepts of Southern honor and the equality of the slave states within the Union. In his first public address, on July 4, 1849, Miles asserted that the attempt to pass the Wilmot Proviso represented a Northern society "deliberately, intentionally, and advisedly" working to destroy the South. Miles, who never owned a slave, nevertheless considered African American slavery "a part of ourselves," inextricably tied to every facet of Southern society. The rising tide of antislavery and abolitionism in the North represented an attack on "all

[13]L. M. Keitt to Francis Lieber, Jan. 18, Sept. 2, 1846, Francis Lieber Papers, Huntington Library, San Marino, Calif.; Walther, *Fire-Eaters*, p. 166.

[14]Robert Barnwell, *Love of Order: South Carolina's First Secession Crisis* (Chapel Hill, N.C., 1982); Walther, *Fire-Eaters*, pp. 166–67; *Charleston Mercury*, Mar. 27, Oct. 16, 1850; June 19, Aug. 8, Sept. 4, 18, 20, 1851.

Fig. 5. Lawrence M. Keitt. *(Prints and Photographs Division, Library of Congress)*

our institutions, our liberties, nay, our very existence." Nevertheless, Miles supported the Cooperationists from 1850 to 1852. With that sectional crisis over, Miles turned all his energies to his college, but his prominence in Charleston launched his political career. In 1855 he won election as mayor of Charleston. The next year he parlayed his record of police and budget reform, and his accomplishments in public health and sanitation, into a successful run for Congress. Sectional issues dominated his campaign, particularly the intertwined issues of the rise of the new antislavery Republican Party and the struggle between pro- and antislavery forces to take hold of Kansas Territory. Miles argued that if the Republican presidential candidate, John C. Frémont, won the presidency in 1856 or if Congress blocked slavery from Kansas, then the only lasting safety for the South lay in a Southern confederacy.[15] Although a latecomer to fire-eating, relative to Wigfall and Keitt, the thirty-two-year-old Miles would prove every bit as radical.

Louis Wigfall's journey to the Senate was a long and faltering one. After squandering his inheritance and acquiring a sizable debt, he hoped to recoup his losses through his law practice, but he had trouble with the business part of that undertaking. He grew so depressed that at one point he considered suicide. Between 1839 and 1840, Wigfall became embroiled in a series of insults, fights, and duels. The most noteworthy of these involved another hotheaded secessionist from Edgefield, Preston Brooks (fig. 7). Wigfall and Brooks got into a fistfight in June 1840 over the words and conduct of their respective friends during a recent duel. Brooks then challenged Wigfall to a duel. But before that took place, Wigfall mortally wounded another man in an exchange of gunfire in Edgefield, which resulted in yet another duel. In November 1840 that affair ended with a bloodless exchange of shots. One week later at the same site, Wigfall met Brooks for their duel. Both missed with their initial shots, but during the second round Brooks hit Wigfall in the thigh as Wigfall's shot struck Brooks through the hip. Ever since that incident Brooks had required the aid of a cane to walk, and infamously used that cane in 1856 to bludgeon nearly to death Massachusetts Republican Charles Sumner on the floor of the U.S. Senate. As he repeatedly struck Sumner, none other than Laurence Keitt held aloft his own ornamental cane to prevent others from stopping the bloodbath. (Keitt told his fiancée that Brooks "combined in happy proportion freedom of speech and freedom of the cudgel." Two years later on the House floor, Keitt attacked Pennsylvania Republican Galusha Grow by leaping straight for his throat, thereby triggered a melee

[15]Walther, *Fire-Eaters*, pp. 272–81; William Porcher Miles, *Oration Delivered before the Fourth of July Association* (Charleston, S.C., 1849), p. 17 (slavery "a part of ourselves"); pp. 19–20, 22–23, 29–30 ("deliberately, intentionally, and advisedly").

Fig. 6. William Porcher Miles. *(Prints and Photographs Division, Library of Congress)*

FIG. 7. Preston Brooks. *(Prints and Photographs Division, Library of Congress)*

that involved at least six other congressmen.) By 1846, Louis and Charlotte Wigfall lost their home, slaves, and other property to a sheriff's sale.[16]

[16]Walther, *Fire-Eaters*, pp. 163–64; 175–78. For Keitt, see Keitt to Sue Sparks, May 29, 1856, Keitt Papers, WPL; *New York Times*, Feb. 8, 1858.

Wigfall then did what thousands had done before and after him as they, too, washed out in the East: he moved to Texas in 1846. Settling in Marshall in East Texas, he rapidly distinguished himself as an attorney and got involved in politics, gaining election to the state assembly in 1850 and speaking out against the Compromise of 1850 and the Union. His secessionism gestated nicely in the Texas heat and humidity. Wigfall won a seat in the U.S. Senate in 1859. He waited impatiently in the state capitol building as the assembly members voted. Confident of victory and quite drunk, Wigfall loudly called his opponents a bunch of "hayseeds" who had no business there. Supposedly when Unionist Sam Houston learned of Wigfall's victory, he replied, "Thank God this country is so great and strong, it can bear even that." Senator Wigfall took his seat on January 4, 1860.[17]

Between Louis Wigfall's selection as senator and the time he took his seat in the second session of the ill-fated Thirty-Sixth Congress, that body found itself bogged down by the controversy surrounding Republican John Sherman's candidacy for Speaker of the House and John Brown's raid on Harpers Ferry, Virginia. The escalating tensions in the country and the more frequent acts of violence both outside and inside Congress led Porcher Miles to arm himself on the floor of Congress—and he was not the only member to do so.[18] He also became the inside man on the speakership issue for his governor, William Gist, who wrote to Miles about his willingness to use force to oust John Sherman. If Miles agreed, Gist wrote, "write or telegraph me, & I will have a Regiment near Washington in the shortest possible time."[19]

Miles also attempted to direct affairs between South Carolina and Virginia in the wake of John Brown. Governor Gist appointed a special commission to go to Virginia in an effort to convince the Old Dominion to secede and lead the South toward a slaveholding Confederacy. Miles wrote to one of the commissioners that if they could coax Virginia to secede:

> If Virginia could only now be induced to withdraw from the Union unless every demand of the South were satisfied and some *absolute* security be given

---

[17]Walther, *Fire-Eaters*, pp. 169–72.

[18]David Potter, *The Impending Crisis, 1848–1861* (New York, 1976), p. 389; D. H. Hamilton to Miles, Dec. 3, 1859; A. Huger to Miles, Dec. 12, 1859, both in Miles Papers, Southern Historical Collection, University of North Carolina, Chapel Hill (hereafter SHC). For more on Miles and the speakership controversy, see Walther, *Fire-Eaters*, pp. 286–87; on the impact of John Brown's raid, see Paul Finkelman, ed., *His Soul Goes Marching On: Responses to John Brown and the Harpers Ferry Raid* (Charlottesville, Va., 1995).

[19]William Gist to Miles, Dec. 20, 1859, Miles Papers, SHC.

> for the future, the South would have a glorious start given her path of *independence*, which we all so ardently desire. . . . If you can only urge our Carolina views in such a manner as to imbue Virginia with it—(and at present she is in the best condition to be impregnated)—we may soon hope to see the fruit . . . in the sturdy and healthy offspring of whose birth we would be so justly proud—a Southern Confederacy. This would indeed be a worthy heir of the joint glory of the two commonwealths to spring from the loins of the Palmetto State![20]

Virginia did not secede, and John Sherman withdrew his name from consideration for Speaker; the spirit of resistance, at least in the Upper South, seemed to have vanished. Miles concluded that the only hope of triggering secession now lay in the election of a Republican as president. By early February 1860, Miles decided that Virginia was nearly hopeless, and therefore, "We, *further South* must act and 'drag her along.'"[21]

During a heated debate on the House floor on April 5, 1860, Miles's anger toward Northerners manifested itself after Owen Lovejoy, a Republican from Illinois, complained about Southerners' refusal to permit any serious discussion or debate over slavery. Lovejoy explained that as an American citizen he could travel to England and discuss matters of church and state, monarchy and republicanism, "but I cannot go into a slave State and open my lips in regard to the question about slavery." Miles angrily asked of Lovejoy, "can you go to England and incite the laboring classes to murder the aristocracy, or to assassinate the Queen?"[22]

Later in April, the Democratic Party assembled in Charleston for their presidential nominating convention. Alabama's premier secessionist, William L. Yancey, led a nearly unified Southern delegation there, pledged to stop Northern Democrat Stephen A. Douglas from gaining his party's nomination and insisting instead that the party first commit itself to active promotion of the expansion of slavery into the western territories, and then find a suitable candidate. Yancey's dogged insistence split the party in two. Over

---

[20]Miles to Christopher G. Memminger, Jan. 10, 15, 1860, in Christopher G. Memminger Papers, SHC.

[21]Miles to Memminger, Jan. 23, 1860 (Republican president); Miles to Memminger, Feb. 3, 1860, Memminger Papers, SHC.

[22]*Congressional Globe*, 36th Cong., 1st sess., app., p. 205. Two quite different studies help frame Miles's remarks: see Clement Eaton, *The Freedom-of-Thought Struggle in the Old South* (New York, 1964), and Eugene Genovese, *Slaveholders' Dilemma: Freedom and Progress in Southern Conservative Thought, 1820–1860* (Columbia, S.C., 1994).

the next several weeks, Douglas received the nod from Northern Democrats, while Southern Democrats nominated John C. Breckinridge, vice president to James Buchanan, and Joseph Lane, a secessionist from North Carolina who went on to become a U.S. senator from Oregon.[23]

After Congress recessed, in May Miles returned home and delivered a short speech to rally the spirit of resistance in Charleston. He proclaimed that the coming presidential election pitted "power against principle—the majority against the minority, regardless of constitutional barriers." As a South Carolinian, Miles promised that he owed allegiance to no other "nation" and called upon his listeners to join him in resisting the election of a Republican president rather than submit to "ruin and vassalage" within the Union.[24]

In the summer heat of Charleston, Miles joined Barnwell Rhett at a public meeting to support the Southern Democratic ticket of Breckinridge and Lane. Miles asked, "Will you allow a sectional, fanatical party, whose creed is hatred of the South . . . to establish their dynasty over you?" Nothing but degradation and inequality would follow. The time had passed for more meetings, resolutions, and compromises. "I am sick at heart of the endless talk and bluster of the South." If Carolinians were in earnest, they must act. Rather than hold out an olive branch, "we ought rather to be preparing to grasp the sword."[25]

Laurence Keitt was enjoying his European honeymoon with his beloved bride, Sue Sparks, when he learned of John Brown's raid, and rushed back to Washington. Poor Sue wrote, "Disappointed, disappointed. And the cause, *Politics*. How I *hate* the word." On the House floor Keitt declared, "There is an indissoluble connection between the principles of the Republican Party . . . and their ultimate consummation in blood and rapine on the soil of Virginia." Only days later Keitt received shocking news: his brother, Dr. William J. Keitt of Ocala, Florida, had been murdered in his sickbed by several of his own slaves, who slit his throat. Unable to believe that his or anyone's slaves were anything but happy and content when left to the care of their masters, Laurence Keitt concluded that both his brother's killing and John Brown's raid were the logical result of Republicans' antislavery agitation. To a friend in South Carolina, Keitt explained, "Our Negroes

[23]See Walther, *William Lowndes Yancey*, pp. 228–52.

[24]*Charleston Mercury*, May 21, 1860.

[25]*Charleston Mercury*, July 10 (with Rhett), 14, 1860.

are being enlisted in politics. I confess this new feature alarms me. . . . If Northern men get access to our Negroes to advise poison and the torch, we must prevent it at every hazard." Like Miles, Keitt now demanded immediate secession if a Republican won the presidency in 1860, an election he called "life or Death."[26]

By the end of summer in 1860, Keitt concluded, "a whole world lies between the North and the South, both upon slavery, and the character of the government." With a Republican victory in the offing, Keitt warned that the South should expect more John Brown raids and the emancipation of its slaves, "though it be over burning homes and butchered masters." Slavery must be preserved in the South, Keitt argued, essential as it was for civilization, sanctioned as so many white Southerners believed by scriptures. Yet even if slavery was, as abolitionists claimed, a "product of rapine and violence; even if it be the hideous wrong the Abolitionists declare it to be," Keitt concluded, "still the South is wedded to it in eternal union."[27] And to Porcher Miles, Keitt confided in October, if South Carolina seceded he would abandon politics. "I intend to take the field."[28]

Not long after Louis Wigfall was seated in the Senate, he announced, "The humbuggery of the sacredness of the Union has had its day."[29] He taunted Northerners, daring them to fulfill the threats of some that they would attack and subdue Southern states that might secede. Clearly having learned nothing but viciousness from his spate of fights and duels in the 1840s, Senator Wigfall proclaimed, "Blood is a very common fluid. It is worth very little. A man is killed; it does not amount to much; it is really a matter of small consequence to him, to his family, or to the country."[30] After Congress adjourned in April, Wigfall traveled back to Texas and spent much of the summer campaigning for the Southern Democratic nominee for president. Like Keitt and Miles, he harped on the necessity to secede if a Republican were elected. He blamed Republican "John Brown men" for a recent

[26]Sue Keitt to "Dear Mar," Dec. 4, 1859; Laurence Keitt to Sue Keitt, Jan. 29, 1860, in Keitt Papers, WPL; *Congressional Globe*, 36th Cong., 1st sess., p. 220 (Republicans and John Brown); R. B. Rhett Jr. to Miles Jan. 24, 1860 (brother's murder), Miles Papers, SHC; Keitt to James H. Hammond, Aug. 4, Sept. 10 (Negroes are being enlisted), Oct. 23 ("life or death"), 1860, James Henry Hammond Papers, Library of Congress.

[27]Keitt to William M. Murray, Sept. 22, 1860, in *Charleston Mercury*, Sept. 27, 1860.

[28]Keitt to Miles, Oct. 3, 1860, Miles Papers, SHC.

[29]*Congressional Globe*, 36th Cong., 1st sess., pp. 322, 1301 (quote).

[30]Ibid., pp. 1301–2.

spate of mysterious fires that plagued the Lone Star State.[31] At a gathering in Tyler on September 3, 1860, Wigfall asked, "Is any one stupid enough to suppose that Mr. Yancey or Mr. Rhett can dissolve this Union? Can it be done except by the people?" And would the people ever consider it unless the Union had become a curse? Did not the people have a right to live under a government of their choosing, to alter, amend, reform, or abolish forms of government "when they see fit? If not, are they free?" All that bound together the Union now was "sickly sentimentality. . . . It is unworthy of freemen."[32]

These three fire-eaters were at their respective homes when they learned of Lincoln's election. Laurence Keitt traveled to Columbia, South Carolina, and told a crowd, "Take your destinies in your own hands, and shatter this accursed Union." He raced toward Charleston and there pledged to carry both Orangeburg and Beaufort Districts in honor of Barnwell Rhett. Keitt used language just like Rhett's more than a generation before when he asserted that submitting to the Union was tantamount to slavery, "and when I am called upon to choose whether I will be a traitor or a slave, God help me—*I am a traitor!*" Keitt vowed to tear down the Union "from turret to foundation-stone." As a delegate to his state's approaching secession convention, he kept that promise.[33]

Months before Lincoln's election, Porcher Miles contracted typhoid fever, which forced him from South Carolina to the late summer coolness of Newport, Rhode Island. But Miles came back to Charleston in order to vote for Breckinridge and to await election results, though still in very poor health. By December 17 he attended his state's secession convention. "Let us act if we mean to act without talking. Let it be 'a word and a blow'—but a blow first." And on December 20, 1860, Miles, Keitt, and Barnwell Rhett celebrated in the streets of Charleston as the convention unanimously declared the withdrawal of the state from the Union.[34]

The moment that South Carolina seceded it both recalled its congressional delegation and triggered a confrontation with the federal government on many levels, among them the question of ownership of the many federal

---

[31]Marshall, *Texas Republican*, Aug. 4, 11, Oct. 20, 1860.

[32]"Speech of Louis T. Wigfall, on the Pending Political Issues, Delivered at Tyler, Smith County, Texas, September 3, 1860," pp. 17–18 (Yancey and Rhett), 23 (sentimentality).

[33]*Charleston Mercury*, Nov. 13, 21, 1860; Merchant, "Keitt," pp. 337–40.

[34]Miles to James Hammond, Aug. 5, 1860, Hammond Papers, Library of Congress; Miles to R. N. Gourdin, Dec. 10, 1860, Gourdin Papers, Robert Woodruff Library, Emory University, Atlanta, Ga.; Daniel, "William Porcher Miles," p. 89.

forts in and around Charleston harbor. Miles and Keitt began negotiations over the forts with President James Buchanan. They insisted on a transfer of all military installations to Carolina officials, but promised to attack them if Buchanan tried to reinforce the forts.[35] And in that case, Miles was ready "to give Uncle Sam a warm reception."[36] And after their election to the new Confederate Congress early in 1861, Miles and Keitt joined Louis Wigfall as aides-de-camp to General P. G. T. Beauregard, commander of Confederate forces in Charleston harbor.[37]

Louis Wigfall joyfully returned to the Senate in December 1860. He asserted that states had the right to withdraw from the Union "with or without cause." He argued that the Declaration of Independence provided that "every people have a right to live under such form of government that suits them. If this government does not suit us, we will leave it. When we leave it"—notice that he said *when*—"we will not leave it as rebels, nor as traitors."[38] From the Senate, Wigfall urged Carolinians to seize all federal munitions and military installations within their borders, and announced that were he still a Carolinian, he would relish the opportunity to begin a war against federal forces, "and raise the cry, 'to your tents, oh Israel, and to the God of battles be the issue.' "[39]

By the end of January 1861, five other states had seceded and with South Carolina prepared to send delegates to Montgomery, Alabama, to form a provisional government for the Confederate States of America. Unionists

---

[35]John McQueen, William Porcher Miles, M. L. Bonham, W. W. Boyce, and Lawrence [*sic*] Keitt to James Buchanan, Dec. 9, 1860, James Buchanan to Robert W. Barnwell, James H. Adams, and James L. Orr, Dec. 30, 1860, in *Correspondence between Commissioners of the State of South Carolina to the Government at Washington and the President of the United States* (Charleston, S.C., 1861), pp. 5–11.

[36]Miles to M. L. Bonham, Dec. 23, 1860, in James L. Orr Papers, SHC; W. P. Miles to Howell Cobb, Jan. 4, 1861, in U. B. Phillips, ed., *Correspondence of Robert Toombs, Alexander H. Stephens, and Howell Cobb* (Washington, D.C., 1913), pp. 528–29.

[37]Miles to W. W. Corcoran, Aug. 7, 1874, P. G. T. Beauregard to the Board of Trustees of the Johns Hopkins University, Aug. 23, 1874, in *Letters and Testimonials Recommending Mr. Wm. Porcher Miles, of Virginia, for the Presidency of the Hopkins University, Baltimore, Md.* (Charleston, S.C., 1874), pp. 5–8, 26–27; W. P. Miles to W. Ballard Preston, Nov. 11, 1861, in Preston Family Papers, Virginia Historical Society, Richmond, Va.; Edward McCrady and Samuel A. Ashe, *Cyclopedia of Eminent and Representative Men of the Carolinas*, 2 vols. (Madison, Wisc., 1892), 1:660–61.

[38]*Congressional Globe*, 36th Cong., 2d sess., pp. 13, 14 (to your tents).

[39]Ibid., p. 14.

scrambled to propose compromise efforts to preclude civil war, and that broke Wigfall's frail patience:

> You denounce us, degrade us, deride us, tell us we shall live under a Government that we say is not tasteful to us; you tell us that we are degraded, that we are not your equals. . . . And when we say to you, if we cannot live together in peace, we will separate, you say we shall not; and then, because I do not choose to make a ninny of myself, because I do not choose to stultify myself, and vote for resolutions that mean nothing, in order that Senators may telegraph over the country that all is peace and quiet—because I do not choose to do that, or to be led by the nose as tenderly as asses are, I am charged with a conspiracy . . . to dissolve the Union.

Wigfall vowed that in fact, "I would burst it; I would fracture it, splinter it into more fragments than gunpowder would blow glass."[40]

Texans gathered in Austin, and on February 1 issued their secession ordinance. Unlike Keitt and Miles, Wigfall decided to remain in the federal Senate even though he had been elected to go to Montgomery. He would stay and speak and vote and debate "if it suits my convenience."[41] And it suited his convenience to annoy, antagonize, and insult his Northern colleagues. After Zachariah Chandler of Michigan said that rather than listen to proponents of disunion he would move west and live with Native Americans, Wigfall fired back, "God Forbid! I hope not. They have suffered enough from their contact with whites."[42] Recalling President Buchanan's failed effort in January to send a supply ship to federal troops at Fort Sumter, Wigfall gloated, "The Star of the West swaggered into Charleston harbor, received a blow planted full in the face, and staggered out. Your flag has been insulted; redress it, if you dare. You have submitted to it for two months, and you will submit to it for ever. . . . You tell us you will keep us in the Union. Try the experiment."[43]

But Wigfall's rearguard actions were not confined to words; he actively gathered military and political intelligence in Washington and transmitted that information to Confederate officials. Wigfall also established a recruiting station in Baltimore to gather men and arms for the Confederacy and

[40]Ibid., p. 667.
[41]Ibid., p. 1442.
[42]Ibid., p. 1372.
[43]Ibid., p. 1373.

arranged for their transportation south. The *New York Tribune* protested Wigfall's use of the congressional franking privilege and the U.S. mail "to hatch and promote treason" while he drew his pay from the federal government.[44] Only the lure of combat and glory made Wigfall leave the capital. On April 13, 1861, Senator Wigfall commandeered a small boat and ordered its African American oarsmen to row swiftly across Charleston Harbor to Fort Sumter. In the midst of continued bombardment, he reached a wharf and, with a white handkerchief tied to the end of his sword, climbed through an embrasure and into the fort. He insisted on meeting the commander, Major Robert Anderson. After all parties agreed to terms of surrender, Wigfall returned to his boat and a hero's welcome in Charleston.[45]

South Carolina unionist Benjamin F. Perry noted in the 1850s that his state's secessionists were "a set of young enthusiasts inspired with notions of personal honor to be defended and individual glory, fame and military laurels to be acquired."[46] That description certainly matched the lives, words, and actions of the three most prominent secessionists in the Thirty-Sixth Congress. Colonel Laurence Keitt lost his life in combat at Cold Harbor, Virginia, in 1864. He was thirty-nine. Louis Wigfall fled the country for London, afraid of possible capture and execution for treason. He and his family headed back to Marshall, Texas, but on February 18, 1874, he died from an undisclosed cause and was buried in Galveston. Porcher Miles abandoned politics for plantation life, an ironic career for a man who never owned a slave and who inadvertently helped destroy the institution that he had hoped to preserve. His application for president of the new Johns Hopkins University of Baltimore in 1874 was rejected because of his past. By 1882 he had acquired Houmas House plantation in Louisiana and became one of the wealthiest men in the South. He continued to consider himself "an old fashioned, strait out, 'strict construction' Democrat, bred in the South Carolina school of John C. Calhoun and State Rights." He still did not consider the United States to be a nation, "but a 'Confe[de]racy of States.'" He died in 1899.[47] But the most significant mark these three have left on history was that, as United States congressmen, they helped propel the country into a bloodletting that lasted four years, an event so huge and complex that it reverberates well into the twenty-first century.

---

[44]Walther, *Fire-Eaters*, pp. 188–89.

[45]Ibid., p. 160.

[46]Benjamin Perry, quoted in Barnwell, *Love of Order*, p. 150.

[47]Walther, *Fire-Eaters*, pp. 192–93 (Keitt), 189–91 (Wigfall), 291–96 (Miles).

Lesley J. Gordon

"These Zouaves Will Never Support Us"

Cowardice, Congress, and the First Battle of Bull Run

THE FIRST BATTLE of Bull Run is remembered for many things, but one of the most dramatic images is that of panicked Union soldiers fleeing wildly from the battle. Indeed, one of the earliest pictures from the battle that the Northern public saw was in the pages of *Harper's Weekly*, entitled "Charge of the Black Horse Cavalry upon the Fire Zouaves at the Battle of Bull Run." In this illustration (fig. 1), billows of smoke rise as Confederate cavalrymen, atop black horses, stampede through lines of Zouaves, some of them stripped bare-chested and fighting for their lives, others running from the field; still others had fallen on the field. It is a powerful image and one that had to have made an impression on anyone who saw it when it was published less than a month after the battle.[1]

The Fire Zouaves, or the 11th New York, were not just any regiment. Raised by Elmer E. Ellsworth, a personal friend and law associate of Abraham Lincoln, the regiment was composed of New York City firemen, famous before they fired a single shot in combat. And the Battle of Bull Run was not just any battle. It was the first large-scale engagement of the American Civil War, and it ended in a disastrous federal defeat. The war, as we well

[1] *Harper's Weekly*, Aug. 10, 1861. There is some controversy, despite the caption, whether this picture accurately shows the 11th New York or the 14th Brooklyn. The author thanks Harry Smeltzer for help in the original conception of this chapter and his editorial feedback. Robert Williams also gave additional assistance in tracking information on the history of the Fire Zouaves.

FIG. 1. "Charge of the Black Horse Cavalry upon the Fire Zouaves at the Battle of Bull Run," wood engraving in *Harper's Weekly*, August 10, 1861 (https://babel.hathitrust .org/cgi/pt?id=mdp.39015085429630;view=1up;seq=9). *(Courtesy HathiTrust)*

know now, would continue for four long years, with other Union debacles, many much worse, with far greater bloodshed; but in Bull Run's immediate aftermath bitter accusations of cowardice arose, made against this specific unit of soldiers. These were serious charges, alleging that the members of the 11th New York lacked the character of brave and reliable fighters. When one looks back at those allegations as they manifested themselves during the investigation by the Joint Committee on the Conduct of the War, the following question comes into focus: Why did the Fire Zouaves seemingly become one of the Union's very first scapegoats?

The Fire Zouaves

The 11th New York, also known as the First Fire Zouaves, New York Militia, consisted primarily of New York City firemen, enlisting initially as "three months men," but eventually extending their service for the duration of the war. Their commander, Colonel Elmer E. Ellsworth (fig. 2), had created an elite Chicago Zouave unit with colorful uniforms emulating French North

FIG. 2. Colonel Elmer E. Ellsworth. *(Prints and Photographs Division, Library of Congress)*

African troops who toured the country in 1860, impressing crowds with their gymnastic abilities and precision drill. When the war began, Ellsworth chose New York City firemen as his ideal recruits: "I want the New York Firemen," Ellsworth famously declared, "for there are no more effective men in the country, and none with whom I can do so much. They are sleeping on a volcano at Washington and I want men who can go into a fight now."[2]

A history of the unit published in 1889 claimed that every "engine house was turned into a recruiting station. In some cases as many as eighteen and twenty men volunteered out of a single company, and the question was not who were to go, but who were to be so unfortunate as to be left behind. It thus took but a few days to rally the eleven hundred men that pushed onto Annapolis, but it was not the number so much as the extraordinary spirit and dash of its members that characterized this representative regiment." Colonel Ellsworth, using his Washington connections, convinced military authorities to arm and rush his Zouaves to the capital immediately.[3]

This excitement combined with elevated hopes for their success in battle. Historian Bruce Catton once remarked that the Fire Zouaves not only dressed uniquely; there were exceptionally high expectations for their performance in battle. Catton stated: "as firemen its members were supposed to be more than ordinarily brave and indomitable."[4] These Fire Zouaves, with their French Algerian–inspired uniforms and gymnastics-centered training, represented a unique combination of the masculine and the feminine to nineteenth-century Americans. These were firemen after all—undeniably manly and daring—yet they wore dapper uniforms with short trimmed gray coats and denim trousers, scarlet red undershirts, and colorful sashes and firefighter badges. Many also donned fez-styled hats and gaiters.[5] Most were Irish and working class, which challenged the more staid and reserved middle-class Northern masculinity, but this fact only

---

[2]Quoted in Charles A. Ingraham, *Elmer E. Ellsworth and the Zouaves of '61* (Chicago, 1925), p. 127.

[3]http://www.usgennet.org/usa/ny/state/fire/41-50/ch42pt1.html, accessed May 3, 2010.

[4]Bruce Catton, introduction to Leonard Metcalf, "So Eager Were We All," *American Heritage* 16 (June 1965):36–37.

[5]It should be noted that the soldiers of the 11th New York were not wearing the complete Zouave uniform on the day of the battle. The original uniforms they had been provided had faded and worn out, and many refused to wear the standard federal issue. Many mixed and matched, keeping the federal blue trousers, and retaining the fez and their own undershirts when they entered the fray on July 21. See http://www.myrtle-avenue.com/firezou/impression.html, accessed July 5, 2010. At least one source states that the "Zouave drill uniform was too conspicuous for the kind of fighting which was ahead." Thus the New Yorkers wore a variation of the U.S. federal regulation uniform. See Ruth Randall Painter, *Colonel Elmer Ellsworth: A Biography of Lincoln's Friend and First Hero of the Civil War* (Boston, 1960), p. 231. An extended discussion of the specifics of their uniform can be found at http://www.myrtle-avenue.com/firezou/impression.html, accessed July 6, 2010.

heightened their potential for aggressiveness in battle. Surely they would make formidable warriors.[6]

Yet the firemen also had a reputation for rabble-rousing, bravado, and willfulness. Before they even left New York, Ellsworth struggled to instill discipline, and had to request acting Assistant Quartermaster Chester Arthur for support to handle the unruly firemen, even having some individuals arrested. When the Zouaves arrived in Washington, their antics continued. While quartered in the United States Capitol, members held raucous mock sessions and swung from ropes suspended in the unfinished rotunda. Residents of the District of Columbia accused the firemen of deliberately setting fires so they could put them out. A reporter for the *Philadelphia Press* remarked: "They have had two days of extensive, expensive and extreme fight, fun and frolic."[7]

Indeed, letters by Zouaves to New York papers only affirmed their rowdy reputation. In one missive, a Zouave described an evening in May: "Last night the Colonel sent a detachment to the city to pick up stragglers. It seems that about a dozen, tired of being kept in camp, crossed the river in fishing-boats, and were seen in the streets of Washington. Word was immediately sent to the camp, and probably all will be arrested before morning as deserters."[8] In another, a Zouave wrote, "Matters and things jog along quietly in camp, with the exception of sundry growls respecting the quality of the rations delivered to the men. Our men are a peculiar class, and although they are capable of and will endure all the necessary privations and hardships that any men on earth will or can, they are intelligent enough to perceive when and where a screw is loose, and will not quietly submit to be imposed upon in the most trifling degree. Hence the grumbling in regard to the provisions."[9]

There were also stinging accusations that the firemen were deliberately setting Washington houses and fences ablaze so that they could show off their fire-dousing skills. At one point, their unruliness led to a direct reprimand

[6]Kristie Ross refers to Zouaves as "gender neutral" in her essay, "Arranging a Doll's House: Refined Women as Union Nurses," in Catherine Clinton and Nina Silber, eds., *Divided Houses: Gender and the Civil War* (New York, 1992), pp. 105–6. The best discussions exploring competing notions of manhood during the nineteenth century include Gail Bederman, *Manliness and Civilization: A Cultural History of Gender and Race in the United States, 1880–1917* (Chicago, 1995), and Amy Greenberg, *Manifest Manhood and the Antebellum American Empire* (Cambridge, U.K., 2005).

[7]Quoted in Ingraham, *Elmer E. Ellsworth*, p. 135. See also p. 134.

[8]Letter to the editor, *New York Leader*, May 17, 1861 (http://dmna.state.ny.us/ . . . /infantry/11thInfReg.htm, accessed May 3, 2010).

[9]http://dmna.state.ny.us/ . . . /infantry/11thInfReg.htm, accessed May 3, 2010.

from General Joseph K. Mansfield, commander of the Department of Washington, who wrote Colonel Ellsworth that he was "entitled to fuel," but that he would have to be "careful not to burn fences, as some have already been burnt."[10] Ellsworth, though, convinced that it was just a handful of rowdies besmirching the reputation of his Zouaves, refused to "take seriously the insubordinations of his men."[11] The colonel paid the costs of the damage out of his own pocket, and punished a handful of men from the ranks.[12] Writing his fiancée Carrie Spafford that spring, Ellsworth affirmed: "All are well—Stories you hear about regiment are all false."[13]

Ellsworth was determined to prove his detractors wrong. When the 11th New York was formally mustered into service on May 7 in Washington, D.C., they lined up in front of a large crowd, with President Lincoln, his son Tad, and other military and political officials in attendance. Colonel Ellsworth publicly vowed, in the words of his biographer, that he would "disgrace the men of the regiment who brought obloquy upon the command and upon the New York Fire Department."[14]

Just a few weeks later, the regiment was hit with unexpected tragedy. Their beloved Colonel Ellsworth was shot and killed on May 24, 1861, during the Union's occupation of Alexandria, Virginia. The Union had one of its earliest martyrs, and the Fire Zouaves gained even greater public attention. Lincoln was especially shaken by young Ellsworth's death. According to one account, "The President burst into tears at the news of the Union's first war casualty. 'Excuse me but I cannot talk. I will make no apology, gentlemen, for my weakness but I knew Ellsworth well, and held him in great regard,'" said the president to a senator who interrupted his grief. Mary's cousin, Elizabeth Grimsley, wrote her family that Ellsworth "was a great pet in the family and Mr. Lincoln feels it very much."[15]

All of these events preceded the Battle of Bull Run on July 21, 1861: the Fire Zouaves' dramatic beginnings in New York City, stinging accusations

---

[10]Joseph K. Mansfield to Elmer Ellsworth, May 9, 1861, quoted in Ingraham, *Elmer E. Ellsworth*, p. 136.

[11]Ibid. In one letter Ellsworth wrote Spafford, "We have sent back but 6—and the men do well." Quoted in Painter, *Colonel Elmer Ellsworth*, p. 239.

[12]Ingraham, *Elmer E. Ellsworth*, p. 136.

[13]Elmer E. Ellsworth to Carrie M. Spafford, [May 1861], quoted in ibid., p. 140.

[14]Ibid., p. 136.

[15]http://www.mrlincolnswhitehouse.org/inside.asp?ID=39&subjectID=2, accessed May 3, 2010. Thus, the implication was that 11th New York was Lincoln's "pet regiment."

of unruliness in Washington, D.C., and the loss of their much-loved commander in Alexandria. The 11th New York, like every other green regiment that hot July Sunday, faced the daunting test of whether they would exhibit "cool courage" in combat.[16] A reporter observed an officer addressing the regiment as they prepared to leave for Washington, who declared that "no one doubted their bravery." However, "many feared about their order and discipline, and they must show now that they could be as good soldiers as they were brave men. The Zouaves "cheered their reply."[17]

The First Battle of Bull Run

In the early morning hours of July 21, Union troops commanded by General Irvin McDowell collided with Confederate troops led by Confederate General P. G. T. Beauregard near Manassas Junction, some twenty-five miles southwest of Washington. Until 3 P.M., it appeared that the battle would prove a decisive Union victory. McDowell's troops managed to press the rebels and take essential positions on high ground, but after a bold stand by Southern General Thomas J. Jackson, and a lull in the fighting, fresh Confederate reinforcements arrived to shift the entire momentum of battle.

The 11th New York had been up since midnight, marching and exhausted, and in the afternoon was ordered to support artillery at Henry House Hill.[18] Private Leonard Metcalf of the 11th New York later recalled those fateful moments. He heard someone declare: "Come on boys and show them what New York can do!" "And with that," he stated, "the pet lambs were led to the slaughter." The Zouaves were "crashing through the cornfield, singing and whistling around our ears, making the air blue and sulphurous with smoke, came a storm of bullets upon us from the woods in front." Colonel Farnham shouted at them to get down, just in time to escape the second volley of bullets. No more orders came down the line, but soldiers rose to fire and then lay

---

[16]Gerald Linderman, *Embattled Courage: The Experience of Combat in the American Civil War* (New York, 1987), p. 76.

[17]*New York Times*, May 3, 1861.

[18]The 11th New York was part of Colonel Samuel P. Heintzelman's 3rd Division and Colonel Orlando B. Willcox's 2nd Brigade.

down to reload. Metcalf wrote: "Some started toward the woods on their own account, crawling slowly along in hopes to get sight of the foe."[19]

By all accounts, those moments on Henry House Hill were brutally chaotic, and eventually the regiment did break, with men fleeing, some milling about as the fight raged, and still others continuing to fight in small groups, and fighting courageously. Screams of "Remember Ellsworth" and "Avenge Ellsworth" were heard through the din. A few sources do attest to the fact that the regiment, or at least parts of it, joined with other soldiers and tried to regain the hill several times, but were beaten back by the tenacious Confederates. When the Fire Zouaves finally took stock of their casualties for the day, they were stunningly high. Numbers vary, but the *Official Records* lists forty-eight killed, seventy-five wounded, sixty-five missing or captured: 188 total. Many of the captured were imprisoned in Castle Pinckney in Charleston Harbor (fig. 3).[20]

Early published reports, both written and illustrated, stressed their tragic losses. Journalist Henry J. Raymond described the retreat after having left the field of battle to send off a dispatch. He suddenly encountered the Fire Zouaves' quartermaster, "who told me, bursting into tears, that his Regiment had been utterly cut to pieces, that the Colonel and Lieutenant-Colonel were both killed, and that our troops had actually been repulsed. I still tried to proceed, but the advancing columns rendered it impossible, and I turned about. Leaving my carriage, I went to a high point of ground and saw, by the dense cloud of dust which rose over each of the three roads by which the three columns of the army had advanced, that they were all on the retreat."[21] Seven days later the dramatic print showing the attack of the Confederate "black horse cavalry" smashing the 11th New York's ranks appeared in the same publication.[22] The firsthand descriptions by two Zouaves published alongside the illustration, however, stressed their tenacious belligerence in the face of the Confederate cavalrymen's attack. One of the soldiers professed: "No quarter, no halting, no flinching now, marked the rapid and death-dealing blows of our men as they closed in upon the

[19]Metcalf, "So Eager Were We All," pp. 36–37.

[20]*The War of the Rebellion: A Compilation of the Official Records of the Union and Confederate Armies*, 69 vols. (Washington, D.C., 1880–1900), ser. 1, vol. 2, p. 405 (hereafter *O.R.*).

[21]*Harper's Weekly*, Aug. 3, 1861. Raymond was a reporter for the *New York Times*.

[22]*Harper's Weekly*, Aug. 10, 1861.

FIG. 3. Captured Fire Zouaves from the battle of Bull Run imprisoned at Castle Pinckney, Charleston Harbor. *(Prints and Photographs Division, Library of Congress)*

foe, in their madness and desperation. Our brave fellows fell, the ranks filled up, the sabers, bowie-knives, and bayonets glistened in the sunlight, horse after horse went down, platoon after platoon disappeared—the rattle of musketry, the screams of the rebels, the shout of 'Remember Ellsworth!'"[23] Yet there was no denying the heavy toll they endured. A report from the *New York Times* stated: "I will mention here that the Fire Zouaves fought like tigers and were fearfully cut up."[24]

---

[23]Quoted in ibid.

[24]*New York Times,* July 23, 1861. The paper further stated: "Our men fought with determined vigor, and accomplished results worthy of veterans. The Seventy-first, the Zouaves, the Sixty-ninth, and the Fourteenth Militia, are most frequently mentioned as among the New-York regiments that most resolutely contested the field." In another account published the next day: "Later in the evening, however, we learned that the War Department had received dispatches announcing that three of the rebel batteries were taken, and that the New-York Firemen Zouaves, the Sixty-ninth, the Seventy-ninth and Thirteenth Regiments had shown in the attacks of these batteries as much entrain as French soldiers" (*New York Times,* July 24, 1861).

The Joint Committee on the Conduct of War

These published accounts delineate the broken and beaten ranks of the once-proud Fire Zouaves. But it would be behind closed doors without a single member of the unit present where serious charges of cowardice arose, directed against the 11th New York. These allegations came about during the proceedings of the Joint Committee on the Conduct of War (CCW).

In the aftermath of Bull Run, the humiliating federal defeat at Ball's Bluff in October (which resulted in the death of Colonel Edward Baker, a U.S. senator), and the Union loss at Wilson's Creek in Missouri in August, Congress created the Joint Committee on the Conduct of War in December 1861. Its members included Senators Ben Wade (R-Ohio), Zachariah Chandler (R-Mich.), Andrew Johnson (D-Tenn.), and Representatives John Covode (R-Penn.), George Washington Julian (R-Ind.), Daniel Gooch (R-Mass.), and Moses F. Odell (D-N.Y.). Senator Wade, a noted Radical Republican, was named chairman. Proceedings were conducted in secret in the Committee on Territories room in the Capitol basement.[25]

The committee's role was largely investigative; it had no real power to legislate, yet it remained in existence throughout the conflict, making recommendations and issuing its judgments on federal military operations.[26] To this day, the CCW's existence and influence remain controversial. Several articles and an entire book have been written on the CCW, discussing the bitter tensions between political and military officials. Brian Holden Reid concluded, "The Joint Committee was a significant example of Congress asserting its authority in wartime."[27] Reid observed: "It is now considered to have had little power of any substance, although it could make a nuisance of itself by searching for scapegoats."[28] In addition, the committee has traditionally been seen as the "thorn in Lincoln's side."[29]

Most recently, historian Bruce Tap criticized the CCW for its sham of bipartisanship, its biased views on war and against West Point commanders,

[25]Bruce Tap, *Over Lincoln's Shoulder: The Committee on the Conduct of the War* (Lawrence, Kans., 1998), p. 35.

[26]Ibid., p. 34.

[27]Brian Holden Reid, "Historians and the Joint Committee on the Conduct of the War," *Civil War History* 38 (1992):335.

[28]Ibid., p. 337.

[29]Quoted in ibid., p. 340.

and its ham-fisted attempts at interfering with military planning. Tap further condemned members of the committee for their "simplistic, amateurish, and unrealistic views on warfare." He wrote: "Echoing popular misconceptions, they believed the South could be defeated in a single battle."[30] Tap asserted: "In many respects, the committee's view on military affairs reflected popular prejudices against an educated, professional soldiery. The idea that high morale or 'determination itself' would be sufficient to produce military victory prevailed. The popular view that courage and moral purity would suffice for training and discipline was much to the committee's liking."[31] The committee members, all civilians of course, certainly represented societal expectations not just of the war, but also the cultural mores of the time and place. They were not professional soldiers, but neither were the majority of volunteers in the ranks.

The CCW began taking sworn testimony from battle participants in late December 1861 and continued into the summer of 1862. Referring to the defeat as the "disaster at Bull Run," congressmen questioned officers about what went wrong for the Union Army that fateful day. More than thirty-five witnesses, including Generals Irvin McDowell and Robert Patterson, as well as division and brigade commanders—all commissioned officers and no enlisted men—recounted their memories. The committee was keen to understand why the Union army fought at all on Sunday when Beauregard clearly had been reinforced by Johnston. They were not interested in "particulars" and frequently urged military witnesses to simply summarize. Several of the officers also remarked on the toll the heavy marching had taken on the green troops.[32] The question asked repeatedly of witnesses was: "To what do you attribute the disaster to our army in that battle?"[33] The congressmen did not want extended details, but they did want their witnesses to answer as "military men."[34]

---

[30]Tap, *Over Lincoln's Shoulder*, p. 45.

[31]Ibid., pp. 44–45.

[32]*Report of the Joint Committee on the Conduct of the War in Three Parts* (Washington, D.C, 1863), p. 63 (hereafter *CCW*).

[33]Ibid., p. 160.

[34]Congressmen repeatedly qualified their questions with this phrase. For example, Congressman Moses Odell asked Colonel David Birney of the 23rd Pennsylvania: "Do you think as a military man that Johnston could have been held or fought better from Bunker Hill than from Charlestown?" See ibid., p. 168. In another example,

In the congressional investigations, the bipartisan committee became especially focused on two factors: General Robert Patterson's apparent failure to prevent Joseph E. Johnston from slipping away from the Shenandoah Valley to reinforce Beauregard and McDowell's decision to fight on Sunday despite delays in getting his men into place.[35]

In their responses, officers repeatedly affirmed the "rawness" of the troops, and their undisciplined condition, their fatigue from marching, and their tiredness the day of the battle. Some remarked that the men were not properly supplied.[36] Commanders also noted that many volunteers were "three month men" whose enlistments were about to expire.[37] Several asserted the difficulties of maneuvering large numbers of untrained men, or blamed the lack of reinforcements. Certainly, some indirectly or directly censured Generals McDowell and Patterson for failures in the planning or execution of the campaign.

General McDowell himself stressed the greenness of his troops and the difficulties of maneuver that prevented him from executing his plans: "There was not a man there," McDowell declared, "who had ever maneuvered troops in large bodies. There was not one in the army; I did not believe there was one in the whole country; at least, I knew there was no one then who had ever handled 30,000 troops. I had seen them handled abroad in reviews and marches, but I had never handled that number, and no one here had. I wanted very much a little time; all of us wanted it. We did not have a bit of it." Lincoln's famed response to McDowell even before the battle began was,

---

Republican senator and chair of the committee Ben Wade asked Colonel R. Butler Price, who at the time of the battle was a major and an aide to General Patterson, "Do you suppose, as a military man—I ask your opinion as a military man—that General Scott could fix, beyond a doubt, upon a day when he could attack the enemy with such an army, the two being so far apart? Could he fix with certainty that he would fight on a particular day?" (ibid., p. 187). Wade continued to use this phrase in his questioning of Price.

[35]Montgomery Meigs was the final witness, recalled on July 14, 1862, to discuss the question of troop supplies. The committee was investigating the Battle of Ball's Bluff at the same time.

[36]Colonel Davies, of the 16th New York, implied that McDowell had not instilled enough discipline in the troops leading up to the battle. He stated in his testimony generally of the soldiers: "But they had been loafing around a great deal; had been out a great deal of nights, and had been broken of their rest, and had not had full rations. They were not altogether in a prime condition for fighting." See *CCW*, p. 182.

[37]For example, General Samuel P. Heintzelman gave this reason during his testimony. See ibid., p. 32.

"You are green, it is true; but they are green, also; you are all green alike." The general explained to the committee that his plan was simple, marching his troops forward in four lines; but knowing communication would be difficult, if not impossible, given the terrain, he had expected that each column would be strong enough to "hold its own."[38]

In their discussion of the federal rout on Sunday afternoon, several military commanders pointed to the exhaustion of the troops, their inexperience, and their unfamiliarity with military commands. But very few officers blamed outright cowardice as the cause. The response of Colonel Thomas A. Davies of the 16th New York Volunteers was typical. When Chairman Wade asked Davies, "What led to the final defeat, as near as you could ascertain on the ground?" Davies responded, "I can tell you what I think is the cause of the whole defeat of that day. The troops were raw; the men had been accustomed to look to their colonels as the only men to give them commands. They had never been taught the succession of officers, which is necessary to understand upon the battle-field. They did not understand the command devolving in succession upon the colonel, lieutenant colonel, major, and the captains, in their order of rank. The officers did not themselves know what to do; they were themselves raw and green." Davies continued, explaining that when a colonel was killed or wounded, neither the subordinate officers nor the men in the ranks knew what to do, so they often fled the field. It was not abject cowardice, the colonel reasoned, "or fear of fighting, but because, having lost their colonels, they supposed they were out of the battle. I consider that the great cause of our army being put in rout on the right wing."[39]

Indeed, Brigadier General Daniel Tyler, who was second in command to McDowell during the battle, also discussed the poor preparation of the troops, which he believed led to the "disaster." He told the committee: "The first great trouble was the want of discipline and instruction in the troops. The troops needed that regimental and brigade instruction which would have enabled them to act together in masses with advantage." "There was," Tyler insisted, "a great want of instruction and professional knowledge among the officers—the company and regimental officers."[40]

---

[38]Ibid., p 38.

[39]Ibid., p. 181.

[40]Ibid., p. 198. Tyler was being questioned by Chairman Wade.

The CCW and the Zouaves

As the days of testimony lengthened, however, the congressmen and officers appeared to grow more focused on a specific moment in the sloping field near the Henry House around 2:30 P.M. General McDowell had ordered Captain James B. Ricketts's Company I, 1st U.S. Artillery, and Captain Charles Griffin's Battery D, 5th U. S. Artillery, to advance forward to Henry House Hill, and the cannoneers subsequently came under heavy fire. To provide infantry support, the chief of artillery, Major William Barry, ordered into action the 11th New York along with the 1st Minnesota, the 14th Brooklyn, and a battalion of marines. But it was the actions and "character" of the 11th New York at this particular moment of the battle that seemed to attract considerable attention from the witnesses and their questioners during these proceedings.

It was during the testimony of General Samuel P. Heintzelman that the performance of the Zouaves first seemed to come under scrutiny. Heintzelman, a West Pointer with experience in the Mexican and Seminole Wars, commanded their division at Bull Run and personally accompanied the Zouaves in their movement to support the artillery position. He testified on December 24, 1861: "I went up, after the zouaves arrived, on the right of the batteries with them. As I rose to cross the ridge, I saw beyond a line of the enemy drawn up at a shoulder-arms, dressed in citizen's clothes. It did not strike me at first who they were. But I just checked my horse and looked at them. I saw in an instant that they were a party of the enemy's troops, and I turned to the zouaves and ordered them to charge them." In response, the New Yorkers moved up "some 20 paces and they fired, and both parties broke and run. Just at this moment some 30 or 40 of the enemy's cavalry came out through an old field and charged the rear of the zouaves. The zouaves turned upon them and emptied some five or six saddles, and the cavalry broke and run."[41] When asked if the unit later rallied, Heintzelman observed, "Not as a regiment. Many of the officers and men joined other regiments, or fought on their own hook."[42]

Major Barry, promoted to general by the time of the hearings, was also sharply critical of the 11th New York during his testimony on January 7, 1862.

---

[41]Ibid., p. 30.

[42]Ibid., p. 31. Heintzelman was being questioned by Senator Chandler.

When asked by Congressman Gooch what "condition" the Fire Zouaves were in at the time he had ordered them to assist the artillery batteries, Barry responded that he perceived them to be "an efficient regiment." "I thought so," he explained. But he admitted that he "knew very little of them, except by newspaper reports. I knew what New York firemen were, and I supposed there was fight and pluck in them. I was struck with the manner they marched forward, very handsomely in line of battle. I rode with the major of the regiment—now colonel of the regiment. They marched up very handsomely in line of battle, passed the various obstacles they met in the usual tactical manner. I thought they did very well, and was very much disappointed and surprised when they broke."[43] Overall, Barry told the committee that he believed the main cause for the military failure that day was "the uninstructed state of our troops. The troops were raw; many of the officers were indolent, and they did not all behave themselves as they should have done on that day. I think that was one cause. All troops are liable to panics. But the great fault I found with our men was that after they had fallen back some distance, and were out of the enemy's fire, they could not be rallied. I look upon that as a difficulty inseparable from green troops. And in rallying men we need the assistance of the regimental and company officers very much, and that assistance was not rendered in many cases."[44]

But it was in the testimony of Captain Charles Griffin and General Andrew Porter that the attacks on the Fire Zouaves became most negative. Captain Griffin testified on January 14, 1862. Griffin, who commanded Battery D, 5th U.S. Regular Artillery, carefully recounted the situation on the afternoon of July 21 on Henry House Hill. Major Barry, Griffin was assured, would support his battery when it was ordered to advance. However, as the Confederates turned to fire on the position, the Zouaves faltered and failed. Griffin initially attributed the unit's collapse to several factors: the numbers of recently reinforced enemy they faced, duplicity by the Confederates, a general "disorganized state," and pure exhaustion.[45]

Later in his testimony, when questioned by Chairman Wade, Griffin grew more critical and singled out the 11th New York. Chairman Wade stated: "You attribute the disaster in that part of the field where you were

[43]Ibid., p. 143.

[44]Ibid., pp. 142–43.

[45]Ibid., p. 171 ("disorganized state").

principally to a mistake in the place where you were to be posted, to having no support of infantry, and to a mistake as to the character of the regiment that appeared there?" Griffin responded that he thought they should have chosen a different location and that Ricketts's battery ought not to have been moved. Wade pressed him further: "Suppose you had been supported, what would then have been the consequence?" Griffin was unequivocal: "If we had been properly supported, we would not have lost our batteries." But Wade wanted to know if the guns could have been saved if supported by the Zouaves. "Five hundred men," Griffin reasoned, "are not enough to support eleven pieces of artillery. The Zouaves could not have supported us. They were not support enough. Five hundred men are not enough to support eleven pieces of artillery."[46] In this exchange, the point of contention was clearly not *who* was ordered to support the artillery battery but how many.

Yet in later questioning by New York Democratic Congressman Moses Odell, the captain grew more accusatory. Odell asked Griffin about a conversation he and Major Barry had had "in reference to the character of the regiment that came out in front of you." Griffin was confident of what he said, and that he spoken directly to Barry, close enough for him to hear it: "There could be no mistake about it," the captain told the committee, "because we had two or three conversations in reference to the support—in reference to the Zouaves more immediately. When I countermarched my pieces, after they had turned off, and moved up on the hill, my last words were, 'These Zouaves will never support us.'" Odell asked why Griffin thought such a thing. And Griffin's response was devastating: "I had seen them on the field in a state of disorganization, and I did not think they had the moral courage to fight. I do not think that any troops that will go through the country in a disorganized state, thieving and robbing, are brave men. They were all running around the field in any way. They were in no kind of order. We got them collected together in some kind of order when we moved on the hill; but before that they were in no kind of order. At least, that is my recollection of it." Chairman Wade proposed, "You do not believe in the maxim, 'The worse the man the better the soldier'?" The Captain answered: "No, sir; I do not. I believe in the maxim that he who is universally cruel to a fallen foe is a coward."[47]

---

[46]Ibid., p. 170.

[47]Ibid., p. 174.

Similarly, during his testimony on January 21, 1862, General Andrew Porter, commanding the 1st Brigade of the 2nd Division, made a point of noting that even though some units initially broke, they then rallied and performed well. He singled out the 14th Brooklyn: "The volunteer regiments were constantly breaking. They would break, and then we would rally two or three regiments and bring them up again. The New York 14th (Brooklyn) that behaved so well was broken nearly all to pieces at the first fire. But they rallied again and went up with Griffin's battery, and stood their ground remarkably well."[48] He did not say anything positive, however, about the 11th New York. Porter blamed the officers and the arrival of Confederate reinforcements, and not the men in the federal ranks for failing that Sunday afternoon: "Our troops could not stand the attacking of the enemy; they were played out quite early. The men were exhausted—somehow or other they seemed to have no heart in the matter. The officers were more to blame than the men."[49] But when asked directly, "Do you consider that Griffin's battery had sufficient support at that time?" Porter responded, "The troops were not at all reliable. If they had been reliable, and could have been kept up to their work, I should think there was sufficient support."[50]

Indeed, Griffin's and Porter's allegations were affirmed on January 28, 1862, by Lieutenant Horatio Reed of Griffin's battery. When asked by Republican Congressman Gooch, "Did the panic on the field commence immediately after the capture of those batteries?" Reed answered almost matter-of-factly, "Well, sir, the Ellsworth zouaves were ordered to support us, but they ran away before that."[51]

Colonel William W. Averell (who was Porter's assistant adjutant general at the battle) blasted the Zouaves, but also the marines, stating on January 28: "Their officers were standing behind them keeping them in ranks; but the destruction of the battery was so complete that the marines and zouaves seemed to be struck with such astonishment, such consternation, that they could not do anything. There were probably 100 muskets fired from the zouaves and marines—not over that; and they, of course, fired too high. They were below the battery, and where the battery was we could not see more than half of the bodies of the rebels, and what they did fire was

[48]Ibid., p. 210.
[49]Ibid., p. 211.
[50]Ibid.
[51]Ibid.

ineffective. They began to break and run down the hill, and nothing could stop them, and then the enemy rushed right over there like a lowering cloud—right over the hill."[52] Averell pointed to this moment as the "turning point of the affair" and the "start of the panic."[53]

Several weeks went by, and General James B. Ricketts (who was an artillery captain at the time of the battle) appeared for questioning on April 3, 1862. Again, the committee returned to the moment on Henry House Hill and the issue of support for the artillery. Chairman Wade asked Ricketts whether there was adequate infantry to sustain his artillery battery. Ricketts responded bluntly: "At that time I knew of no support. I was told a support was ordered. One regiment, the Fire Zouaves, I know came up to support me, and, when I saw them in confusion, I rode up to them and said something cheering to them. I had not much time to speak to them, but I thought I would say a little something cheering to them, as it might have some effect upon them."[54] Congressman George Julian then returned to this: "What kind of support did you receive from the Fire Zouaves?" Ricketts answered: "Well, sir, these Fire Zouaves came up to the ground, but they soon got into confusion and left."

But Democrat Odell sought more; he asked whether their failure was due to "want of proper directions from their officers. Ricketts was careful in his answer: "I should judge, from the manner in which the men stood there, and from their not being properly in line, that it was from want of officers; either that their officers were ignorant of their duty at that time, or that they were not there. I cannot say how that was." "Our men really behaved very gallantly," Ricketts assured the congressmen, "up to a certain time."[55]

But Ricketts's and the other commanders' words had already done their damage. At first the implication seemed to be that green officers and men and insufficient troops were to blame for the Union setback at Henry House Hill, which proved a tactical turning point in the daylong battle. Yet, in

[52]Ibid., p. 216.

[53]Ibid. Historian John Hennessy writes: "Years later historians would point to the 33d Virginia's capture of Griffin's two guns as the turning point of the battle, and indeed it was. But that was hardly apparent to Colonel Cummings, General Jackson or anyone else on July 21." See John Hennessy, *The First Battle of Manassas: An End to Innocence, July 18–21, 1861* (Lynchburg, Va., 1989), p. 86.

[54]*CCW*, p. 243.

[55]Ibid., p. 246.

follow-up questions, almost every officer returned to pointing the finger at the "character" and reliability of one specific regiment: the 11th New York.

Nonetheless, by several of these very same officers' own admission, the Fire Zouaves were not the only soldiers to falter in the battle. In fact, the 1st Minnesota also broke during those fateful moments on Henry House Hill, as did a battalion of marines. The fight on the hill shifted hands at least four times before the Confederates finally claimed victory, and several units fell back, including Confederates. Yet it was the Fire Zouaves who were singled out during the congressional hearings and harshly blamed by commanding officers.[56] And even though remnants of the unit regrouped and continued to fight, even valiantly, this was hardly mentioned.

The military reports filed by the same officers do not offer anything dramatically contradictory in their assessment of the 11th New York's poor performance. These reports, often written just days after the battle, allow us to consider how officers were beginning to make sense of the defeat in its immediate aftermath. And we can see whether their leaders had somehow been coaxed or prodded by the questioning of the congressmen.

Major William F. Barry, chief of artillery, wrote his just two days after Bull Run: "The zouaves, catching sight of the cavalry a few moments before they were upon them, broke ranks to such a degree that the cavalry dashed through without doing them much harm. The zouaves gave them a scattering fire as they passed, which emptied five saddles and killed three horses." He added: "The Eleventh and Fourteenth Regiments instantly broke and fled in confusion to the rear, and in spite of the repeated and earnest efforts of Colonel Heintzelman with the latter, and myself with the former, refused to rally and return to the support of the batteries."[57]

General Andrew Porter's report, dated July 25, 1861, stated: "The evanescent courage of the zouaves prompted them to fire perhaps a hundred shots, when they broke and fled, leaving the batteries open to a charge of the enemy's cavalry, which took place immediately." He added: "All further efforts were futile; the words, gestures, and threats of our officers were thrown away upon men who had lost all presence of mind and only longed for absence of body. Some of our noblest and best officers lost their lives in

[56]For a description of both the 1st Minnesota's and 11th New York's performance that day, see Hennessy, *First Battle of Manassas*, pp. 82–83.

[57]Report of Major William F. Barry, Fifth U.S. Artillery, Chief of Artillery, July 23, 1861, *O.R.*, ser. 1, vol. 2, p. 347.

trying to rally them." But he went on to note the courageous performance of other units including the 27th, 38th, and 69th New York. He also stated that the marines and 14th New York Militia, though broken, rallied and made a stand. He made no such mention of the Zouaves.[58]

General Samuel Heintzelman's report too, written on July 31, was just as highly critical of the green troops' performance: "Such a rout I never witnessed before. No efforts could induce a single regiment to form after the retreat was commenced. Our artillery was served admirably, and did much execution. Some of the volunteer regiments behaved very well, and much excuse can be made for those who fled, as few of the enemy could at any time be seen. Raw troops cannot be expected to stand long against an unseen enemy." But about the Zouaves, he noted, he could not say very much as he had no real accounting: "I have been unable to obtain any report from the zouaves, as Colonel Farnham was wounded, and is sick in the hospital. I have only the list of the killed and wounded. Since the retreat more than three-fourths of the zouaves have disappeared."[59]

General Orlando Willcox, the brigade commander, though wounded and then captured on the field, did not file a report until September 1862, long after the committee had completed its interviews. In his opinion, Willcox commented that the Zouaves, "though broken as a regiment," did "good service, under my own eyes, in the woods, and detachments of them joined other regiments in the fight."[60]

Aftermath

The regiment would never recover its strength or its reputation. Zouaves returned home to New York, with or without authorization. In August 1861, some three hundred members of the unit met in New York City to air

[58]Report of Col. Andrew Porter, Sixteenth U. S. Infantry, Commanding 2nd Division, 1st Brigade, July 25, 1861, ibid., p. 385.

[59]Report of Gen. Samuel P. Heintzelman, Seventeenth U. S. Infantry, commanding Third Division. HDQRS. 3rd Div. Dept. Northeastern Virginia, Washington, July 31, 1861. See ibid., p. 404. Heintzelman was an 1826 West Point graduate with experience in the Seminole Wars and Mexican-American War. Colonel Farnham would die in August 1861.

[60]O. B. Willcox, brigadier general, late colonel 1st Michigan Infantry, to Brigadier General L. Thomas, adjutant-general, U.S. Army, Sept. 3, 1862. Ibid., p. 409. Willcox did not testify before the committee.

their grievances. A *New York Times* article entitled "Return of the Fire Zouaves; Meeting of the Discontented Statement of Grievances," listed their complaints: "That, to sum up all, the regiment has been treated with bad faith; fed to the dogs; deprived of the credit of what they did on the field of battle; stigmatized as deserters for doing as their officers told them, and kept out of their pay for an unreasonable length of time." The Zouaves complained of the extension of their service from three months to the war's duration, of the change in treatment after Ellsworth died, the loss of their distinctive Zouave uniforms and style of drill, and lack of pay, promised arms, and adequate food. The article further stated that the men were also upset by negative statements made against them by Colonel Heintzelman "as to the conduct of the regiment on the field of battle." The Zouaves deemed them to be "grossly incorrect."[61]

There were attempts to refill the ranks with new recruits, but this largely failed. The 11th New York served in the Department of Virginia, witness to the famous naval battle at Hampton Roads, but was formally mustered out of service on June 2, 1862, almost an entire year before the CCW issued its final report and published the damning testimony against the regiment.

So the question remains: Why? Why was the 11th New York singled out for its "character" and alleged cowardly behavior during these proceedings where congressmen first began to challenge the decisions and plans of military leaders. Why dwell on the performance of a single unit? And why did the officers, who initially began to complain about the regiment in their military reports, allow such allegations to spill out months later in front of members of Congress, when the 11th New York was far removed from active campaigning?

At a present-day reenactment website devoted to the unit, the web surfer will read: "The battle of Bull Run was a cataclysmic disaster for the Union army, and a dismayed public was looking for people to blame. In this flurry of criticism, the Fire Zouaves did not escape freely. Accusations of cowardice and poor leadership were leveled at the regiment, some commanders

[61] *New York Times*, Aug. 15, 1861. The paper reported that the Zouaves claimed "That they took from fifty to sixty pistols of the Black Horse Cavalry, which they have now, and killed and wounded many of them having M.V.G., supposed to stand for 'Mount Vernon Guards,' on their hats." And further: "That the Ricketts Battery was not deserted by the Zouaves, but was disabled only because the horses and gunners were killed. That the Zouaves did actually bring off several of the guns."

going so far as to say they ran after firing only one volley. As far as can be determined, the blame for the Union rout does not rest squarely on anyone's shoulders. Many conspicuous acts of valor were performed that day, particularly among the 11th New York, but the regiment was not the proud organization it once was [afterward]."[62]

Perhaps it is true that these Fire Zouaves, with their boasting, well-connected colonel, and raucous behavior, were destined for a harsh lesson in the realities of war. But we also know that many other units similarly disappointed that day.

There may also be some subtle political tension behind the CCW proceedings and their focus on the 11th New York. Although it is clear from the *O.R.* that many of these commanders had not dramatically changed their views of the Zouaves' performance at Bull Run, the congressmen may have permitted the 11th New York to emerge as the sole unit of soldiers singled out during the proceedings for political purposes. This, after all, was a unit associated, at least initially through their slain colonel, with Lincoln, who by the time of the proceedings, December 1861–July 1862, was increasingly under fire from both Radical Republicans and Democrats for his handling of the war. And these were Irish immigrants. Could it be that some of the frustrations voiced against them was also part of broader cultural anxieties about immigration and class? After all, the men participating in the congressional proceedings were powerful military and political players, still unsure what this war meant to the future of American society.

We do not know for sure. We do know that the no one from the Fire Zouaves was there during the CCW proceedings to defend them: no one from their ranks, and not one of their officers. Instead, in a bitter and ironic twist, there was no one to support *them* when they were accused by officers of shameful cowardice before a rapt audience of politicians.

---

[62]From http://www.myrtle-avenue.com/firezou/impression.html, accessed May 3, 2010.

Paul Finkelman

The Summer of '62

Congress, Slavery, and a Revolution in Federal Law

SECESSION AND THE war that followed were about slavery and race. At the time everyone, North and South, knew this. Lincoln would later recall that at the beginning of the war, "One-eighth of the whole population were colored slaves, not distributed generally over the Union, but localized in the southern part of it. These slaves constituted a peculiar and powerful interest. All knew that this interest was somehow the cause of the war. To strengthen, perpetuate, and extend this interest was the object for which the insurgents would rend the Union even by war, while the Government claimed no right to do more than to restrict the territorial enlargement of it."[1] Lincoln had hardly taken office when Alexander Stephens, the Confederate vice president, made this point, although with an emphasis on racial theory and proslavery ideology: "Our new [Confederate] government is founded . . . its foundations are laid, its corner-stone rests, upon the great truth that the negro is not equal to the white man; that slavery—subordination to the superior race—is his natural and normal condition. This, our new government, is the first, in the history of the world, based upon this great physical, philosophical, and moral truth."[2]

---

[1]Abraham Lincoln, "Second Inaugural Address," in Roy P. Basler, ed., *The Collected Works of Abraham Lincoln*, 9 vols. (New Brunswick, N.J., 1953–55), 8:332–33 (hereafter *Collected Works*).

[2]Alexander Stephens, "The Cornerstone Speech," Mar. 21, 1861, in Henry Cleveland, *Alexander H. Stephens, in Public and Private: With Letters and Speeches, before, during, and since the War* (Philadelphia, 1886), pp. 717–29 (http://www.TeachingAmericanHistory.org/library/index.asp?documentprint=76).

Facing the secession of seven states and the possibility of war when he entered the White House, Lincoln asserted that his only goal was to preserve the Union and publicly disavowed harming slavery in the South. Lincoln maintained this position when the war began after the fall of Fort Sumter on April 13; however, within four months both Congress and the Lincoln administration began to accept that slavery and race caused secession and the war. In the next year, both Congress and the president would dismantle slavery and initiate a revolution in race relations. As this chapter demonstrates, the key moment in this transition would be the summer of 1862, when Congress vigorously attacked slavery and substantially altered race relations. The burst of antislavery and egalitarian activity in the summer of '62 culminated with Lincoln issuing the Preliminary Emancipation Proclamation on September 22, just as fall was beginning.

When he entered the White House in March 1861, and six weeks later when the war began, President Lincoln was determined not to make the conflict about slavery or race. Lincoln's primary focus was to preserve the nation and bring the seceding states back into the Union. Because he knew slavery was the cause of secession, in his first inaugural Lincoln promised to do nothing to harm slavery where it existed. He hoped this policy would lead the states of the Deep South to reconsider their position and return to their proper place in the Union. In addition to this political reason, Lincoln also believed this was the constitutionally proper position. In his inaugural address he asserted, "I have no purpose, directly or indirectly, to interfere with the institution of slavery in the States where it exists. I believe I have no lawful right to do so, and I have no inclination to do so."[3] Presumably, neither did Congress. In the first few months of the war the president made no overt moves against slavery. Congress, which was not in session, naturally did not move against slavery.

From the beginning of the war the administration faced mounting pressure to take a different approach that connected four issues: to acknowledge that the war *was* about slavery, to move toward emancipation, to alter the racial status quo, and to allow blacks to serve in the army. However the war had hardly begun when events overtook policy and forced the administration to take a position on slavery and emancipation.

---

[3]Abraham Lincoln, "First Inaugural Address—Final Text," Mar. 4, 1861, *Collected Works*, 4:263.

The war began on April 12, 1861, with the bombardment of Fort Sumter, which surrendered on April 13. On the 15th, Lincoln issued a proclamation, noting that "the laws of the United States" were "opposed" and "obstructed" by "combinations too powerful to be suppressed by the ordinary course of judicial proceedings or by the powers vested in the Marshals by law." He asked the states to provide 75,000 militia troops to quell the rebellion "and to cause the laws to be duly executed."[4] The next day Burr Porter, who had served as a major in the Ottoman army during the Crimean War, urged Secretary of War Simon Cameron to "raise as soon as practicable, two regiments of infantry from the free colored people of the border States."[5] Such a move was not "practicable" at that time, because it would doubtless have immediately pushed the Border States into the Confederacy. But this letter illustrates that from the beginning of the war black military service was on the table. Of course, no one knew when it would be "practicable" to enlist black troops, and tied to that, when it would be practical to strike at the cause of secession and the reason for the Confederacy: slavery. But as this letter indicates, from day one of the war thoughtful Unionists were considering these issues.

Soon other Northerners pushed for enlisting blacks and emancipation. They argued that destroying slavery was necessary both to win the war and to preserve the Union. In May the nation's leading black abolitionist, Frederick Douglass, explained in an editorial titled "How to End the War" that "*The simple way, then, to put an end to the savage and desolating war now waged by the slaveholders, is to strike down slavery itself,* the primal cause of that war."[6] He further urged that blacks be enlisted in the cause:

> LET THE SLAVES AND FREE COLORED PEOPLE BE CALLED INTO SERVICE, AND FORMED INTO A LIBERATING ARMY, to march into the South and raise the banner of Emancipation among the slaves. The South having brought revolution and war upon the country, and having elected and consented to play at that fearful game, she has no right to complain if some good as well as calamity shall result from her own act and deed.[7]

---

[4]Abraham Lincoln, "Proclamation Calling Militia and Convening Congress (Apr. 15, 1861)," in *Collected Works*, 4:331.

[5]Burr Porter to Simon Cameron, Apr. 16, 1861, U.S. War Department, *The War of the Rebellion: The Official Records of the Union and Confederate Armies* (Washington, D.C., 1880), ser. 3, vol. 1, p. 77 (hereafter *O.R.*).

[6]Frederick Douglass, "How to End the War," *Douglass' Monthly* (May 1861). Italics in the original.

[7]Ibid. Capitalization in the original.

In June 1861 Douglass extended this argument, noting that emancipation would not only aid the Union cause—it would also cripple the enemy. He said the administration might "evade and equivocate," but in the end "slavery is not only the cause of the beginning of this war, but slavery is the sole support of the rebel cause. It is, so to speak, the *very stomach* of this rebellion."[8] Because slavery was the cause of the war, abolition was the best way to end the war. "We wage war against slaveholding rebels, and yet protect and augment the motive which has moved the slaveholders to rebellion. We strike at the effect, and leave the cause unharmed. . . . This war with the slaveholders can never be brought to a desirable termination until slavery, the guilty causes of all our national troubles, has been totally and forever abolished."[9] Other abolitionists, black and white, also pushed for movement against slavery, but the administration mostly ignored them. However, circumstances on the ground in Virginia—what Lincoln would later would call the "mere friction and abrasion" of the "incidents of war"—soon altered public policy.[10]

The circumstances are well known—the arrival at Fortress Monroe in Virginia of three slaves owned by Confederate Colonel Charles Mallory, who had been using these slaves to help build fortifications for the troops under his command. A day after Mallory's slaves "delivered themselves up" to General Benjamin F. Butler's "picket guard,"[11] Butler faced what was perhaps the most surreal spectacle of the war, when Confederate Major M. B. Carey appeared under a flag of truce, demanding the return of the fugitive slaves. Major Carey, identifying himself as Colonel Mallory's agent, told Butler he was obligated to return the slaves under the Fugitive Slave Clause of the Constitution and the Fugitive Slave Law of 1850. Butler told Carey to come back the next day.

---

[8]"Substance of a Lecture Delivered by Frederick Douglass at Zion Church, Sunday, June 30," *Douglass' Monthly* (Aug. 1861). Italics in the original.

[9]Ibid.

[10]"Appeal to Border State Representatives to Favor Compensated Emancipation," July 12, 1862, *Collected Works*, 5:317–18. In this statement Lincoln unsuccessfully urged Border State representatives to support compensated emancipation in their states—with the federal government footing the bill. Otherwise, he warned that through "friction and abrasion," slavery "will be gone and you will have nothing valuable in lieu of it."

[11]Major General Benjamin F. Butler to Lieutenant General Winfield Scott, May 24/25, 1861, *O.R.*, ser. 2, vol. 1, p. 752. See also Chandra Manning, "Military Emancipation before the Emancipation Proclamation: Overcoming Structural Obstacles," in this volume.

A successful Massachusetts lawyer before the war, Butler devoted some thought to the issue. After reading as much as he could on the law of war, Butler concluded that the fugitive slaves were "contrabands of war,"[12] no different than weapons, horses, or wagons being used by the enemy. Because Colonel Mallory had used these slaves to build fortifications, General Butler considered them to be military "property" that could legitimately be taken from the enemy. Butler also told Major Carey "that the fugitive slave act did not affect a foreign country, which Virginia claimed to be and she must reckon it one of the infelicities of her position that in so far at least she was taken at her word."[13] With a marvelous touch of irony, Butler offered to return the slaves to Colonel Mallory if he would come to Fortress Monroe and "take the oath of allegiance to the Constitution of the United States."[14] But until Mallory took such an oath (which Butler knew would never happen), his former slaves were "contrabands of war" and could not be returned.[15]

Butler hired these three former slaves as laborers for the army and they soon came to be known as "contrabands." Overnight he had begun to turn slaves into free workers. The War Department immediately approved Butler's actions, while admonishing him to not seek out slaves to liberate. The administration "reserved for future determination" the "final disposition" of the status of the contrabands. But it was obvious to anyone who understood what was happening that the three former slaves would never be returned to bondage, and that in his ad hoc way, Butler had singlehandedly changed U.S. policy. Taking slaves away from Mallory and other Confederates served the dual purposes of depriving the enemy of labor while providing labor for the United States. Even Northern opponents of abolition supported this policy.[16]

By the middle of the summer there were about 850 former slaves at Fortress Monroe, while more runaway slaves—newly minted contrabands—had

---

[12]Benjamin F. Butler, *Butler's Book* (Boston, 1892), pp. 256–57. On slavery and the law of war, see Paul Finkelman, "Francis Lieber and the Modern Law of War," *University of Chicago Law Review* 80 (2013):2116–21.

[13]Major General Benjamin F. Butler to Lieutenant General Winfield Scott, May 24/25, 1861, *O.R.*, ser. 2, vol. 1, p. 752.

[14]Ibid.

[15]Butler, *Butler's Book*, pp. 256–57.

[16]For a full discussion of these events, see Paul Finkelman, "Lincoln v. The Proslavery Constitution: How a Railroad Lawyer's Constitutional Theory Made Him the Great Emancipator," *St. Mary's Law Journal* 47 (2015):63, 109–13. Eric Foner, *The Fiery Trial: Abraham Lincoln and American Slavery* (New York, 2010), p. 170. Simon Cameron, Secretary of War, to General Benjamin F. Butler, May 30, 1861, *O.R.*, ser. 2, vol. 1, pp. 754–55.

emerged at other bases. Lincoln joked about "Butler's fugitive slave law," and clearly approved of the policy. In August, Congress would provide support for this policy in the First Confiscation Act. Thus, early on in the war, the realities of the conflict led to a de facto emancipation policy, although on a very limited scale. It only involved slaves who *could* reach U.S. Army lines, which would always be a very small percentage of the three and a half million or so people held in bondage in the Confederate states. It was initially not backed by legislation nor aggressively implemented. But *if* slaves managed to reach the army, the army was authorized to (but did not have to) give them sanctuary.

Eventually, Lincoln would use the contraband theory as the basis of the Emancipation Proclamation. If General Butler could emancipate three slaves as a military measure in order to deprive the Confederates of labor, then Lincoln would ultimately determine that he could emancipate three million slaves for the same purpose.[17] But before he could accomplish this, Congress would move against slavery and racism in a variety of ways.

Congress, the Civil War, and Slavery: 1861

In understanding how Congress operated during the war, we need to look at what it did, and also at what the Congress did not do. For example, in the early days of the war Lincoln on his own authority suspended habeas corpus from Washington, D.C., to New York City. Chief Justice Roger B. Taney claimed that this exceeded the president's authority and that only Congress could suspend the writ.[18] Other critics of Lincoln voiced the same opinion. Lincoln argued that the Constitution only specified that there be an invasion or rebellion and that the public safety required a suspension, but did not specify whether the executive branch or the legislative branch could

[17]There were about four million slaves in the United States on the eve of the war. Just under 500,000 were in the four loyal slave states, the District of Columbia, and that part of Virginia that became West Virginia. The Emancipation Proclamation of January 1, 1863, did not apply to the loyal slave states or to Tennessee and parts of Louisiana and Virginia, which means that it applied to about three and a quarter million slaves.

[18]*Ex parte Merryman*, 17 F. Cas. 144 (C.C.D. Md. 1861) (No. 9487). For a history of this case, see Brian McGinty, *The Body of John Merryman: Abraham Lincoln and the Suspension of Habeas Corpus* (Cambridge, Mass., 2011), and Jonathan W. White, *Abraham Lincoln and Treason in the Civil War: The Trials of John Merryman* (Baton Rouge, 2011).

suspend the writ. Since Congress was not in session when the war began, Lincoln acted on his own. When Congress met in July it might have passed a law repealing the suspension, or a resolution condemning it. Or Congress might have passed a law authorizing the suspension. It did none of these, leaving the suspension in place, which in effect ratified Lincoln's actions.

Similarly, Congress might have rejected the contraband policy and passed a law ordering the military to return slaves to Confederate masters. But again, Congress did not act in that way. Instead, Congress passed the Confiscation Act of 1861, now known as the First Confiscation Act. This law allowed for the emancipation of some slaves owned by Confederates, and in effect endorsed the contraband policy.[19] This was the first time in U.S. history that Congress had passed any law specifically allowing the government to take slaves from their masters and not return them.

The law declared that any personal or real property used in "the insurrection against the Government of the United States," was "hereby declared to be lawful subject of prize and capture wherever found; and it shall be the duty of the President of the United States to cause the same to be seized, confiscated, and condemned." Such property could be secured to the United States through a condemnation procedure in the federal courts. This was cumbersome and could not be accomplished quickly. It could also not be done on a mass scale because there were a limited number of courts, judges, and U.S. attorneys to bring claims against Confederate property owners.[20]

The last section of the act, section 4, directed entirely at slaves, was more innovative and intriguing. The language of the section tracked the Fugitive Slave Clause of the Constitution[21] and can be understood as a modification of the Fugitive Slave Act of 1850.[22] Section 4 declared that the owner of

[19]"An Act to Confiscate Property Used for Insurrectionary Purposes [First Confiscation Act]," Act of Aug. 6, 1861, 12 Stat. 319 (1863).

[20]Ibid., secs. 1–3.

[21]"No Person held to Service or Labour in one State, under the Laws thereof, escaping into another, shall, in Consequence of any Law or Regulation therein, be discharged from such Service or Labour, but shall be delivered up on Claim of the Party to whom such Service or Labour may be due." U.S. Constitution, Art. IV, sec. 2, cl. 3.

[22]"An Act to Amend, and Supplementary to, the Act Entitled 'An Act Respecting Fugitives from Justice, and Persons Escaping from the Service of Their Masters,' Approved February Twelfth, One Thousand Seven Hundred and Ninety-Three," Sept. 18, 1850, 9 Stat. 462 (1862).

"any person claimed to be held to labor or service under the law of any State" would "forfeit his claim to such labor" if the slave was used "to take up arms against the United States," or "to work or to be employed in or upon any fort, navy yard, dock, armory, ship, entrenchment, or in any military or naval service whatsoever, against the Government and lawful authority of the United States."[23] This obviously mirrored Butler's policy.

The meaning of this act was clear, although it failed to spell out any specific process. Slaves used by the Confederacy were "forfeit[ted]." The act did not say what would happen to such slaves, but the logic of federal law and the war made the end result obvious. The United States was not claiming the slaves and planning to "own" them, the way the government was taking ownership of other confiscated Confederate property. The United States did not own any slaves and had no rules for owning the forfeited slaves. These slaves would in effect now own themselves. Nor did the law require any proceeding, factual determination, or court intervention to accomplish this, as was required for the confiscation of other kinds of Confederate property. Under this law any slaves found working for the Confederacy, serving their masters in the army, or working in any military capacity were simply forfeited, with the army presumably seizing them, freeing them, and then mostly likely employing them, for wages, to work for the United States.

The language did not declare that the slave was free, but asserted that if a master tried to recover his slave, "it shall be a full and sufficient answer to such claim that the person whose service or labor is claimed had been employed in hostile service against the Government of the United States, contrary to the provisions of this act."[24] The language seems to assume that the now former slaves would be attached to the army or the government as free employees, or perhaps would be working on their own. Because they were immune from recapture, under the law such former slaves were de facto free.

The Confiscation Act was both an affirmation and an expansion of General Butler's contraband policy, which Lincoln and Secretary of War Cameron had tentatively endorsed in May. The War Department endorsement had allowed commanders in the field to free slaves used for military purposes

---

[23]First Confiscation Act, sec. 4. For an analysis of this section and its historiography, see James Oakes, "Reluctant to Emancipate? Another Look at the First Confiscation Act," *Journal of the Civil War Era* 3 (2013):458–66.

[24]First Confiscation Act, sec. 4.

who escaped to the army. But the statute authorized the army to actively confiscate slaves used by the Confederacy, whether or not they had escaped from their bondage or sought refuge with the army. In addition, Butler's action had been only an ad hoc policy invented by a general and endorsed by the executive branch. The new procedures were now the law of the land.

The Confiscation Act did not create a program to end slavery because it only applied to slaves actually being used for the Confederate war effort. But the law created a powerful weapon to be used against the Confederacy and slavery. Furthermore, it opened the door to more attacks on slavery. The law applied to slaves in the Confederate Army or working on Confederate military bases, "or in any military or naval service whatsoever, against the Government and lawful authority of the United States." A determined military officer could have construed that last sentence to include any slave used in any industry or mine, or to produce any agricultural products (food, tobacco, cotton, animals, or forage for animals) that might be used by the Confederate Army. In effect, that could include almost all the slaves in the South. Such creative interpretations or applications of the law would never be necessary, because events of the next year would accelerate the war against slavery. But the Confiscation Act of 1861 was an important step in turning the war for the Union into a war for freedom. It helped make the war a "people's contest" for all the people in the nation, including those of African ancestry.

Two days after Lincoln signed the Confiscation Act, the administration formally endorsed Butler's contraband policy. Secretary of War Cameron told General Butler that President Lincoln understood that "in States wholly or partially under insurrectionary control" the laws could not be enforced, and it was "equally obvious that rights dependent on the laws of the States within which military operations are conducted must be necessarily subordinated to the military exigencies created by the insurrection if not wholly forfeited by the treasonable conduct of the parties claiming them." Most importantly, "rights to services" could "form no exception" to "this general rule."[25] This was actually an expansion of the new Confiscation Act, because it would allow the army to protect the liberty of any slave—even one not involved in military activity—if protecting such a slave was in the interest

[25]Foner, *Fiery Trial*, pp. 170, 171. Simon Cameron to Benjamin F. Butler, Aug. 8, 1861, *O.R.*, ser. 2, vol. 1, pp. 761–62.

of "military operations" or necessary for the "military exigencies created by the insurrection," even where the slaves were not "forfeited by the treasonable conduct" of their masters.

From the beginning of the conflict Lincoln had publicly asserted that his only goal was to suppress the rebellion and preserve the nation. The Constitution did not allow the president or Congress to interfere with slavery in the states, and the administration continued to assert that it was not planning to end slavery or interfere with it. However, military necessity and the actual conditions on the ground, such as slaves running away to army camps, were changing the understanding of what the Constitution permitted. By the beginning of August, commanders in the field (like Butler), the War Department, the president, and Congress all understood this, even if none of the leaders of the nation were willing to publicly articulate it.

Congress, Slavery, and Equality in Federal Jurisdictions

Congress adjourned on August 6, 1861, the day that the Confiscation Act became law. In the months that followed, the war dragged on with few successes for the United States for the rest of the summer. This changed in late 1861, and from then until the following July would be "one of the brightest periods of the war for the North." In November 1861 Admiral Samuel F. Du Pont successfully seized the South Carolina Sea Islands with the important naval base at Port Royal. Once established, the United States would never be dislodged from this beachhead on the South Carolina coast. At least some of the war would now be fought in the Confederate heartland.[26] Although no one knew it at the time, this was the beginning of the shrinking of the Confederacy. By the end of April, the navy and army had captured or sealed off every Confederate port on the Atlantic except Charleston, South Carolina, and Wilmington, North Carolina. In the West, the

[26]James McPherson, *Battle Cry of Freedom: The Civil War Era* (New York, 1988), p. 368. One of the important results of this was the liberation of thousands of slaves on the Sea Islands, many of whom would later be enlisted when the United States began to organize black regiments in late 1862. See David Dudley Cornish, *The Sable Arm: Negro Troops in the Union Army, 1861–1865* (New York, 1966), and Willie Lee Rose, *Rehearsal for Reconstruction: The Port Royal Experiment* (New York, 1976).

United States won a series of crucial victories that completely altered the military and political situation in the Ohio and Mississippi Valleys. In February 1862, troops under Ulysses S. Grant took Fort Henry and Fort Donelson, capturing 12,000 Confederates and establishing a U.S. presence in the Confederate state of Tennessee. Instead of a Confederate army threatening Kentucky, the United States Army was now bivouacked in Confederate Tennessee. The U.S. victory at Pea Ridge in Arkansas ended Confederate hopes of capturing Missouri and turning it into a Confederate state, and a month later the United States won an important but bloody victory at Shiloh, in southwestern Tennessee. In April, Memphis fell, and on May 1 General Benjamin Butler, who had developed the contraband policy while a commander in Virginia, marched into New Orleans. By June a good piece of Tennessee as well as the cities of New Orleans, Baton Rouge, Natchez, and smaller river towns in Mississippi, Louisiana, and Arkansas were firmly under U.S. control.

As the prospects for military success multiplied, Congress, meeting from December 2, 1861, to July 17, 1862, began a revolution in American race relations. This burst of antislavery energy would culminate in Lincoln's Preliminary Emancipation Proclamation in September 1862 and the final Emancipation Proclamation on January 1, 1863. But well before Lincoln announced his plans to end slavery in the Confederacy, Congress passed laws to abolish slavery in the District of Columbia,[27] end slavery in all the federal territories,[28] allow for the confiscation of slaves owned by those in rebellion,[29] formally and emphatically free all slaves who escaped to the U.S. Army,[30] prohibit the army from returning fugitive slaves to any masters and provide for court martials for any officers allowing this to happen,[31] allow for the enlistment of black soldiers,[32] and create public schools for

[27] "An Act for the Release of Certain Persons Held to Service or Labor in the District of Columbia," Apr. 16, 1862, 12 Stat. 376 (1863). See Kate Masur, *An Example for All the Land: Emancipation and the Struggle over Equality in Washington, D.C.* (Chapel Hill, N.C., 2010).

[28] "An Act to Secure Freedom to All Persons within the Territories of the United States," Act of June 19, 1862, 12 Stat. 432 (1863).

[29] "An Act to Suppress Insurrection, to Punish Treason and Rebellion, to Seize and Confiscate the Property of Rebels, and for Other Purposes," Act of July 17, 1862, 12 Stat. 589 (1863) (hereafter/Second Confiscation Act).

[30] Second Confiscation Act.

[31] "An Act to Make an Additional Article of War," Act of Mar. 13, 1862, 12 Stat. 354 (1863).

[32] "Act to Amend the Act Calling Forth the Militia to Execute the Laws of the Union, Suppress Insurrections, and Repel Invasions, Approved February Twenty-Eight,

African American children in the District of Columbia.[33] The timing of these moves by Congress and the president undermine claims that the moves against slavery were the result of desperation and the fear that the United States might lose the war. Congress moved against slavery in the wake of military success, as did Lincoln when he issued the Preliminary Emancipation Proclamation after the important U.S. victory at Antietam.

All of these laws were incremental and situational. But taken together they reveal the revolutionary change in Congress and federal law that began with the First Confiscation Act and would continue through the end of Reconstruction. This was all possible because of the war, the ideology of the Republican Party at this time—which would eventually be known as the Party of Lincoln—and the absence of most proslavery Southerners from Congress. The heart of this revolution in federal law came in the summer of 1862.

Congress's first move against slavery was the passage in March of "An Act to Make an Additional Article of War." This innocuous-sounding law prohibited the army from returning fugitive slaves to any masters and provided for court martials for any officers allowing this to happen. The law did not apply only to fugitives from the Confederacy, who had been taken care of through General Butler's contraband policy and the First Confiscation Act. This law meant that the army would not help return fugitives from the loyal slave states as well. Some officers had been returning runaway slaves to their masters, especially in Kentucky and what would become West Virginia. But now they were prohibited from doing so and would be court martialed if they violated this new regulation. This law modified the practice under the Fugitive Slave Law of 1850, in which slaves had been removed from the North with the help of the state militias, the regular army, the marines, and the coast guard.[34]

Seventeen Hundred and Ninety-Five, and Acts Amendatory Thereof, and for Other Purposes [Militia Act of 1862]," Act of July 17, 1862, 12 Stat. 597, 599 (1863). Section 12 explicitly provides for the enlistment of African Americans.

[33]"An Act Providing for the Education of Colored Children in the Cities of Washington and Georgetown, District of Columbia, and for Other Purposes," Act of May 21, 1862, 12 Stat. 407 (1863) (hereafter D.C. School Act). For a discussion of the politics surrounding this law, see Masur, *An Example for All the Land*, pp. 26–27.

[34]"An Act to Make an Additional Article of War," Act of Mar. 13, 1862, 12 Stat. 354 (1863). For an example of the use of the military in this way, see Paul Finkelman, "Legal Ethics and Fugitive Slaves: The Anthony Burns Case, Judge Loring, and Abolitionist Attorneys," *Cardozo Law Review* 17 (1996):1793.

Prohibiting the army from participating in the return of fugitive slaves did not raise any significant constitutional issues. The Fugitive Slave Law still protected loyal masters, but they could not ask the army for help in recovering their slaves, and presumably could not recover them from military bases. While the Supreme Court had always endorsed the right of masters to recover fugitive slaves,[35] there was certainly nothing unconstitutional about Congress and the president determining what soldiers might spend their time doing and what they might be prohibited from doing. Indeed, in his remarkably proslavery decision in *Prigg v. Pennsylvania*, Justice Joseph Story had discussed the possibility that the Congress might repeal the Fugitive Slave Law of 1793. Story argued that masters would still have a common law right to recover their slaves under the Fugitive Slave Clause of the Constitution, even if Congress repealed the federal law that provided support for them in recovering their slaves. The implications of *Prigg* were clear: Congress could, if it so chose, repeal laws helping masters recover their fugitives. In 1862 Congress took a step in that direction. This law was at most an indirect assault on slavery, but it did indicate a new direction for American policy. The federal government would no longer expend its resources or energy protecting slavery.

In early April, with a nonbinding joint resolution of the House and Senate, Congress took another step toward ending slavery. In terms of public policy, this resolution was stunning and dramatic. The resolution consisted of one long sentence: "*Be it resolved by the Senate and House of Representatives of the United States of America in Congress assembled,* That the United States ought to cooperate with any State which may adopt gradual abolishment of slavery, giving to such State pecuniary aid, to be used by such State in its discretion, to compensate for the inconveniences, public and private, produced by such change of system."[36] Never before had Congress attempted to interfere with slavery in the states where it already existed. Never before had Congress taken the position that slavery ought to be abolished anywhere. Now it was actually offering to pay for the costs in the loyal slave

---

[35] *Prigg v. Pennsylvania*, 41 U.S. (16 Pet.) 539 (1842). For a more detailed discussion of these issues, see Paul Finkelman, *Supreme Injustice: Slavery in the Nation's Highest Court* (Cambridge, Mass., 2018).

[36] Joint Resolution Declaring That the United States Ought to Cooperate with, Affording Pecuniary Aid to Any State Which May Adopt the Gradual Abolition of Slavery, Passed Apr. 10, 1862, 12 Stat. 617 (1863).

states—Delaware, Kentucky, Maryland, and Missouri—if they would end slavery. Presumably, this offer would also have been available to any Confederate state that sought to rejoin the Union, although everyone knew this was unlikely to ever happen.

Less than a week after passing this resolution, Congress applied its logic to the national capital, where it had plenary power to end slavery. The "Act for the Release of Certain Persons Held to Service or Labor in the District of Columbia"[37] was a huge step forward in turning the war for the Union into a war for freedom. For the first time in American history an act of Congress mandated the actual emancipation of slaves. All other limitations on slavery had been taken to prevent slavery from spreading to new places, and often, as was the case in territorial Indiana and Illinois, the ban did not actually end slavery in those places.[38] But this was different. Here Congress passed a law, the president signed it, and slavery came to an end.

The law began with an emphatic statement: "That all persons held to service or labor within the District of Columbia by reason of African descent are hereby discharged and freed of and from all claim to such service or labor; and from and after the passage of this act neither slavery nor involuntary servitude, except for crime, whereof the party shall be duly convicted, shall hereafter exist in said District."[39] Following this were eleven sections spelling out a compensation scheme for owners. Congress recognized that slaves were "property" and thus could not be taken from their owners without just compensation and due process.

But even while recognizing the need to pay compensation, as the Fifth Amendment required, Congress took some property without any compensation. The law immediately freed all slaves in the District, while the compensation process was set to take place over a period of nine months. Thus, masters lost the use of their slaves immediately but were not

---

[37]"An Act for the Release of Certain Persons Held to Service or Labor in the District of Columbia," Act of Apr., 16, 1862, 12 Stat. 376 (1863) (hereafter D.C. Emancipation Act).

[38]Paul Finkelman, *Slavery and the Founders: Race and Liberty in the Age of Jefferson*, 3rd ed. (New York, 2014), pp. 46–101 (describing how slavery continued in Indiana and Illinois long after the passage of the Northwest Ordinance); Paul Finkelman, "Almost a Free State: The Indiana Constitution of 1816 and the Problem of Slavery," *Indiana Magazine of History* 111 (2015):64 (describing how slavery lingered in Indiana and how the Indiana courts dealt with it).

[39]D.C. Emancipation Act, para. 1. This paragraph serves as "section 1" of the law, and the next paragraph is designated as "section 2," but the act does not call the first paragraph "section 1."

compensated until later.[40] The act also denied compensation to anyone who was not "loyal" or who had in any way aided the rebellion. Thus, some people in Washington would have lost their slave property without any compensation because of their public endorsement of secession or their overt acts supporting the rebellion. Any slaves brought into the District after the passage of the act would be free without any compensation to the owner. The law also punished kidnapping of the now free black population and repealed existing laws "inconsistent with the provisions of this act."[41] Thus, slavery came to an end in the nation's capital.

A month after ending slavery in the District, Congress reorganized the city's public school system, which had suffered from neglect and underfunding throughout the city's history. The elaborate bill provided for a school board and taxing of all white property owners. Under the law, "any white resident of said county shall be privileged to place his or her child or ward at any" school in the county.[42] However, the law also provided that the city set up public schools for African American children.

The next day Congress passed a separate law just for the creation of publicly funded schools for blacks. The law required that these schools be funded by taxes collected "from the real and personal property . . . owned by persons of color." This set the stage for a huge funding differential between schools for whites and those for blacks. A subsequent act would place partial control of the schools in the hands of the secretary of the interior. By placing public education in the control of the national government (and at this time the Lincoln administration) Congress prevented local officials, in what was essentially a Southern city, from interfering with or preventing the creation of schools for blacks.[43] In spite of its inadequacies, the law provided greater access to public education for blacks than in a number of Northern states, and it created the only public school system for blacks south of the Mason-Dixon line. From a modern perspective, this was an

---

[40]Ibid., sec. 4.

[41]Ibid., secs. 2, 3, 10, and 12.

[42]"An Act to Provide for the Public Instruction of Youth in Primary Schools throughout the County of Washington, in the District of Columbia, without the Limits of the Cities of Washington and Georgetown," Act of May 20, 1862, 12 Stat. 394 (1863) (hereafter Primary Schools Act).

[43]D.C. School Act; "An Act Relating to Schools for the Education of Colored in the Cities of Washington and Georgetown, in the District of Columbia," Act of July 11, 1862, 12 Stat. 537 (1863). Masur, *An Example for All the Land*, p. 28.

inadequate, segregated system of schools; from the perspective of 1862, it was an enormous step forward in providing education for African Americans, especially in the wake of district-wide emancipation that had taken place a month earlier.

The final section of the law was even more remarkable, and stunningly progressive, even by modern standards. The law provided:

> That all Persons of Color in the District of Columbia, or in the corporate limits of the cities of Washington and Georgetown, shall be subject and amenable to the same laws and ordinances as free white persons are or may be subject or amenable; that they shall be tried for any offences against the laws in the same manner as free white persons are or may be tried for the same offences; and that upon being legally convicted of any crime or offences against any law or ordinance, such persons of color shall be liable to the same penalty or punishment, and no other, as would be imposed or inflicted upon free white persons for the same crime or offence; and all acts or parts of acts inconsistent with the provisions of this act are hereby repealed.[44]

This provision can be understood as the precursor to the Equal Protection Clause of the Fourteenth Amendment and as a major step in the Republican movement toward racial equality. While the school portion of this bill created segregated schools that would not be funded on the same basis as schools for whites, section 4 of the law mandated equality in criminal prosecutions. This was the first provision of its kind in the history of the national government: a promise of equal protection of the laws for blacks charged with crimes.

Having abolished slavery in the District, provided schools for the children of the newly free slaves, and guaranteed that the criminal laws of the District would not discriminate against blacks, Congress turned to the other jurisdiction where it had plenary power to dismantle slavery: the federal territories. Ending slavery in the territories was perhaps theoretically more problematic than in the District of Columbia, since Chief Justice Taney had held in *Dred Scott v. Sandford* (1857) that Congress had no authority to end slavery, or even prohibit it, in the territories. But the Republican Party had made ending slavery in the territories a major component of its program, and almost all Republicans agreed with Lincoln that Taney's analysis of the territories clause of the Constitution was *dicta*, wrong, and insulting. Chief

[44] D.C. School Act, sec. 4.

Justice Taney had dismissed the lawsuit in *Dred Scott* for lack of jurisdiction, asserting that blacks could never be citizens of the United States and thus Dred Scott could not sue in federal court under diversity jurisdiction. Because he dismissed the suit, most Republicans argued that everything he said about the territories was *dicta*, and had no precedential authority. If there was no case before the Court because Dred Scott could not legally bring the suit, then the Court could not rule on any substantive issues, including congressional power over slavery in the territories.

In addition to the *dicta* argument, Taney's claims that Congress had no power to pass any laws for the governance of the territories flew in the face of the Territories Clause of Article IV. No scholars have ever found any plausible argument to support Taney's position since then. At the time, Lincoln and other Republicans confidently believed they had the power to regulate the territories and end slavery in them. They believed Taney's argument was flatly wrong, and since they also considered it *dicta*, they saw no reason to defer to it.

The Republicans in Congress thus acted on *their* theory of the Constitution and simply ignored Taney's *dicta*. The act was straightforward: "That from and after the passage of this act there shall be neither slavery nor involuntary servitude in any of the Territories of the United States now existing, or which may at any time hereafter be formed or acquired by the United States, otherwise than in punishment of crimes whereof the party shall have been duly convicted."[45] With one sentence Congress had undone a key aspect of the holding in *Dred Scott* and reversed public policy on slavery in the territories dating from the Confederation period.

The abolition of slavery in the territories did, however, raise at least one legitimate constitutional question. There were very few slaves in the federal territories at this time, but unlike their counterparts in the District of Columbia, masters in the territories did not receive any compensation when Congress emancipated their slaves.[46] From the perspective of the slave

---

[45]"An Act to Secure Freedom to All Persons within the Territories of the United States," Act of June 19, 1862, 12 Stat. 432 (1863).

[46]In 1860 there were only fifty-nine slaves in the Utah Territory (http://mapmaker.rutgers.edu/REFERENCE/Hist_Pop_stats.pdf); the census reported no slaves in New Mexico, but it seems likely that some of the sixty-four African Americans in the territory were slaves (http://mapmaker.rutgers.edu/REFERENCE/Hist_Pop_stats.pdf); Nebraska had fifteen slaves, according to the census (http://mapmaker.rutgers.edu/REFERENCE/Hist_Pop_stats.pdf). There are no slaves recorded in any other territories, although there

owners, this was clearly a taking of "private property . . . for public use, without just compensation,"[47] in violation of the Fifth Amendment. However, Republicans had long argued that slavery was "contrary to natural right,"[48] inconsistent with the law of nature, and violated the precepts of the Declaration of Independence. They argued that "[w]herever it exists at all, it exists only in the virtue of positive law."[49] Senator Charles Sumner captured the essence of this in the title of his 1852 speech "Freedom National; Slavery Sectional."[50] Similarly, Lincoln succinctly made the same point in a speech on the Kansas-Nebraska Act, noting that slavery was "a gross outrage on the law of nature."[51] These Republican leaders endorsed the theory, originating in Lord Mansfield's 1772 decision in *Somerset v. Stewart*, that slavery could only exist where there was positive law—that is, statutes—that created it and protected it. Without such formally enacted laws, slavery could not exist and slaves became free where there were no laws to keep them in bondage. Under this theory, the status of slaves in the territories differed markedly from the status of slaves in the District of Columbia.

While the Compromise of 1850 and the Kansas-Nebraska Act of 1854 had not prohibited slavery in the territories—and thus implicitly allowed the institution in most of the western territories—neither had these acts contained language establishing or legalizing slavery in the territories. Thus, the Republican position reflected the idea that slavery still could not legitimately exist in the territories. The situation had been different in the District of Columbia because in that city there had been extensive legislation creating and protecting slavery. Thus, compensation was necessary. But if slavery had never actually been created by Congress in the territories, then slavery never legally existed in them, and slaves brought into the territories were technically free because there were no laws holding them in bondage.

---

were a substantial number of slaves in the Indian Territory, which would eventually become Oklahoma; there are no census figures for Oklahoma for that period.

47U.S. Constitution, Amend. V.

48Salmon P. Chase, *Speech of Salmon P. Chase, in the Case of the Colored Woman, Matilda* (Cincinnati, 1837), p. 8. Chase made this argument in 1837, when he was an antislavery Democrat. In the 1850s he helped organize the Republican Party in Ohio, and in 1861 he became secretary of the Treasury under Lincoln. In 1865 he would become chief justice of the U.S. Supreme Court.

49Ibid.

50Charles Sumner, *Freedom National; Slavery Sectional* (Boston, 1852).

51Abraham Lincoln, Speech at Springfield, Illinois, Oct. 4, 1854, *Collected Works*, 2:245.

Race, Slavery, and Foreign Relations

In the summer of '62, Congress spent some of its energy on slavery-related issues that were tangential to the war effort or ending slavery in the United States, but were symbolically important to Congress's revolution in race relations. In June Congress authorized the president to develop formal diplomatic relations with Haiti and Liberia, nations governed by former slaves and their descendants.[52] Starting with the administration of Thomas Jefferson, the United States had treated Haiti as a pariah nation, without any diplomatic relations,[53] and Southern power in Congress had prevented any change since then. Similarly, Southerners blocked any diplomatic recognition of Liberia. With most Southerners no longer in Congress, this situation had changed.

Diplomatic relations with either country would have led to an African or a person of African ancestry presenting diplomatic credentials to the president of the United States. This would have been a shocking assault on the racial etiquette of the nation's capital. All presidents before Lincoln (with the possible exception of John Adams and John Quincy Adams) would have opposed meeting with a black man on terms of equality or in a diplomatic setting. It is important to note that before the election of Lincoln only four presidents—John Adams, John Quincy Adams, Millard Fillmore, and Franklin Pierce—had been neither slave owners nor come from slave-owning families. While never personally involved with slavery, Fillmore and Pierce were proslavery Northern doughfaces who opposed any sort of racial equality. The other Northern presidents, Martin Van Buren, William Henry Harrison, and James Buchanan, who were from New York, Ohio, and Pennsylvania, respectively, had grown up in slaveholding families, and the first two personally owned slaves at some point in their lives. All other presidents had been Southern slave owners.[54] The idea of a black diplomat in the

[52]"An Act to Authorize the President of the United State to Appoint Diplomatic Representatives to the Republics of Hayti and Liberia, Respectively," Act of June 5, 1862, 12 Stat. 421 (1863).

[53]Finkelman, *Slavery and the Founders*, pp. 78–82.

[54]Van Buren's father owned six slaves in Kinderhook, New York. Van Buren himself owned a slave named Tom. Tom escaped and was caught ten years later. When he was caught, Van Buren simply sold him to the captor for $50 (http://www.american-presidents.org/2009/11/martin-van-buren-and-slavery.html). Buchanan's father owned slaves, and as an adult the future president was tangentially (at least) connected to slaveholding. The *Franklin Repository* (Mercersburg, Penn.), Apr. 2, 1816, contains an advertisement for Buchanan's father, also named James Buchanan, selling the labor of his "stout healthy

nation's capital—attending receptions, meeting with government officials, being accorded dignity and respect—would simply have been unacceptable to the Washington establishment and the residents of the White House.

Black envoys from Haiti or Liberia would have had diplomatic immunity. Under that immunity, they could have denounced slavery in the District of Columbia and other places, and been legally able to speak out against slavery in the South. Such speech would have violated the laws of the District and of all fifteen slave states that existed in 1860. Thus, before the Republican victory of 1860 and the subsequent exodus of most slave state senators and representatives, it would have been impossible to recognize the black republics of Haiti and Liberia.

In April, the Senate ratified a treaty with Great Britain to cooperate in suppressing the African slave trade. Previous administrations would not have negotiated such a treaty, nor would the Senate, with a large number of Southerners sitting in it, have ratified the treaty.[55] Under the treaty, and the implementing legislation, the United States would appoint judges and arbitrators to reside in New York City, Sierra Leone, and the Cape of Good Hope to adjudicate seizures of ships involved in the illegal African slave trade. The treaty allowed warships of both nations to interdict ships of both nations. Thus, under this treaty illegal slavers could not fly an American flag and hope to avoid capture, knowing that the U.S. Navy was mostly tied up with the war against the Confederacy, and might not have the ships or manpower to also patrol the coast of Africa. British ships could now stop suspected slavers flying the American flag in international waters.

In July, a month after opening diplomatic relations with the world's two black republics, Congress authorized the appointment of three judges and three arbitrators to fulfill the obligations of a newly ratified bilateral treaty with

---

Negro boy who has about six years to serve." The same paper, February 19, 1822, contains notice of the sale of the senior Buchanan's estate, including "The time of a small active coloured Girl who has almost five years to serve." I thank Patrick Clarke, the director of President James Buchanan's Wheatland, for copies of these advertisements. William Henry Harrison, who was from Ohio when elected president, came from a planter family in Virginia, and had owned slaves in Virginia and when he first moved to Ohio.

[55]Ibid.; "Treaty between the United States and Great Britain for the Suppression of the Slave Trade. Concluded at Washington, April 7, 1862. Ratifications Exchanged at London, May 25, 1862. Proclaimed by the President of the United States, June 7, 1862," Apr. 7, 1862, 12 Stat. 1225 (1863).

Great Britain to suppress the African slave trade.[56] While Southerners in Congress always claimed they opposed the illegal African trade, they consistently blocked legislation to adequately fund naval and diplomatic efforts to suppress it. Some did this on principle, because they believed that slavery was legitimate, and therefore the trade must be legitimate. Others doubtless opposed vigorous suppression of the trade because their constituents benefited from illegal importations, which were popular in much of the Deep South. This treaty and the implementing legislation was an important step in suppressing the African trade. The treaty and its implementation were only possible because the delegations from eleven slave states were no longer in Congress.

Federal Law beyond Slavery

In addition to laws directly related to slavery and race, in the summer of '62 Congress passed a number of laws that were indirectly connected to the struggle against human bondage. These laws illustrated the remarkable change in constitutional theory and legislative politics that came with secession and the war, and collectively they signaled that Southern secession had fundamentally changed the United States. Secession led to the exit of twenty-one Southern senators[57] and almost seventy Southern House members.[58] Without these proslavery legislators, the Congress ran more smoothly and was able to accomplish all sorts of things that the slave state representatives had stopped in the past. Some of these laws had nothing directly to do with slavery but were important to reshaping America. Before the war, Southerners had opposed much of this legislation because the laws were likely to lead to new free states, might help develop the North, or were seen as implying federal powers that might someday be used to harm slavery. But with most Southerners no longer in Congress, the legislative agenda had changed. Thus, in the summer of 1862, Congress created the Department

[56]"An Act to Carry into Effect the Treaty between the United States and Her Britannic Majesty for the Suppression of the African Slave-Trade," Act of July 11, 1862, 12 Stat. 531 (1863).

[57]Eleven slave states seceded, but one Southern senator, Andrew Johnson of Tennessee, refused to resign his position or to join the Confederacy.

[58]In the previous Congress the seceding states had a total of sixty-eight members of the House of Representatives.

of Agriculture,[59] passed the Homestead Act,[60] upgraded public education in the District of Columbia,[61] passed legislation for the creation of the transcontinental railroad,[62] and passed laws to create land grant colleges.[63]

A month after banning slavery in the territories, Congress also banned polygamy in the territories, with a law directed at the members of the Church of Jesus Christ of Latter-Day Saints (better known as the Mormons) in Utah.[64] Mormons, who constituted almost all the settlers in Utah, actively practiced polygamy, which they called "plural marriage." At first glance this ban on polygamy hardly seems like a statute that should have been tied to secession or the evolution of a Congress with few slave owners in it. But opposition to polygamy was actually tied to proslavery and antislavery politics. Southerners were not advocates of polygamy, but feared that any regulation of the "domestic institutions" of any territory or state would set a precedent for interfering with slavery. Thus, they opposed any federal law regulating marriage in Utah.

While never explicitly part of the political debate, Southerners may have been particularly sensitive about any federal regulation or even discussion of sexual morality, because so many Southern white men—including many in Congress and some in the executive branch—had fathered children with their slaves and were well known to keep a slave mistress in Washington. In addition, most Mormons in Utah were Democrats, some owned slaves, and their church did not allow full participation for free blacks. Thus for a host of reasons, Southerners and Democrats in Congress fought any limitations on Mormon polygamy. On the other hand, in 1856, the Republican Party platform condemned both slavery and polygamy: "Resolved: That the

59"An Act to Establish a Department of Agriculture [Department of Agriculture Act]," Act of May 15, 1862, 12 Stat. 387 (1863).

60"An Act to Secure Homesteads to Actual Settlers on the Public Domain [Homestead Act]," Act of May 20, 1862, 12 Stat. 392 (1863).

61Primary Schools Act. It is worth noting that only North Carolina had even a rudimentary system of public schools in the South.

62"An Act to Aid in the Construction of a Railroad and Telegraph Line from the Missouri River to the Pacific Ocean, and to Secure to the Government the Use of the Same for Postal, Military, and Other Purposes [Pacific Railroad Act]," Act of July 1, 1862, 12 Stat. 489 (1863).

63"An Act Donating Public Lands to the Several States and Territories Which May Provide Colleges for the Benefit of Agriculture and Mechanic Arts [Morrill Land Grant College Act]," Act of July 2, 1862, 12 Stat. 503 (1863).

64"An Act to Punish and Prevent the Practice of Polygamy in the Territories of the United States and Other Places and Disapproving and Annulling Certain Acts of the Legislative Assembly of the Territory of Utah [Morrill Anti-Polygamy Act]," Act of July 1, 1862, 12 Stat. 501 (1863).

Constitution confers upon Congress sovereign powers over the Territories of the United States for their government; and that in the exercise of this power, it is both the right and the imperative duty of Congress to prohibit in the Territories those twin relics of barbarism—Polygamy, and Slavery."[65] Having prohibited slavery in the territories the previous month, the Republicans were now able to end the other "relic of barbarism" in the territories, polygamy.

The Pacific Railroad Act[66] also had implications for slavery. Tying the West Coast to the East Coast with trains and a telegraph system would speed the settlement of the West and lead to new states—more than likely free states. Before 1861, Southerners had opposed these policies because they feared this outcome. Similarly, they opposed a Homestead Act, which would encourage settlers with relatively few assets to move west and claim land. Most people at the time believed that it was easier for Southerners to settle the West because they could bring slave laborers to help with the initial tasks of clearing land, cultivating it, and building houses. A Southern settler with only a few slaves had a huge advantage over a free state settler who had no labor to command. In addition, slave owners had more wealth to buy land. Thus if land was sold to settlers, the South would have an advantage in settling the West. But the Homestead Act, which gave land to settlers for free undercut many of these advantages.[67]

Southerners had also been generally reluctant to support federally sponsored internal improvements, such as roads and canals. The transcontinental railroad, the new Department of Agriculture,[68] and the system of land-grant colleges were precisely the kind of governmental innovations that threatened the South and at least indirectly threatened slavery. In the summer of '62, Congress moved forward on all of these innovations. None of them directly threatened slavery, but all of them did so indirectly.

Slavery in the Confederacy and Blacks in the Army: The True Revolution of the Summer of '62

The final acts of Congress to dismantle slavery in this revolutionary summer were the passage of the Second Confiscation Act and the Militia Act

[65]http://www.presidency.ucsb.edu/ws/?pid=29619.

[66]Pacific Railroad Act.

[67]Homestead Act.

[68]Department of Agriculture Act.

at the very end of the congressional session.[69] The new Confiscation Act contained a variety of provisions for the emancipation of slaves owned by Confederate officials and military officers, anyone convicted of treason against the United States, anyone who might "assist, or engage in any rebellion or insurrection against the authority of the United States, or the laws thereof, or shall give aid or comfort thereto, or shall engage in, or give aid and comfort to, any such existing rebellion or insurrection," "anyone who having held an office of honor, trust, or profit in the United States . . . shall hereafter hold an office in the so-called confederate states of America," and anyone living in the loyal slave states who gave any aid or comfort to the Confederacy. In addition, all slaves escaping to the army, or captured by the army, who were owned by anyone who supported the rebellion were explicitly declared "forever free of their servitude, and not held as slaves." Any slaves escaping into the United States, or within the United States, would not be returned to their masters unless the owner could "first make oath" that the claimant "has not borne arms against the United States in the present rebellion, nor in any way given aid and comfort thereto." However, under this law no member of the U.S. Army or Navy was permitted to return a fugitive slave.[70] This provision reaffirmed the law passed in March 1862 that prohibited the army from returning fugitive slaves. Most of these provisions required some sort of judicial hearing to prove that the slave owner had in fact committed treason or supported the rebellion in some other way. Nevertheless, it is possible to imagine freeing slaves after summary proceedings against slave owners captured while wearing Confederate uniforms or performing duties for the Confederate government.

Having taken steps to dismantle slavery within the Confederacy, Congress then empowered the president "to employ as many persons of African descent as he may deem necessary and proper for the suppression of this rebellion, and for this purpose he may organize and use them in such manner as he may judge best for the public welfare." Presumably, this would have included enlisting them in the army. In a sop to conservatives, the law allowed, but did not require, the president "to make provision for the transportation, colonization, and settlement, in some tropical country beyond the

[69]Second Confiscation Act; Militia Act of 1862, ch. 201. Again, section 12 explicitly provides for the enlistment of African Americans.

[70]Second Confiscation Act, secs. 2, 5, 6, 9, and 10.

limits of the United States, of such persons of the African race, made free by the provisions of this act, as may be willing to emigrate, having first obtained the consent of the government of said country to their protection and settlement within the same, with all the rights and privileges of freemen."[71] A similar provision had been in the District of Columbia Emancipation Act, but that law included some funding for the expatriation of former slaves. This law contained no funding. But none of this really mattered. President Lincoln never took any steps to move blacks outside the United States, and no blacks ever stepped forward to seek transportation.

Following the Second Confiscation Act, Congress passed the Militia Act of 1862. The law resolved any ambiguity in the Confiscation Act about the enlistment of black troops. The Militia Act of 1792 had limited militia service to "every free able-bodied white male citizen."[72] But the Militia Act of 1862 authorized "the enrolment of . . . all able-bodied male citizens between ages of eighteen and forty-five."[73] The word "white" was now gone. This was a quiet but dramatic change in American law. It theoretically meant that blacks could now be in the army.[74] In *Dred Scott*, Chief Justice Taney had held that blacks were not citizens of the United States, but at this point Congress refused to give any deference to Taney's decision. Furthermore, there might have been a few loopholes, even if Congress deferred to Taney's argument. In *Dred Scott*, Taney had made a distinction between state and federal citizenship, conceding that blacks could be citizens of states. Militias were organized at the state level, so it was plausible to conclude that the states would now be free to enroll blacks if they chose. By this time, blacks could vote or hold office in eight Northern states, so they were presumably citizens. But, since many citizens were denied the franchise—women are the most obvious example—it was plausible to argue that blacks were also citizens in other Northern states, even if they could not vote.[75] Furthermore,

[71]Second Confiscation Act, secs. 11 and 12.

[72]"An Act More Effectually to Provide for the National Defence by Establishing an Uniform Militia throughout the United States," Act of May 8, 1792, 1 Stat. 271 (1845).

[73]Militia Act of 1862, unnumbered sec. 1.

[74]It is also worth noting that Native Americans served in the army as well, most notably General Grant's staff officer Lieutenant Colonel (and later Brevet Brigadier General) Ely S. Parker of the Seneca Nation. Parker was allowed to join the army in 1863, in part as a result of the Militia Act of 1862.

[75]There was no clear definition of citizenship in the United States at this time, and thus it is impossible to know who was a "citizen" and who was not. No Northern state ever defined what a citizen was, or what the legal status was of its free black inhabitants.

while the Militia Act designated who had to be in the militia—able-bodied male citizens of any race between ages eighteen and forty-five—it did not limit militia service to those groups. Throughout the United States, immigrants served in the militia even though they were not yet citizens. Under this theory, by eliminating the word "white" from the militia law, Congress essentially allowed for the enlistment of blacks, whether they were citizens or not.[76]

Any doubts about the meaning of this law with regard to the enlistment of blacks were resolved by sections 12 and 13 of the law. Section 12 authorized the president to "to receive into the service of the United States, for the purpose of constructing intrenchments, or performing camp service, or any other labor, or any military or naval service for which they may be found competent, persons of African descent, and such persons shall be enrolled and organized under such regulations, not inconsistent with the Constitution and laws, as the President may prescribe."[77] The first part of this clause imagined blacks as laborers working for the military, as they had been doing since the advent of General Butler's contraband policy. Indeed, this can be seen as a further codification of that policy. But the clause clearly went further, allowing "persons of African descent" to serve in "any military or naval service for which they may be found competent." Blacks had fought in colonial militias, in the Revolutionary armies, and in the War of 1812 (in spite of the language of the 1792 Militia Act). Certainly they were "competent" to serve in the army. Now the president was authorized to recruit them. About a month after signing this law, the Lincoln administration would begin to do just that. On August 25, Secretary of War Edwin M. Stanton would authorize Brigadier General Rufus Saxton, headquartered in Hilton Head, South Carolina, to begin to enlist and train black troops.[78] This was an immediate and clear implementation of the revolutionary actions of Congress.

Blacks could vote on the same basis as whites in Massachusetts, Rhode Island, New Hampshire, Vermont, and Maine, and they could vote in New York if they owned property, although by this time whites did not need to own property to vote. Blacks could vote in school funding elections in Michigan, and in Ohio blacks could hold public office even though they could not vote. John Mercer Langston had held elected office in Ohio in the 1850s.

[76]Militia Act of 1862, unnumbered sec. 1.

[77]Militia Act of 1862, sec. 12.

[78]Letter from Edwin M. Stanton to Brigadier General Saxton, Aug. 25, 1862, *O.R.*, ser. 1, vol. 14, pp. 377, 377–78.

The next section of the Militia Act was even more far-reaching. The text is worth quoting in full:

> Sec. 13. *And be it further enacted,* That when any man or boy of African descent, who by the laws of any State shall owe service or labor to any person who, during the present rebellion, has levied war or has borne arms against the United States, or adhered to their enemies by giving them aid and comfort, shall render any such service as is provided for in this act, he, his mother and his wife and children, shall forever thereafter be free, any law, usage, or custom whatsoever to the contrary notwithstanding: *Provided,* That the mother, wife and children of such man or boy of African descent shall not be made free by the operation of this act except where such mother, wife or children owe service or labor to some person who, during the present rebellion, has borne arms against the United States or adhered to their enemies by giving them aid and comfort.[79]

While not stated, the legal presumption was that every slave owner in the Confederacy had given "aid and comfort" to the rebellion, and thus from that point forward, any slave in a Confederate state joining the army would bring freedom to his mother, wife, and children. This was by far the strongest attack yet on slavery in the Confederacy.

Unfortunately, Congress did not fully think through all the implications of this law, because the act did not emancipate siblings, fathers, or grandparents of slaves. Nor did Congress deal adequately with the salaries for black soldiers. The Militia Act provided that blacks would receive the same pay as laborers, which meant they were paid less than white soldiers. The law paid them only ten dollars a month, and three dollars of this would be deducted for clothing. There are plausible explanations for this obviously discriminatory policy. First, Congress may have assumed blacks that would be enrolled as laborers rather than soldiers, and thus they were being paid according to that job status. But this flies in the face of the language that allowed blacks to serve in any capacity in the military. Alternatively, Congress may have assumed that former slaves would be unable to manage their own affairs (and purchase their own clothes), and thus the military had to do it for them. The paternalistic and racist implications of such an analysis are obvious. Moreover, some black soldiers were free when the war began, and thus understood both the money economy and the need to

[79]Militia Act of 1862, sec. 13.

support themselves. The third possibility is that Congress simply did not think black soldiers were worth as much as white soldiers. As James McPherson notes, the unequal salary was a "concession to prejudice."[80] Whatever the motivation, this part of the law was roundly condemned by black leaders, black soldiers, and their white allies. In 1864 Congress equalized pay and gave black soldiers some back pay.[81] In 1865 a new statute authorized further back pay for all soldiers recruited by Major General David Hunter and Brigadier General Rufus Saxton in South Carolina in 1862, and to all other black soldiers "in every case where it shall be made to appear to the satisfaction of the Secretary of War that any regiment of colored troops has been mustered into the service of the United States, under any assurance by the President or the Secretary of War, that the non-commissioned officers and privates of such regiment should be paid the same as other troops of the same arm of the service, shall, from the date of their enlistment, receive the same pay and allowances as are allowed by law to other volunteers in the military service."[82]

But even with the discrimination in pay, the law was a remarkable assault on slavery. Throughout the Confederacy—as well as in the loyal slave states—the U.S. Army could begin to recruit slaves to fight for the nation while at the same time fighting to end slavery. Slaves joining the army would bring freedom to many of their family members, and this freedom would be enforced by the army itself. Even without the Emancipation Proclamation, the Militia Act, combined with the Second Confiscation Act, would have significantly undermined slavery in the Confederacy and in the loyal slave states. Furthermore, by authorizing the emancipation of slaves throughout the Confederacy and allowing the enlistment of black troops, Congress and President Lincoln had fundamentally altered the nature of the war. The

---

[80]McPherson, *Battle Cry of Freedom*, p. 789.

[81]"An Act Making Appropriations for the Support of the Army for the Year Ending the Thirtieth of June, Eighteen Hundred and Sixty-Five, and for Other Purposes," Act of June 15, 1864, 13 Stat. 126 (1866), secs. 2–4. The law provided full back pay for blacks who had been free when the war began or who had enlisted in 1863 through their state militias, but all others—most of whom had been slaves when the war began, received back pay only from Jan. 1, 1864.

[82]"An Act to Amend the Several Acts Heretofore Passed to Provide for the Enrolling and Calling Out the National Forces, and for Other Purposes," Act of March 3, 1865, 13 Stat. 487 (1866). For a discussion of the politics of these laws, see Herman Belz, "Law, Politics, and Race in the Struggle for Equal Pay during the Civil War," *Civil War History* 22 (1976):197–213.

war was now clearly a crusade against slavery, even if for political reasons neither Congress nor the president was willing to say so.

Beyond the Summer of '62

In the next three years Congress continued to pass laws that challenged slavery and racism. The president, however, took the lead with the Emancipation Proclamation, offered as a preliminary document in September 1862 and the final document on January 1, 1863.[83] The end of slavery was now the official goal of the United States of America. A year and a half later Congress repealed the Fugitive Slave Laws of 1793 and 1850. Masters in Kentucky, Delaware, and a few other places still held on to their slaves, but they could no longer expect help from the national government in tracking those who acted on their own to achieve self-emancipation.[84] One of the most draconian and unfair laws in U.S. history was now relegated to the dustbin of history. Seven months later Congress passed the Thirteenth Amendment, sending it on to the states. Its language was simple and direct: "Neither slavery nor involuntary servitude, except as a punishment for crime whereof the party shall have been duly convicted, shall exist within the United States, or any place subject to their jurisdiction." In an entirely new and innovative change in constitutional law, the amendment granted Congress "power to enforce this article by appropriate legislation."[85] By December 1865 slavery would be over in the United States.

Meanwhile, Congress pushed on other fronts to alter the landscape of American race relations. Shortly after Lincoln issued the final Emancipation Proclamation, Congress incorporated the National Association for the Relief of Destitute Colored Women and Children, granting it the use of up to one hundred acres of land in the District of Columbia.[86] Never before

[83]"By the President of the United States of America: A Proclamation [Preliminary Emancipation Proclamation]," Sept. 22, 1862, 12 Stat. 1267 (1863), and "By the President of the United States of America: A Proclamation [Final Emancipation Proclamation]," Jan. 1, 1863, 12 Stat. 1268 (1863).

[84]"An Act to Repeal the Fugitive Slave Act of Eighteen Hundred and Fifty, and All Acts and Part of Acts for the Rendition of Fugitive Slaves," Act of June 28, 1864, 13 Stat. 200 (1866).

[85]"A Resolution Submitting to the Legislatures of the Several States a Proposition to Amend the Constitution of the United States," Feb. 1, 1865, 13 Stat. 567 (1866).

[86]"An Act to Incorporate the National Association for the Relief of Destitute Colored Women and Children," Act of Feb. 14, 1863, 12 Stat. 650 (1863).

had Congress issued articles of incorporation to benefit African Americans, nor had it allocated federal property for such a purpose. A month later Congress incorporated the Institution for the Education of Colored Youth in the District of Columbia, in order to "educate and improve the moral and intellectual condition of such of the colored youth of the nation."[87] Seven years earlier Chief Justice Taney had told the nation that under the Constitution blacks could "claim none of the rights and privileges which that instrument provides for and secures to citizens of the United States. On the contrary [he found they were] a subordinate and inferior class of beings, who had been subjugated by the dominant race, and, whether emancipated or not, yet remained subject to their authority, and had no rights or privileges but such as those who held the power and the Government might choose to grant them." Later in the opinion, he asserted that at the founding they "had for more than a century before been regarded as beings of an inferior order, and altogether unfit to associate with the white race, either in social or political relations," and as such they were "so far inferior, that they had no rights which the white man was bound to respect; and that the negro might justly and lawfully be reduced to slavery for his benefit."[88] Now they suddenly had rights, including the right to be educated in the nation's capital.

On the same day that Congress chartered the Institution for the Education of Colored Youth, all blacks in the city gained another right: the right to ride streetcars on an equal basis with whites. In rechartering the Washington and Alexandria Railroad, Congress added a single sentence to the charter that can be seen as the first federal civil rights law in American history, although it applied to only one transportation company: "*And provided, also,* That no person shall be excluded from the cars on account of color."[89] In 1864 Congress chartered a new streetcar company in the District of Columbia, the Metropolitan Railroad. This charter contained a slightly modified and somewhat stronger civil rights protection: "*Provided,* That there shall be no regulation excluding any person from any car on account of

[87]"An Act to Incorporate the Institution for the Education of Colored Youth in the District of Columbia," Act of Mar. 3, 1863, 12 Stat. 796 (1863).

[88]*Dred Scott v. Sandford,* 60 U.S. (19 How.) 393 (1857), pp. 404–5, 407.

[89]"An Act to Extend the Charter of the Alexandria and Washington Railroad Company, and for Other Purposes," Act of Mar. 3, 1863, 12 Stat. 805 (1863).

color."[90] The change in language was significant. The Washington and Alexandria charter might have allowed for a separate car for blacks, but this new provision would prevent exclusion from "any car." But, a year later—the same day Congress created the Freedmen's Bureau—it amended the Metropolitan Railroad charter with a more elaborate and powerful civil rights provision: "*And be it Further enacted*, That the provision prohibiting any exclusion from any car on account of color, already applicable to the Metropolitan Railroad, is hereby extended to every other railroad in the District of Columbia."[91] This appears to be the first federal public accommodations law in the nation's history. It is the origin of the Civil Rights Acts of 1866, 1875, and 1964.

In 1864 Congress authorized the secretary of the treasury to rent out or lease abandoned lands and property across the South and to provide "for the employment and general welfare of all persons within the lines of national military occupation within said insurrectionary states formerly held as slaves, who are or shall become free."[92] This was the first federal law passed to directly provide for the "general welfare" of indigent people on a large scale. Ending slavery required more than just removing the chains of bondage. Congress understood that it meant providing employment and the necessities of life for former slaves. A year later, Congress created the Freedmen's Bureau, to provide "provisions, clothing, and fuel," as well as "immediate and temporary shelter and supply" for recently freed slaves.[93] At the same time, Congress created the Freedmen's Savings Bank to help former slaves save money, accumulate capital, and prepare for their lives as free people in a free economy.[94] On the same day that Congress created the Freedmen's Bureau and the Freedman's Savings Bank, Congress also passed

---

[90]"An Act to Incorporate the 'Metropolitan Railroad Company,' in the District of Columbia," Act of July 1, 1864, 13 Stat. 326 (1866).

[91]"An Act: To Amend an Act Entitled 'An Act to Incorporate the Metropolitan Railroad Company in the District of Columbia,'" Act of Mar. 3, 1865, 13 Stat. 536 (1866). For a detailed and useful discussion of the political maneuvering that led to these charter provisions, see Masur, *An Example for All the Land*, pp. 100–112.

[92]"An Act in Addition to the Several Acts Concerning Commercial Intercourse between Loyal and Insurrectionary States, and to Provide for the Collection of Captured and Abandoned Property, and the Prevention of Frauds in States Declared in Insurrection," Act of July 2, 1864, 13 Stat. 375 (1866).

[93]"An Act to Establish a Bureau for the Freedmen and Refugees," Act of Mar. 3, 1865, 13 Stat. 507 (1866).

[94]"An Act to Incorporate the Freedman's Savings and Trust Company," Act of Mar. 3, 1865, 13 Stat. 510 (1866).

the law noted above, requiring equal access to seating on streetcars in Washington, D.C.[95]

Shortly after this law was passed the war would end, and with it slavery. A new era would emerge, as Congress and the nation made the transition from antislavery to civil rights. Congress would pass numerous laws to protect black freedom in an attempt to fully reconstruct American society. Thus, the foundation of federal civil rights law began in a burst of creative congressional lawmaking in the truly revolutionary summer of '62.

---

[95]"An Act: To Amend an Act Entitled 'An Act to Incorporate the Metropolitan Railroad Company in the District of Columbia,'" Act of Mar. 3, 1865, 13 Stat. 536 (1865).

Fergus M. Bordewich

The Radicals' War

How the Joint Committee on the Conduct of the War Tried to Shape the Course of the Civil War

On July 21, 1861, the unimaginable happened. After a day's fighting at Bull Run, the United States Army collapsed into a mob and fled the battlefield before the shocked eyes of their officers and of tourists who had come down from Washington expecting to see the rebels trounced. Soldiers threw away their packs and their guns, galloped away on mules, raced off in commandeered ambulances, ignoring what officers were still left to give orders. Among the onlookers were several appalled members of Congress. One of them, Ohio Senator Benjamin Franklin Wade (fig. 1), jumped out of his carriage, and with the help of his friend Senator Zachariah Chandler (fig. 2) of Michigan, pushed it over to form a barrier, bellowing at the fleeing soldiers, "Boys, let's stop this damned runaway!"[1]

Wade and Chandler couldn't stop the panic. However, what they saw that day would have a lasting impact on the war, test constitutional doctrine, strain relations between Congress and the president, end the careers of prominent officers in the Union Army, and leave a legacy that stretched forward to the Second World War.

Most Northerners, and their congressmen, had expected the Union—with its immense resources and advantages in manpower—to overwhelm the South in a matter of weeks. No one had been prepared for a defeat, much

[1]Benjamin Wade to Caroline Wade, July 22, 1861, Benjamin F. Wade Papers, Library of Congress, reel 3 (hereafter Wade Papers, LC).

FIG. 1. Senator Benjamin F. Wade of Ohio. *(Brady-Handy Collection, Prints and Photographs Division, Library of Congress)*

FIG. 2. Senator Zachariah Chandler of Michigan. *(Brady-Handy Collection, Prints and Photographs Division, Library of Congress)*

Fig. 3. "Death of Col. Baker" at the Battle of Ball's Bluff. *(Prints and Photographs Division, Library of Congress)*

less on the scale of Bull Run, where the Union forces lost nearly 3,000 men, killed, wounded, and missing. (The Confederates lost about two-thirds as many.) In the months that followed, Union and Confederate troops faced each other warily across the Potomac. In the North, public frustration at the army's inactivity mounted. At last, on October 21, 2,000 Union troops crossed the Potomac River and attacked a Confederate camp near Ball's Bluff (fig. 3), thirty-eight miles up the Potomac from Washington. The result was another humiliating debacle. Half the Union force was killed, wounded, or captured. Among the dead was Senator Edward Baker of Oregon, a personal friend of Abraham Lincoln and the only sitting U.S. senator ever killed in battle.

Coming three months to the day after the demoralizing defeat at Bull Run, Ball's Bluff shocked and outraged the North. Militarily, the battle had no significance; it was little more than a skirmish measured against the prodigious bloodletting to come. Politically, however, its impact was momentous. Added to the military passivity of the previous months, the two defeats spurred widespread fears that the army was infiltrated with traitors, and that high-ranking officers had failed to do their duty at the cost of lives.

It is axiomatic that in wartime, Americans—and other nations, of course—hunt for traitors in their own ranks. One need only think of the harassment of German Americans during World War I and Japanese Americans during World War II, not to mention the persistent hostility toward Muslim Americans since 9/11. During the Civil War, Yankees had more reason for such anxiety. Southern sympathizers known as Copperheads were numerous and politically powerful, especially in the Midwest. Democratic newspapers ranted against the Union war effort and encouraged their readers to resist it. Hundreds of army officers had defected to the Confederacy, and many of those who remained with the Union were conservative Democrats with Southern family connections. When Union generals seemed to shy away from battle, it stoked Northern suspicions, sometimes to the point of paranoia, which persisted through most of the war. In a letter to Ben Wade, a Detroit businessman would warn of "the rank treason that permeates almost our whole army . . . the shiftless manner in which the whole war and its attendants are conducted: the utter discouragement of the friends of the Government and the impudent and defiant conduct of the traitors of the North, who are now more numerous than the traitors of the South."[2]

On December 5, 1861, Chandler—a former Detroit mayor, dry goods merchant, and Underground Railroad activist—called for the creation of a congressional committee to investigate the catastrophes at Bull Run and Ball's Bluff. Radical Republicans such as Chandler, who were defined by their commitment to the immediate emancipation of slaves, civil rights for all African Americans, and a hard war policy, were a minority in their own party. However, with the departure of every Southern senator and congressman except Andrew Johnson of Tennessee, their leverage sharply increased. In late 1861, Republicans controlled the Senate by more than two to one, holding thirty-one of that body's forty-four occupied seats to the Democrats' thirteen. There was no doubt that Chandler would get his committee, but the debate was sharp, as senators advanced arguments that still resonate today.

Republican Senator Lafayette Foster of Connecticut opposed any investigation of the army, asserting that war was best left to the generals, even when what they were doing seemed incompetent to civilians. If there were

[2]E. B. Ward to Benjamin Wade, Feb. 7, 1863, reel 4, Wade Papers, LC.

to be any investigations, he said, the proper time should only be after the war. "We cannot have men in the field fighting a battle, and have them here in our committee rooms testifying as to who was to blame for a disaster," Foster protested. "I believe in letting the military authorities manage the Army. If they manage it badly we shall make a bad matter worse by tampering and interfering, and that is all that will grow out of our action."[3]

In reply, William P. Fessenden of Maine declared that Congress's duty to the voters required it to monitor how military appropriations were spent, and to investigate the army's failures if it was not willing to investigate itself. "What are we to do?" he demanded. "Sit idle during all the period that this war is to progress; or are we manfully to do our duty, and when the occasion presents itself in the progress of the war, inquire in what manner it is conducted?" He added, "We are not under the command of the military of this country. They are under ours as a Congress."[4]

On December 10, Chandler's resolution was passed, creating the Joint Committee on the Conduct of the War. As amended, the bill stipulated that the committee would be composed of five Republicans and two Democrats, reflecting the balance of power in Congress. It provided the committee with a free-ranging mandate to examine not just the two recent defeats but all aspects of the war. The committee would exercise that mandate with vigor for the next three and a half years.[5]

Normally, the senator who proposed a new committee would chair it, but Chandler invited Wade, a lawyer, to take the job instead. Wade was as tough and difficult as any man in the Senate. He was stout and square, as if chiseled from granite, with a powerful voice, a profane vocabulary, and a bulldog obduracy that gave short shrift to evasive witnesses. In an era of intense religiosity, he was an outspoken freethinker, with a manner so blunt and opinionated that it either awed or alienated many of his contemporaries. His enemies called him just about everything from a demagogue and a "political scavenger," to a "Robespierre" and a vulgarian.[6]

At the end of 1861, the Capitol was as much an army camp as it was the seat of government. Rooms had been turned into barracks and sometimes

---

[3] *Congressional Globe* (hereafter *CG*), 37th Cong., 2nd sess., Dec. 5, 1861, pp. 16–17.

[4] Ibid.

[5] Ibid.

[6] Hans L. Trefousse, "The Motivation of a Radical Republican: Benjamin F. Wade," *Ohio History* 73 (1964):63–76.

hospitals. (Zouaves in red pantaloons were once seen swinging from ropes hung from a cornice of the dome.) Building materials had been seized to erect barricades. Mountains of bacon and hams were dumped on the marble floors. Fourteen roaring ovens beneath the west terrace baked a thousand loaves of bread daily. "Things are more unpleasant here every day," Capitol Architect Thomas Walter complained. "The Senate Chamber is alive with lice; it makes my head itch to think of it. . . . The building is like one grand water closet—every hold and every corner is defiled."[7]

It was in this atmosphere that the Joint Committee met. It held 272 sessions in all, in what is now room S-124, off the famous Brumidi Corridor. (The Italian artist Constantino Brumidi was working on his frescoes even as the committee interrogated its witnesses, a few feet away.)

In all, eleven different men served on the committee during its life span. (Membership always included three senators and four representatives.) Wade was by far the most active member. He, Chandler, and Radical Republican Representatives George Julian of Indiana (fig. 4) and Daniel W. Gooch of Massachusetts generally propelled the committee's investigations and set its tone. Its longest-serving Democratic member was Representative Moses Odell of New York, who, like most of the Democrats who served on the committee—they included, briefly, Andrew Johnson, among others—followed the Republicans' lead without demur. Typically for the era, the committee's only staff member was a stenographer.

The committee was controversial from the start. Assessments have generally fallen along ideological lines. In 1863, the Republican *New York Times* praised the committee for its unsparing investigations of military shortcomings, declaring of its revelations, "There is not such another record of dereliction and inefficiency in all military history."[8] Lincoln's biographers and former secretaries, John Hay and John G. Nicolay, writing after the war, said of the committee: "It was often hasty and unjust in its judgment, but always earnest, patriotic and honest; on the whole it must be merited more praise than blame."[9] In later years, however, the committee's reputation sank in tandem with that of the Radical Republicans generally. During the Jim Crow era, for revisionist historians it became a cynosure of political

[7]*The Senate's War* (pamphlet), U.S. Senate Historian's Office, Benjamin Wade file.

[8]*New York Times*, Apr. 7, 1863.

[9]Quoted in Mary Land, "'Bluff' Ben Wade's New England Background," *New England Quarterly* 27 (1954):484–509.

FIG. 4. Congressman George W. Julian of Indiana. *(Brady-Handy Collection, Prints and Photographs Division, Library of Congress)*

meddling and alleged personal vindictiveness. Writing in 1939, the Southern-oriented historian T. Harry Williams condemned the committee for pressuring Lincoln to embrace emancipation, for promoting "mass-hatred" of the Confederacy, and for deliberately fostering a "war psychosis" in the North.[10]

When Senator Harry Truman formed his own Special Committee to Investigate the National Defense Program on the eve of World War II, he was determined to avoid what he regarded as the Civil War committee's negative precedent. A student of history, Truman read the Joint Committee's reports, but he was also guided in his thinking by Robert E. Lee biographer Douglas Southall Freeman, who blamed the Joint Committee for gross interference with the Union war effort, and lambasted its work as "most unpatriotic." Truman wrote, "I became familiar with its mistakes and was determined to avoid the same errors in the conduct of my special committee."[11] Right-wing Republican enemies of the Roosevelt administration, he wrote, "tried to get me to make a Joint Committee out of my committee. Thank goodness I knew my history, and wouldn't do it."[12]

Today, following the sesquicentennial of the Civil War, and nearly half a century after the enactment of civil rights legislation that restored to African Americans the rights that Radical Republicans such as Wade and Chandler demanded and that Union armies made possible by victory on the battlefield, it is time to reexamine what the Joint Committee did—and to extract it from the deep shadow into which later generations cast it. The committee's work, like virtually all political processes, was often imperfect, and its impact was not always clear. The results of its efforts were complex, and in a few cases unfortunate. But they also helped to guide the Union war effort toward victory, and to infuse it with a higher moral meaning than when it began. The committee's actions also helped to turn the war into a racial revolution. Its leading members held views about human rights that were progressive and far ahead of their time. They were remarkably strong-willed men who were determined to shape a war effort that, well into 1862, was at best indifferent to enslaved African Americans, and often frankly

---

[10]Harry Williams, "Benjamin F. Wade and the Atrocity Propaganda of the Civil War," *Ohio State Archaeological and Historical Quarterly* 47 (1939):33–43.

[11]Harry S. Truman, *Memoirs*, vol. 1: *Year of Decisions* (Garden City, N.Y., 1955), p. 168.

[12]Michael David Pearlman, *Truman and MacArthur: Policy, Politics, and the Hunger for Honor and Renown* (Bloomington, Ind., 2008), pp. 21–23.

hostile to them. They also understood, before Abraham Lincoln did, what kind of war would have to be fought to ensure final victory, and what kind of generals would be needed to fight it.

In practice, the committee's day-to-day work consisted mainly in taking testimony from Union Army officers. It would eventually interview almost every major Union military figure including George McClellan, Henry Halleck, Ulysses S. Grant, William Tecumseh Sherman, David Porter, and many others—hundreds in all. Meetings attended by the full committee were rare, and at any given time two or more members might be away doing field research. Testimony was sometimes taken by only a single member, usually Wade. None of the hearings were public. Although those who appeared before the committee were directed not to talk to the press, committee members helped to establish a Washington tradition by strategically leaking documents when it suited them. None of the committee's original members had a military background. (Representative Benjamin F. Loan of Missouri, who joined the committee later, had served two years with the Missouri State Militia.) "Almost to a man, [they] shared a total ignorance of military affairs at the time the war broke out," as Elizabeth Joan Doyle observed in *Congress Investigates*, a history of congressional investigations, voicing what many critics of the committee have deemed a fatal shortcoming.[13]

The committee would eventually produce some 2,000 pages of reports. In the course of its work, the committee probed in often remarkable detail the conduct of Union defeats from First Bull Run to the Petersburg Crater of 1864, the management of the Army of the Potomac and other armies, and the competence and loyalty of senior officers. Not surprisingly, the committee irritated military men by asking often embarrassing questions about their tactics and strategy, logistical problems, motivations, and especially their failures. Why, the committee demanded, for instance, had the Rebels been allowed to blockade the Potomac River below Washington in the autumn of 1861? How had the debacle at Ball's Bluff transpired, and who was responsible for it? How feasible was it to move an army overland into eastern Tennessee, and by what route? Why had McClellan advanced so slowly on Richmond during the Peninsular Campaign of 1862? Had III Corps been needlessly put at risk during the Battle of Gettysburg? Could the

[13]Elizabeth Joan Doyle, "The Conduct of the War, 1861–1865," in Roger A. Bruns et al., eds., *Congress Investigates: A Critical and Documentary History*, 2 vols. (New York, 2011), 1:165–68.

Confederate Army have been destroyed in the days after that battle, and why wasn't it? The committee also considered many other subjects: Confederate atrocities; the abuse of Union prisoners; dishonest contracting for the armed forces; the military administration of Alexandria, Virginia; the development of turreted ironclad ships; the manufacture of cannon; and even the slaughter of friendly Cheyenne Indians at Sand Creek, Colorado. Throughout its deliberations, the committee consistently championed emancipation and the enrollment of black troops into the Union Army, an initiative that conservative officers stoutly resisted for years.[14]

Almost from its inception, the committee leaned hard against the president, nudging, prodding, provoking, and occasionally insulting him. Members of the Joint Committee were particularly impatient with his conciliatory attitude toward the South, his reluctance to embrace a harsh war policy, and his gradualist approach to equality for blacks. While Lincoln's speeches often wove in hints of reconciliation, Wade—typically for congressional Radicals—declared that the war must be carried on until the "absolute, unqualified, and unconditional subjugation of every rebel in the land to the Constitution and the laws," and called for total war until "there is no source from which they can derive revenue or means for the maintenance of the war, except by depriving the people of their property, day after day, year after year, so long as the war shall continue, thus reducing them to poverty and want."[15] Wade at one point dismissed Lincoln's leadership as a "rose-water war."[16] On another occasion, Chandler told Lincoln that he ought to send for Jefferson Davis at once if he was determined to pursue such cautious policies, and that the Radicals would vote neither money nor men until they were used "to promptly crush this accursed rebellion."[17]

The Radicals' criticism of the president never really ceased. In 1864, Lincoln's veto of proposed Reconstruction measures advocated by the Radicals so incensed them that for several months they considered replacing Lincoln at the head of the Republican ticket with either Benjamin Butler or

[14]Joint Committee on the Conduct of the War, *Annual Report 1863* (Washington, D.C., 1863), 1:125ff., 3:9–18 (hereafter JCC); U.S. Senate Report no. 41, 37th Cong., 2nd sess., pp. 9ff.; Sen. Rep. no. 63, 38th Cong., 1st sess., pp. 4–7; Sen. Rep. no. 114, 38th Cong., 2nd sess., p. 121.

[15]Doyle, "Conduct of the War," p. 199.

[16]Land, "Ben Wade's New England Background."

[17]Hans L. Trefousse, *Benjamin Franklin Wade: Radical Republican from Ohio* (New York, 1963), p. 154.

John C. Frémont. Lincoln, Wade wrote in a manifesto published in August of that year, "must understand that our support is of a cause and not of a man."[18]

Every American conflict has brought struggle between Congress and the executive over how much power the president has to wage war, and how he is permitted to exert it. The Constitution ambiguously declares the president to be commander in chief, but empowers Congress to "provide for the common defense," to declare war, and to raise and support armies. It also specifies that Congress possesses the authority "to make all laws which shall be necessary and proper for carrying into execution the foregoing powers."[19] Even Harry Truman, who disliked the Joint Committee, nonetheless recognized the importance of congressional oversight. He wrote: "The power to investigate is necessary to the intelligent exercise of the powers of Congress. This is especially true in wartime, when the Congress must delegate many of its powers. Only by investigation can it review the exercise of them and ascertain how and to what extent they should be modified."[20]

Lincoln, in his capacity as commander in chief, created an army, financed it out of Treasury funds, proclaimed a blockade of Southern ports, suspended the writ of habeas corpus, and imposed other war measures without congressional authorization, claiming that all this fell under implicit presidential powers during a period of unprecedented national emergency. Meanwhile, the Joint Committee asserted a right both to advise the president and to participate in guiding the war effort itself. Wade declared that his "arm would fall off before [he would] surrender one jot or tittle of [legislative] power," adding, "I cannot bear to hear with complacency the doctrine urged that, the moment war is declared . . . Congress loses all power to regulate the rights of war." The president might be commander in chief, Wade said, "but Congress, the legislative power sitting superior to him or any other magistrate in the nation, may regulate, modify, and direct whatever principles they please [that] their commander in chief shall act upon and execute."[21]

Despite such sentiments, the committee generally maintained amicable relations with Lincoln and his cabinet, who regularly complied with

---

[18]Ibid., p. 226.

[19]Theodore Wilson, "The Truman Committee on War Mobilization, 1941–44," cited in Bruns, *Congress Investigates*, 1:636.

[20]Truman, *Memoirs*, 1:168.

[21]Ibid., 1:169.

committee requests for meetings and information. During the Thirty-Seventh Congress alone, members of the committee met alone with the president at least eight times. We are today accustomed to a dominant executive, an "imperial presidency," as it is often described; nineteenth-century Americans were not. Lincoln himself was a product of an era of legislative dominance. He never complained of any infringement on the office of the president. Although Lincoln was often annoyed by the committee's pressure—he once complained that it was an "improvised vigilant[e] committee"—he never refused to cooperate with it.[22]

Lincoln's reluctance to challenge his generals—most particularly the battle-averse George B. McClellan—certainly encouraged the committee to press aggressively for more forceful action. In his *Reminiscences*, George W. Julian recalled a meeting with Lincoln and several members of his cabinet in early 1862:

> The most striking fact revealed by the discussion which took place was that neither the president nor his advisors seemed to have any definite information respecting the management of the war, or the failure of our forces to make any forward movement. We were greatly surprised to learn that Mr. Lincoln himself did not think he had any right to know. Our grand armies were ready and eager to march, and the whole country was waiting for some decisive movement; but during the delightful months of October, November and December, they had been kept idle for some reason which no man could explain.[23]

An odor of political partisanship has colored much of the later writing about the committee's work. It is true enough that the officers the committee challenged most severely were Democrats, and those it favored were usually Republicans. In a speech indicative of Radical sentiments that Julian delivered to the House of Representatives in February 1863, he declared flatly that the Republican Party stood for freedom while the Democrats stood for slavery. "Not only is it that rebels are Democrats, but so are rebel sympathizers, whether in the North or the South," he asserted. "Loyalty and Republicanism go hand in hand throughout the Union, as perfectly as treason and slavery." He further charged that "Democratic policy"—by which he meant sympathy toward the South, tolerance for slavery, and a hesitant

---

[22] Ibid., 1:172.

[23] George W. Julian, *Speeches on Political Questions* (New York, 1872), pp. 201–3.

war strategy—had infected the Lincoln administration, and was responsible for the army's litany of "blunders, misjudgments, and defeats." To the committee's Radical members, as well as to many other Northerners, Democratic politics and incompetent tactics seemed to go hand in hand.[24]

The committee issued its first report on April 3, 1863, a few weeks before the Battle of Chancellorsville. Its assessment of the eastern theater of war was scathing. "Had the success of the Army of the Potomac during this period corresponded with the success of our arms in other parts of the country, there is reason to believe that the termination of the campaign of 1862 would have seen the rebellion well-nigh, if not entirely, overthrown," it declared. The report was, on the whole, thorough and illuminating. However, its investigation of the Ball's Bluff debacle, in particular its targeting of General Charles P. Stone, gave rise to persistent accusations of witch-hunting fanaticism that dogged its work ever after. The Massachusetts-born Stone was a career army officer—and a Democrat—who in the first weeks of the war had been lionized for successfully organizing Washington's defenses. As a division commander, he had ordered the crossing of the Potomac at Ball's Bluff. The committee's investigation revealed shocking ineptitude and miscommunication among a number of senior officers, including Stone. It also found, among other things, that only three leaky boats were on hand to transport the 2,000 federal troops across the river, which virtually guaranteed that they would be trapped and butchered by the Rebel guns on the bluffs above. A parade of witnesses from various Union regiments told the committee that for weeks before the battle Stone had sent "packages" and letters across the river, personally visited with Rebel officers, permitted the enemy to erect fortifications that he could have prevented, returned fugitive slaves to their masters, and cultivated the friendship of secessionists on the Maryland side of the river. Much of this was rumor, and some of it, though accurate, was misconstrued. After the debacle, however, Stone was tagged as a likely traitor, as well as an incompetent. Many of his troops refused to serve any longer under his command. Colonel George Tompkins of the 2nd New York told the committee that Stone seemed to be "too well-liked" by secessionists in the vicinity, while Lieutenant Philip J. Downey of the same regiment testified, "I thought he was more of a Secesh than anything else."[25]

---

[24] *CG*, 37th Cong., 1st sess., Feb. 18, 1863, pp. 1064–65.
[25] JCC, 1863, 1:9–18, 295–301, 373.

Stone did not help himself when he was called to testify before the committee, and when questioned about his strategy before the battle, loftily replied, "If I had any plans, I should not wish to tell them, even to my aide-de-camp."[26] Stone's commander, George McClellan, testified that some of the charges—mainly that Stone was rather well liked by the Confederates—were corroborated by a refugee from Leesburg, Virginia, who said he had heard Rebel officers talking about Stone.[27] Stone was arrested and spent six months in a military prison in New York. Although the charges against him were later dropped and he was restored to active service in 1864, his reputation never recovered. If he was guilty of anything, apart from snobbery, it was a degree of professional ineptitude that was shared by most officers in those early months of the war.

By today's standards, the abuse of Stone's civil rights was flagrant. Hearsay evidence was both solicited and accepted, and Wade made it clear that he did not consider the Fifth Amendment valid when it came to testimony before any congressional committee. Stone was never allowed to face his accusers or to see their testimony until 1863. Ball's Bluff demanded a scapegoat, and Stone was made to order. In Joan Doyle's words, "As an example of the worst in investigatory techniques and of character assassination, the handling of General Stone has seldom been equaled."[28] Stone's professional destruction had no discernible impact at all on the war. But it probably encouraged future witnesses to take the Joint Committee seriously. Later in the war, when General George McClellan was called to testify, he wrote to Lincoln, "If I escape alive I will report when I get through." Ever afterward, he referred to the committee's members as "hounds."[29]

By now, however, Ball's Bluff had been far eclipsed by the killing fields of Shiloh, Second Bull Run, Antietam, Fredericksburg, and many less famous but terrible battles. The committee's primary—and far better justified—target in its first report was McClellan (fig. 5), who led the Army of the Potomac from August 1861 to November 1862. The wealthy, breathtakingly arrogant, West Point–trained McClellan was tapped in August 1861 to take charge of the army following two small victories he won in western Virginia.

---

[26]Ibid., p. 267.

[27]Ibid., pp. 509–10.

[28]Doyle, "Conduct of the War," p. 173.

[29]Ibid., pp. 175, 191–92.

FIG. 5. Major General George B. McClellan, c. 1861, carte de visite. *(Prints and Photographs Division, Library of Congress)*

After Bull Run, anyone who could win a battle looked like a potential savior; newspapers extravagantly dubbed him the "Young Napoleon." He amassed troops around Washington, marched, drilled, paraded, built forts, dug trenches, and then marched and drilled some more. As month bled into month, he demanded more time and more troops, always asserting that he was faced with overwhelming numbers of the enemy, when in fact their forces were only a fraction of his own. When he finally crept a little further into northern Virginia, it was revealed that the Confederate fortresses that McClellan had deemed to be impregnable were armed only with "Quaker guns"—wooden logs painted to look like cannon.

Apart from his undeniable talents as a drillmaster, McClellan was an albatross for the Union war effort. No matter how hard Lincoln and the congressional Radicals pushed McClellan through the autumn of 1861 and the winter of 1862, he simply refused to move. Although the Radicals on the Joint Committee had initially supported him, in spite of his Democratic Party affiliation, they now began to wonder if he was afraid to fight, or if he was guilty of something worse. George Julian wrote, "It seemed like a betrayal of the country itself to allow him to hold our grand armies for weeks and months in unexplained idleness, on the naked assumption of his superior wisdom."[30]

At last, under intense political pressure, in May, McClellan struck at the Confederate capital by landing his army on the peninsula that extends between the James and Rappahannock rivers, and then marching on Richmond from the southeast, entrenching virtually every mile of the way, apparently dreading an attack by the enemy. Despite a huge numerical advantage, McClellan was repeatedly outmaneuvered during what came to be known as the Seven Days battles, and was forced ignominiously to reembark his men for the North.

"This is called strategy!" Zachariah Chandler roared on the Senate floor. "One hundred and fifty-eight thousand men, ably handled, can defeat any force the Confederates can raise; and that is the force that went down to the Peninsula. But, sir, it lay in ditches, digging, drinking rotten water, and eating bad food, and sleeping in the mud, until it became greatly reduced in numbers and, of those that were left, very many were injured in health.

---

[30]Julian, *Speeches on Political Questions*, pp. 201–3.

Still they fought, still they conquered in every fight, and still they retreated, because they were ordered to retreat."[31]

The Joint Committee's hearings on the Army of the Potomac over the course of 1862 laid McClellan open to often scathing criticism by his subordinate officers. The testimony delivered by Joseph Hooker, a favorite of the Radicals, who commanded a front-line division on the Peninsula and later superseded McClellan as commander of the Army of the Potomac, was typical.

Q: "To what do you attribute the failure of the Peninsula Campaign?"
A: "I do not hesitate to say that it is to be attributed to the want of generalship on the part of our commander."

Hooker described McClellan as inexplicably disinclined to leave his headquarters in order to examine the situation on the front lines. "General McClellan showed a great indisposition to go forward," he remarked.

Q: "Is it your judgment that you could have gone into Richmond then?"
A: "I think we could have moved right on, and got into Richmond by the second day after that battle [of Williamsburg] without another gun being fired."[32]

Although Hooker was self-interested, he was also pretty much right.

The committee's 1863 report squarely blamed McClellan for, among other things, failing to advance into Virginia in the winter of 1861; for fumbling the Peninsular Campaign; for repeatedly exaggerating the numbers of the enemy he faced; for failing to reinforce General John Pope in the summer of 1862, thus contributing to the Union defeat at Second Bull Run; for failing to crush Robert E. Lee's army at the Battle of Antietam in September 1862; and then for allowing Lee to escape across the Potomac after that battle. In the words of the *Pittsburgh Daily Gazette*, the report "utterly pulverizes General McClellan."[33] On the floor of Congress, George Julian further excoriated the "Young Napoleon" for his conservative politics, declaring, "Every man who loved negro slavery better than his country, and

[31]Walter Buell, "Zachariah Chandler," *Magazine of Western History* 4 (1886):271–78, 338–52, 432–44.

[32]Doyle, "Conduct of the War," pp. 195–97.

[33]Bruce Tap, *Over Lincoln's Shoulder: The Committee on the Conduct of the War* (Lawrence, Kans., 1998), p. 163.

would sooner see the Republic in ruins than the slaves set free, is the zealous advocate and unflinching champion of McClellan."[34]

After Antietam, McClellan was replaced as chief of the Army of the Potomac by IX Corps commander Ambrose Burnside, who considered himself unready, and initially tried to decline the appointment. In December 1862, he proved his instinct correct by mismanaging the battle of Fredericksburg, which cost the Union more than 12,000 casualties. (Confederate casualties numbered 5,300.) Burnside was followed in January 1863 by Joseph "Fighting Joe" Hooker, who had commanded I Corps under McClellan and Burnside. Hooker was crushed in turn by Robert E. Lee at Chancellorsville in May 1863, resulting in another 18,000 Union casualties. (The Confederates lost about 13,000.) In June, Lee launched the Army of Northern Virginia northward to invade Pennsylvania. On June 28, Hooker was abruptly removed from command of the Army of the Potomac and was replaced by the surprised V Corps commander George G. Meade. Meade, though a Democrat, was a largely apolitical professional, but not very likeable. As Bruce Catton put it, he "was crabbed and dyspeptic, a regular army officer who had never cared very much for the volunteer system," and had never won the hearts of his men.[35]

Less than a week after his appointment, Meade led the army to a decisive victory at Gettysburg. The euphoria was brief. Despite Meade's overwhelming numbers and his troops' high morale, he failed to vigorously pursue Lee, who managed to escape to Virginia with his battered army. "I do not believe you appreciate the magnitude of the misfortune involved in Lee's escape," Lincoln wrote to Meade on July 14, in a letter he never sent. "Your golden opportunity is gone, and I am distressed immeasurably because of it."[36] So were the Radicals on the Joint Committee. The squandering of what had seemed like the long-awaited destruction of Lee's army now seemed only to lead to a repeat of George McClellan's hopeless tactics of 1861 and 1862. From then on, Ben Wade and his colleagues, most of whom regarded the bombastic but forceful Hooker's dismissal as a mistake, put Meade in the political hot seat and kept him there for the rest of the war.

---

[34]*CG*, 37th Cong., 1st sess., Feb. 18, 1863, pp. 1064–65.

[35]Bruce Catton, *Glory Road: The Bloody Route from Fredericksburg to Gettysburg* (Garden City, N.Y., 1952), p. 331.

[36]Abraham Lincoln, unsent letter to George G. Meade, July 14, 1863, cited in Harold Holzer, ed., *Lincoln on War* (Chapel Hill, N.C., 2111), p. 199–200.

The committee collected extensive testimony about Meade's behavior before, during, and after Gettysburg. The hearings were dominated by Daniel E. Sickles (fig. 6), one of the most colorful Union generals of the war, and exactly the sort of aggressive citizen soldier the committee liked. In 1859, while a congressman from New York, he shot dead the son of Francis Scott Key in front of witnesses outside the White House—Key had seduced Sickles's wife—but was acquitted as a result of the first successful plea of temporary insanity in American judicial history. Though devoid of military experience, he raised a regiment through his Tammany Hall connections, and steadily ascended to brigade, division, and finally corps command under Hooker and Meade. Unfortunately in Sickles's case, rank was not congruent with competence.

Sickles nearly lost the battle of Gettysburg for the Union on July 2, 1863, when he impulsively advanced III Corps beyond the Union line, leaving it dangerously exposed to Confederate attack. In the subsequent fighting, Sickles was severely wounded, and suffered the amputation of his leg. (The leg is now a prized possession of the National Museum of Health and Medicine in Silver Spring, Maryland.) Despite his disability, and his costly misjudgment at Gettysburg, he was eager to return to service, and was furious when Meade declined to restore him to command of his corps later in 1863.

When called to testify before the Joint Committee, Sickles declared that he "considered it a misfortune to the army" for Hooker to have been replaced by Meade in the first place.[37] He also came close to claiming personal credit for the victory at Gettysburg, asserting that he had begged Meade to concentrate the army at Gettysburg, while Meade seemed afraid to confront Lee head-on. With better justification, he bluntly criticized Meade for failing to destroy the Army of Northern Virginia when for several days the Confederates were trapped with their backs against the flooding Potomac.

He told the committee what it wanted to hear, as in this exchange:

Q: "Could there have been any great hazard to our army in venturing an engagement there?"

[37]JCC, 1865, 1:34ff.

FIG. 6. Major General Daniel Sickles. *(Prints and Photographs Division, Library of Congress)*

A: "No, sir. If we could whip them at Gettysburg, as we did, we could much more easily whip a running and demoralized army, seeking a retreat which was cut off by a swollen river."[38]

When summoned to testify on his own behalf, Meade justified his actions clearly, but not all that convincingly. "Knowing that if I were defeated the whole road to Washington would be open, and all the fruits of my victory at Gettysburg dissipated, I did not feel that I would be right in assuming the responsibility in blindly attacking the enemy without any knowledge of his position," he told the committee. Like McClellan, Meade had a tendency to overestimate the size of his enemy, asserting that he believed that Lee had 110,000 troops on hand after Gettysburg when the actual number was closer to 45,000.[39]

Lincoln and the Radicals were further frustrated by Meade's failure to bring Lee to battle again in the autumn of 1863. Although Sickles was not with the army at the time, the committee elicited his opinions of Meade's actions anyway. The committee characterized his strategy as a "retreat" rather than, as Meade himself described it, maneuver for topographical advantage. The committee asked Sickles:

Q: "In your judgment, was it good generalship to retreat before the enemy in order to find an eligible place to fight a battle? Would that not have more tendency to demoralize our troops than to fight a battle under circumstances perhaps less advantageous?"
A: "I think the army felt humiliated by that retreat."
Q: "To a military man, was it an unacceptable retreat?"
A: "I can discover no good military reason for it."[40]

Bruce Catton, writing in the 1950s, described Meade during this period as "an infinitely weary man," who felt responsibility as a paralyzing weight. "He had been one of the few men who could have lost the war irretrievably in one day, and he had managed to avoid the mistakes that would have lost it. He would continue to avoid mistakes, even if he had to miss opportunity."[41]

Sickles was hardly an unbiased source. The committee collected similarly critical testimony from several other disgruntled officers, including

[38]Ibid, 1:295–97, 300–301.
[39]Ibid, 1:334ff.
[40]Ibid., 1:304
[41]Catton, *Glory Road*, p. 328.

Abner Doubleday, whom Meade had declined to give corps command after Gettysburg; David Birney, who had briefly commanded III Corps after Sickles was wounded, but was then required to yield it to William French; the Hooker loyalist Daniel Butterfield, whom Meade carried over as his chief of staff during the Gettysburg campaign; and Alfred Pleasonton, who had commanded the army's cavalry at Gettysburg and was known to be unfriendly to Meade. Pleasonton was exceptionally caustic:

Q: "What effect is produced on the men by the constant shrinking from an engagement?"
A: "It discourages them very much."
Q: "If the hearts of the leaders of the army are not in the enterprise it is very easy for them not to act with that spirit by which success is generally achieved?"
A: "I do not know any profession in which the character of one man stamps itself more indelibly upon masses of men than in the military profession."
Q: "And the spirit of the commanding general usually diffuses itself through the whole army?"
A: "Yes, sir."[42]

The committee struck hard at Meade again after the Battle of the Crater during the siege of Petersburg in July 1864. After Grant's failure to capture the city and turn the Confederate flank in May, the opposing armies had settled into a stalemate. In an effort to break it, the colonel of a Pennsylvania regiment from that state's coal mining districts proposed digging a mine under the Rebel fortifications, filling it with powder, and blowing a hole in the Confederate line through which Union troops could pour. Meade never liked the idea, scoffed that it would never work, and offered no logistical support. Burnside, from whose lines the mine would extend, embraced it, however. While the miners dug, Burnside drilled his African American division to exploit the anticipated breakthrough. Not only might the mine create a breakthrough that could end the war, it offered an opportunity to showcase the skill and bravery of black troops. Just before the mine was to be detonated, Meade ordered Burnside to replace the black division with a white one, none of whose men had been trained for the assault. The mine was a success, blowing an entire Confederate redoubt into the sky. But the assault was a complete failure, with the untrained Union assault troops

[42]JCC, 1865, 1:360ff.

pouring into the crater and milling around in it until the Confederates regrouped, restored their line, and killed and captured the hapless Federals in droves. The Union lost nearly 4,000 men, the Confederates fewer than half that number. The Joint Committee's report flayed Meade:

> In conclusion they, your committee, must say that in their opinion the cause of the disastrous result of the assault of the 30th of July last is mainly attributable to the fact that the plans and suggestions of the general [Burnside] who had devoted his attention for so long a time to the subject, who had carried to a successful completion the project of mining the enemy's works, and who had carefully selected and drilled his troops for the purpose of securing whatever advantages might be attainable from the explosion of the mine, should have been so entirely disregarded by a general [Meade] who had evinced no faith in the successful prosecution of that work, had aided it by no countenance or open approval, and had assumed the entire direction and control only when it was completed, and the time had come for reaping any advantages that might be derived from it.[43]

While the committee had worked to undermine McClellan, and made clear its unhappiness with Meade, it offered steady support for several generals whose less than lustrous performance on the battlefield has tended to discredit its entire engagement in the war effort. Among these were John C. Frémont, Benjamin F. Butler, Ambrose Burnside, and Joseph Hooker. They were a diverse group. Frémont (fig. 7), an explorer of the West and the 1856 Republican candidate for president, was ambitious, impulsive, and insubordinate. Burnside, though West Point–trained, proved his unfitness for high command at Fredericksburg. Hooker, another West Pointer, was an effective division and corps commander but, like Burnside, out of his depth at the army level.

Members of the committee often waxed enthusiastic over these men long after their limitations had become manifest, typically blaming their problems on cabals of Democratic officers within the army. Zachariah Chandler, for instance, wrote to his wife that Hooker "would fight if he could have a chance but that he cannot have at present as the McClellan men in the Army are down *upon him* & they are today too powerful for him."[44] As late as 1863, George Julian was still calling Frémont "a man of genius and

---

[43]Sen. Rep. no. 1, 37th Cong., 3rd sess., pp. 11–12, 105ff.

[44]Doyle, "Conduct of the War," p. 178.

FIG. 7. Major General John C. Frémont, design drawing for engraving by J. C. Buttre, c. 1862–64. *(Prints and Photographs Division, Library of Congress)*

dauntless courage," and suggesting him as a model for the rest of the army.[45] The committee typically favored officers who embodied, or at least boasted, of their commitment to what Bruce Tap termed "a bold, offensive

[45]*CG*, 37th Cong., 1st sess., Feb. 18, 1863, pp. 1067–69.

style of warfare that appealed to the committee's popular conception of battle."[46] As George Julian put it, "What we need is action—instant, decisive, defiant action—scourging faithless men from power, sweeping away obstacles, and kindling in the popular heart the fires of a new courage and hope."[47] On the other hand, Butler (fig. 8), one of the committee's most favored generals, was a shrewd and tough-minded politician, but sluggish and ineffectual when he actually lumbered into the field. The only time the committee seriously undertook an investigation of one of his misadventures—his fumbled attempt to capture Fort Fisher in Georgia in December 1864—he "left the committee not only convinced of his innocence in the Fort Fisher attack, but even impressed by his presumed military brilliance," in the words of Joan Doyle.[48]

While it is difficult to generalize about these men, one thing most of them had in common was either a commitment to, or at least a willingness to accept, the Radicals' commitment to emancipation. As the military governor of the politically torn Border State of Missouri in 1861, Frémont, a true abolitionist, declared an end to slavery in the state, the first such act of emancipation in American history. (Fearing the complete loss of the already divided state, however, the Lincoln administration rescinded his edict, and removed Frémont from office.) Butler, though a prewar Democrat who had supported Jefferson Davis as the Democratic candidate for president in 1860, created the legal route that led ultimately to the Emancipation Proclamation: in 1861, as the commander of Fortress Monroe in Virginia, he had declared fugitive slaves to be "contraband of war," and thus protected from the claims of their masters, enabling Lincoln to circumvent Congress by defining the proclamation as a war measure. His severity as the military governor of the captured city of New Orleans had also endeared him to the Radicals. Burnside had integrated a division of black troops into his own IX Corps, although it would be badly mangled in the tragically mismanaged Battle of the Crater.

Critics of the Joint Committee have typically focused on its preoccupation with military strategy and personalities. They tend either to omit or to treat as an afterthought the members' fierce, overarching, and uncompromising

---

[46]Tap, *Over Lincoln's Shoulder*, p. 168.

[47]*CG*, 37th Cong., 1st sess., Feb. 18, 1863, pp. 1067–69.

[48]Doyle, "Conduct of the War," p. 184.

Fig. 8. Major General Benjamin F. Butler. *(Prints and Photographs Division, Library of Congress)*

commitment to the human rights of African Americans. To the Radicals themselves, however, the destruction of slavery was not an ancillary concern: it was central to the war's purpose. From the early months of the war, they worried that racist generals such as McClellan, who had no interest in black civil rights, would prevent or reverse the liberation of black Americans, or make agreements with the defeated Confederates that stripped blacks of their hard-won gains.

One of the committee's most forceful reports, and by far the most chilling to read, details its investigation into the cold-blooded massacre of hundreds of disarmed Union soldiers, most of them black, at Fort Pillow, in Tennessee, by Confederate forces under Nathan Bedford Forrest on April 12, 1864.[49] Forrest, a dynamic cavalry commander, and a prewar slave trader—he would later help establish the Ku Klux Klan—led a bold raid as far north as Paducah, Kentucky, and continued to sow disorder as he returned south. Fort Pillow, on the Mississippi River, was poorly designed for defense from the land. It was occupied by about 550 men from two black regiments, the 6th U.S. Heavy Artillery and the 2nd U.S. Light Artillery, and the 13th Tennessee Cavalry, a white Union regiment. The garrison waged a spirited defense, but was quickly overwhelmed.

What followed was by far the worst war crime perpetrated during the Civil War. (Although Sherman's march through Georgia is still treated as a paradigm of wartime "cruelty," battles were few, and apart from the destruction of property it was characterized by almost nothing that would today be considered a war crime.) Confederate forces had murdered black Union soldiers before, but nothing approached the scale of what happened at Fort Pillow. Shouts of "No quarter!" were heard as soon as the Confederates penetrated the fort. Soldiers attempting to surrender were shot, hacked with sabers, and beaten to death with rifle butts. Wounded men were slaughtered indiscriminately where they lay. Several were burned to death in huts. Others were thrown into pits with the dead and buried alive.[50]

Ben Wade and Daniel Gooch of the Joint Committee traveled to Tennessee two weeks after the battle to interview survivors. Their eyewitness observations still make painful reading: "We found evidences of this murder

[49]Sen. Rep. no. 63, 38th Cong., 1st sess., pp. 4ff.
[50]JCC, 1864, p. 14.

and cruelty still most painfully apparent," they reported. "We saw bodies still unburied of some sick men who had been fleeing from the hospital and beaten down and brutally murdered, and their bodies left where they had fallen. We could still see the faces, hands and feet of men, white and black, protruding out of the ground."[51]

A white hotel keeper told the two investigators that he saw the Confederates trap about one hundred soldiers at the bottom of the bluffs along the river. When they begged to be allowed to surrender, "The rebels would reply, 'God damn you, why didn't you surrender before?' and shot them down like dogs." John Hogan, an African American corporal, testified: "I saw Captain Carson [a white officer], and heard some of the enemy ask him if he belonged to a nigger regiment. He told them he did. They asked him how he came here. He told them he was detailed there. Then they told him they would give him a detail and immediately shot him dead."[52]

Without the committee's efforts to record the facts, the Fort Pillow massacre might well have been scrubbed from history. Even so, it was played down, and sometimes discredited entirely, during the long years of Jim Crow politics and Jim Crow historiography, when the role of African American troops was largely airbrushed, not just from the Southern but also the nation's memory.

The Joint Committee's leaders may have been limited in their grasp of tactics and strategy, but they were politically farsighted. They clearly saw political dangers that the generals did not, or at least did not care about. They understood that the feral violence that ran amok at Fort Pillow would still thrive in the postwar South unless Reconstruction was carried out with unbending determination and a sustained commitment to the rights of African Americans. With good reason, the Radicals feared that what had been won in blood on the battlefield would be surrendered by politicians and generals who were in a hurry to yield authority to their former Confederate enemies in the Southern states. By the autumn of 1865, the persecution of Negroes and Union men was in full swing. "The slave holders will have slavery in time," committee member John Covode of Pennsylvania wrote to Ben Wade in September, "unless the government lay a firm hand

[51]Ibid., pp. 6–8.

[52]Ibid., pp. 30–32.

on Louisiana."[53] Even Bedford Forrest, the mass murderer of Fort Pillow, had had the confidence to apply for a federal pardon.

THE MOST THOROUGH modern study of the committee is found in Bruce Tap's *Over Lincoln's Shoulder*, published in 1998. Tap acknowledges that the committee exposed financial mismanagement and abuses, and bolstered Northern resolve to continue the war. However, his judgment of the committee is on the whole harsh and dismissive. "A number of investigations were simply a waste of time, energy and resources," Tap writes, and "amounted to Monday morning quarterbacking." He charges the committee with abandoning objectivity for partisan ends and with failing to offer "practical advice" on how to avoid repeating the mistakes it highlighted. He further says that the committee's members "refused to believe that their ignorance of military affairs was a liability. Passionately committed to action, they refused to defer to the experts." He blames the committee for fostering factionalism in the officer corps, for damaging relations between the military and civilian officials, and for undermining "consensus" by equating Democrats with traitors. Although the committee's unrelenting pressure for action may have forced some generals to act more forcefully, Tap writes, it may also have propelled others, such as Ambrose Burnside, to undertake "foolish, premature" maneuvers such as the suicidal assaults on Marye's Heights at Fredericksburg. "Instead of sowing the seeds of unity, the committee often planted suspicion and discord."[54]

There is certainly some truth in this indictment. No one can imagine that the Union war effort would have fared better if John C. Frémont or Benjamin Butler had been given more important field commands. But the indictment is based in part on arbitrary assumptions: that unity of purpose between civilian politicians and the military was achievable; that consensus between Republicans and Democrats was possible; that the ultimate results of a given investigation could somehow be known before it was undertaken; that "objectivity" was easy to define; that the committee members' lack of military experience was a fatal flaw that should have barred them from questioning serving generals; and that they had a duty to offer remedies for

[53]John Covode to Benjamin Wade, July 11, 1865, reel 6, Wade Papers, LC.
[54]Tap, *Over Lincoln's Shoulder*, pp. 255–59.

the military's shortcomings. But were these really standards that the committee could have, or should have, been expected to meet?

Ben Wade wrote in the committee's 1865 report that the committee "have not sought to accomplish any purpose other than to elicit the truth; to that end have all their labors been directed."[55] While it would be naïve to take Wade's statement of purpose entirely at face value, a close reading of the committee's reports reveals a persistent, determined, and increasingly sophisticated commitment to getting to the bottom of what happened before, during, and after battle, and who was responsible. Precisely what occurred at Ball's Bluff on October 21, 1861? Why did Dan Sickles impulsively push III Corps beyond the Army of the Potomac's Cemetery Ridge line on July 2, 1863? What went on in George Meade's command tent in the days after the Battle of Gettysburg? Or in the chaos of Fort Pillow's capture?

For many of the war's crucial battles—as well as battles that failed to happen, such as Mine Run—the committee's reports provide remarkable and detailed records of what the principal players thought happened. One of the committee's stated goals was to bequeath to posterity a detailed record of military operations. In this it certainly succeeded. In its reports, we hear soldiers, strategists, and eyewitnesses only months or even weeks after the events in which they participated. We hear the real-time voices of heroes and scoundrels alike—some authoritative, others defensive, unreliable, or vengeful, but always immediate—speaking from within the fog of war about orders dispatched but never received, and about decisions—some wise, some foolish—made in the heat of battle.

Ben Wade's biographer Hans Trefousse argued that Lincoln used the committee deliberately to prod cautious generals such as McClellan and Meade into action. Tap, by contrast, suggests that there is little direct evidence to support this contention, and that Lincoln regarded the committee more as a hindrance than as a helpful tool. Lincoln was a canny politician who had nothing to gain by alienating abolitionist congressmen more than he already had. But he did not really need the committee to tell him how to think about the war. In time, his early naïveté, like that of most Northerners, gave way to hard reality. By 1863, the committee's views and Lincoln's inexorably converged. Lincoln was already coming to accept that the war would be long, brutal, and bloody, and that victory required the leadership

---

[55]JCC, 1865, 1:v.

of hard and aggressive men, a journey in the president's strategic thinking that would eventually lead him to Ulysses S. Grant, William T. Sherman, and Philip Sheridan. He also concluded, as the Radicals had long before, that it must also bring about the emancipation of the slaves. "If God wills that [the war] continue, until all the wealth piled up by the bondsman's two hundred and fifty years of unrequited toil shall be sunk, and until every drop of blood drawn with the lash, shall be paid with another drawn with the sword, as was said three thousand years ago, so still it must be said 'the judgements of the Lord are true and righteous altogether,'" Lincoln intoned in his second inaugural address.[56] Wade, Chandler, and their colleagues on the Joint Committee had been saying the same thing, if less eloquently, for four years.

The committee certainly desired to have a direct impact on the war effort. So much is clear from their lines of questioning, particularly of less aggressive generals. But did they? Their actual power is hard to quantify. Committee pressure may well have contributed to Lincoln's eventual firing of McClellan, but the president held on to George Meade until the end of the war, no matter how much the committee attacked him. The committee's outspoken demands for more aggressive generalship may have influenced Ambrose Burnside's decision to launch repeated suicidal assaults against Marye's Heights at Fredericksburg. And the committee's support for Joseph Hooker may have helped secure him the job as Burnside's replacement, but it couldn't keep him in the job after his humiliating defeat at Chancellorsville. Lincoln continued to employ a few generals favored by the Radicals past the point at which their behavior clearly warranted dismissal. Frémont, after his removal from Missouri, was reassigned to the command of a small army in western Virginia, only to be ignominiously trounced by Stonewall Jackson in 1862; he never held a field command again. Without any obvious boost from the committee, Hooker went on to perform well in the western theater in 1863 and 1864. Among them all, Benjamin Butler led the most charmed life of all, continuing to serve into 1865, until the approaching end of the war finally made him expendable.

How much did it matter that the committee's principal members had never served in the army? It disposed them to favor volunteer officers such as Butler, and to sometimes disparage professionals. It's worth noting, too,

[56]Holzer, *Lincoln on War*, p. 280.

that nearly all the soldiers who fought the war were essentially citizen soldiers, including a significant number of generals and countless subordinate officers. Many generals, including Grant and Sherman (though West Point graduates, both had left the military for civilian life in the 1850s), also enjoyed high-level political connections. Lincoln himself began the war with almost no grasp of things military. But by the end of it, through study and observation, he had made himself an expert. The members of the Joint Committee went through a similar process. The tuition was high, but they learned as they went. There is no evidence that the committee's hostility to McClellan, Meade, and other military men seriously impeded the war effort, or that it caused the removal of any commander "of such surpassing brilliance that the war would have ended sooner had he been kept in command," as Doyle put it.[57]

Moreover, the committee was fundamentally right in its analysis of McClellan's, and for that matter Meade's, dilatory tactics, and aversion to full-scale war. McClellan had the men and matériel to capture Richmond in 1862; his failure to exploit his advantages prolonged the war for years. Meade's great victory at Gettysburg was fought as a defensive battle; he was not much more effective on the offensive than McClellan until he came under Grant's direct command in 1864. Meade's failure to follow up his victory at Gettysburg was another of the war's great squandered opportunities. The civilians on the Joint Committee may have gotten some of their generals wrong, but they got their strategy right.

The notion that the Joint Committee spoiled a broad-based Northern consensus on the war is politically naïve. In a democracy, government is rarely unified. The Revolutionary War, the War of 1812, and the Mexican War—not to mention more recent conflicts—all produced deep and long-lasting fissures among Americans. The committee's partisanship must be seen against the backdrop of a widespread and in some states powerful antiwar movement which threatened constantly, until 1864, to undermine the Northern war effort. Northern subversives such as Congressman Clement Vallandigham, an Ohio Democrat, openly advocated disloyalty, while Senator Jesse Bright of Indiana, also a Democrat, was expelled from office in 1862 for dealing with the enemy. As late as the summer of 1864, Lincoln believed that he could not be reelected, and that the Democratic Party was

57 Doyle, "Conduct of the War," p. 178.

likely to make peace with the Confederacy on the South's terms. There were plenty of loyal Northerners who fairly begged Wade and his colleagues to pursue their duties aggressively. "Nothing that you could do would be of more benefit to your country or self than that of unraveling the mysteries of our defeats and protraction of this war," wrote Edgar Conkling, an officer of the National Union Association in Cincinnati.[58]

Wars that are fought without serious oversight are wars that may get out of hand. Generals and presidents lie, obfuscate, manipulate, and suppress or deny unwelcome truths. Would the war in Vietnam have had a better result without aggressive congressional oversight? Or the war in Iraq, with its parade of federal officials and beribboned commanders telling Americans year after year that victory was at hand, and the enemy was just a handful of "dead-enders." Would the Civil War ever have been won had the Joint Committee rallied support behind George McClellan in the name of national "unity," instead of exposing him as the hopeless loser that he was? And would the United States have been better off with conservative Democrats' notion of victory, which might well have left slavery intact? We can thank the Joint Committee on the Conduct of the War, along with hundreds of thousands of Union soldiers who were better than their generals, that we do not know the answer to these questions.

---

[58]Edgar Conkling to Benjamin Wade, May 21, 1865, reel 6, Wade Papers, LC.

Jenny Bourne

We Are Coming, Father Abraham, but How Will You Pay for Us?

RAISING AN ARMY means paying for an army. What Congress and President Abraham Lincoln did to pay for the Civil War forever changed financial markets in the United States. They created a unified currency and a system of national banks, pioneered the use of fiat money, established the direct sale of federal bonds to the public, and, best of all, invented the Internal Revenue Service.

The Largest Army the World Had Ever Seen

The world had never before seen anything to compare to the size of the Union Army. As figure 1 shows, the only armies to come close were Napoleon's troops entering Russia in 1812 and, perhaps not surprisingly, the Russian standing army in 1816. Official enlistments of federal forces totaled 2.8 million soldiers, but many men enlisted more than once, including my great-great-grandfather.[1] The total number of individuals serving

[1]John McDaniel enlisted on the first day of April 1862 in time for the Battle of Shiloh, deserted the following February to put in a crop of corn, and reenlisted two months later to fight at Chancellorsville. He had to join a different regiment because his original one had disbanded due to massive casualties. He mustered out in Raleigh on Apr. 12, 1865.

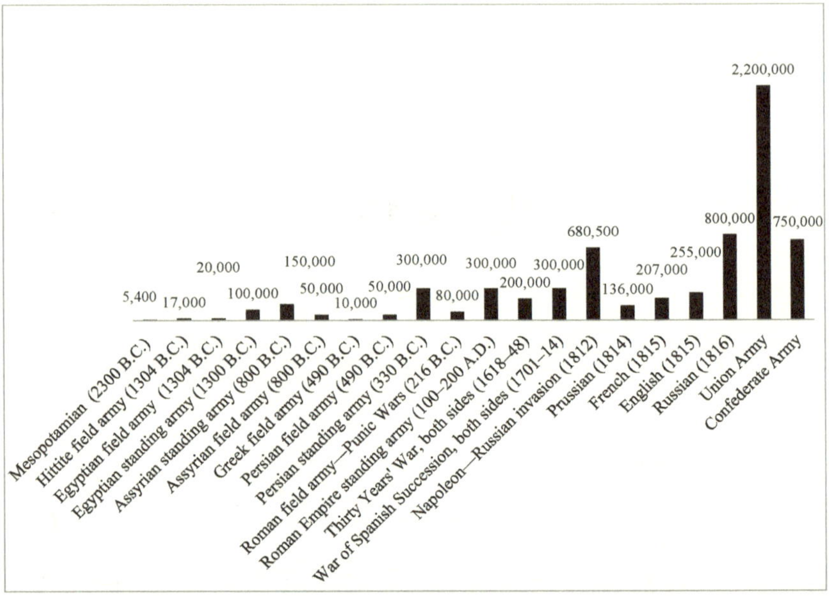

FIG. 1. Size of various armies through time. *(Sources: http://eh.net/encyclopedia/article/eloranta.military, http://napoleonistyka.atspace.com/FRENCH_ARMY.htm#_under_Louis_XIV_the_Sun_King_strength,http://www.au.af.mil/au/awc/awcgate/gabrmetz/gabr0009.htm, http://www.historyofwar.org/articles/wars_spanishsuccession.html)*

the Union is more like 2 million to 2.2 million. By comparison, the best estimate for the number serving the Confederacy is about 750,000.[2]

Figure 2 offers snapshot views of the numbers of soldiers and sailors actually on the rolls at different times during the war. One can see the federal advantage in numbers widening over time—with its payroll likewise expanding. Of course, official numbers don't reveal everything. Absentee rates were high, especially in the South, as figure 3 depicts. But all those troops—absent or not—and their supplies cost a considerable amount.

[2]Thomas Livermore, *Numbers and Losses in the Civil War in America, 1861–1865* (Boston, 1901), is typically cited for official numbers. Other numbers are compiled at http://www.historynet.com/civil-war-soldiers and http://www.civilwarhome.com/armysize.htm.

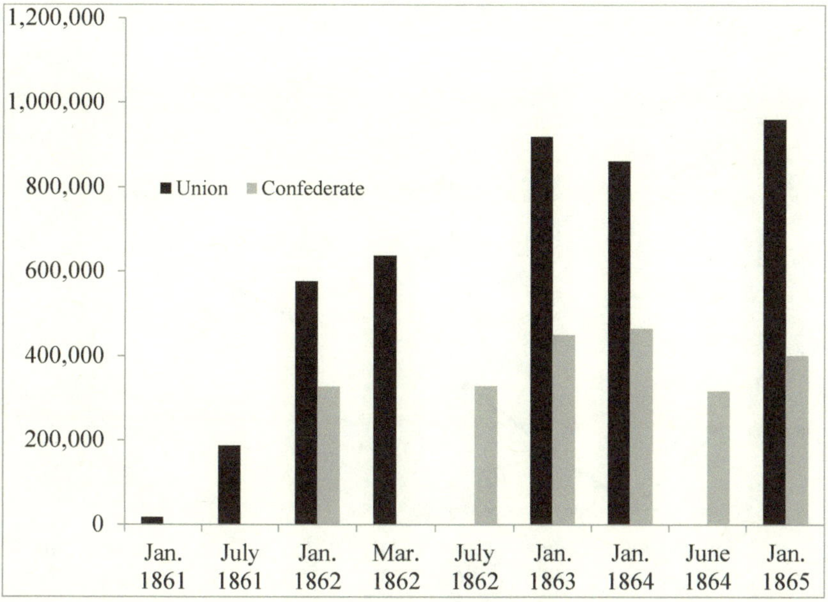

FIG. 2. Official number of troops, January 1861–January 1865. *(Source: http://www.civilwarhome.com/armysize.htm)*

The Largest Government Expenditure the World Had Ever Seen

The U.S. Civil War marks a monetary milestone: for the first time in history, annual spending by an autonomous government exceeded 1 billion units of its own currency.[3] Figure 4 shows the amount of federal government spending from 1857 to 1866. As an interesting aside, the U.S. government—perhaps recalling its most recent conflicts—chose to use the French billion (containing nine zeroes) rather than the English one (containing 12 zeroes).

Union government spending in 1865 was nearly three times that of the United Kingdom, despite similar population sizes. Even more telling, federal government spending constituted more than 30 percent of GDP for the Union in 1865, whereas the same figure was less than 10 percent in England.[4]

---

[3]John Steele Gordon, "The High Cost of War," *Barrons*, Apr. 9, 2011.

[4]Spending for the United States appears in Susan B. Carter, Scott Sigmund Gartner, Michael R. Haines, Alan L. Olmstead, Richard Sutch, and Gavin Wright, eds., *Historical*

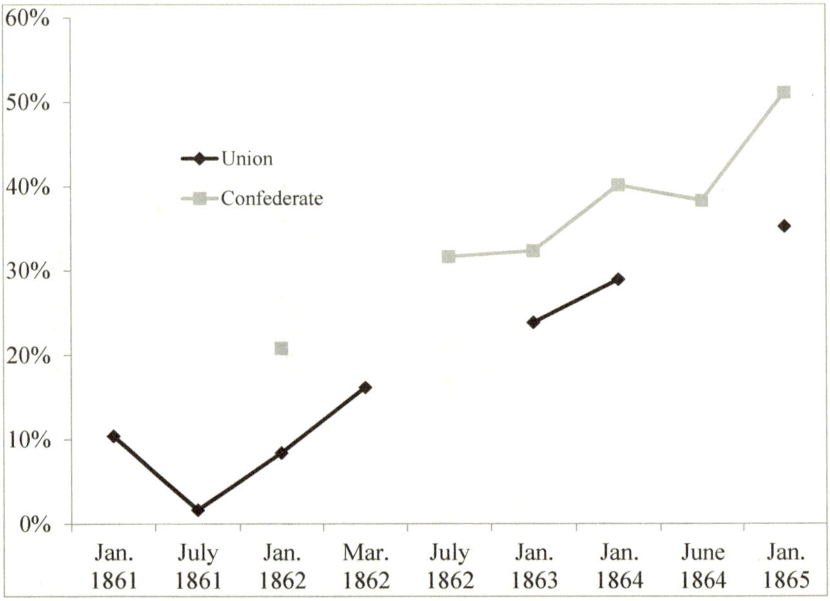

FIG. 3. Percentage of troops absent, January 1861–January 1865. *(Source: E. B. Long,* The Civil War Day by Day: An Almanac, 1861–65 *[New York, 1971])*

Of course, not all government spending went toward the war, but figure 5 shows that much of it did. Economists Claudia Goldin and Frank Lewis have estimated that the direct cost of the war to the North—including government spending at all levels, loss of human capital, and the cost of the draft—was about $3.4 billion in 1860 dollars. Soldiers' pay and matériel accounted for a little more than half of this amount.[5]

Governments have only a few ways to finance their operations: direct taxation (via property, income, excise, and sales taxes, plus import tariffs), deferred taxation in the form of government borrowing, and money

Statistics of the United States, Earliest Times to the Present: Millennial Edition (New York, 2006), ser. Ea636–43 (hereafter *HSUS*). Spending for the United Kingdom is reported at http://www.ukpublicspending.co.uk/uk_year1865_0.html; the dollar–sterling exchange rate for 1865 is listed at http://measuringworth.com/datasets/exchangeglobal/result.php?year_source=1791&year_result=2007&countryE[]=United+Kingdom. For U.S. population figures, see *HSUS*, ser. Aa9–14. For U.K. population size, see *Parliamentary Papers, House of Commons and Command*, vol. 17, p. xxiii (http://books.google.com).

[5]Claudia Goldin and Frank Lewis, "The Economic Cost of the American Civil War: Estimates and Implications," *Journal of Economic History* 35 (June 1975):299. The total of $3.4 billion in 1860 dollars translates into about $96 billion in today's money. To calculate, I used consumer price index information reported at http://www.measuringworth.com/uscpi/.

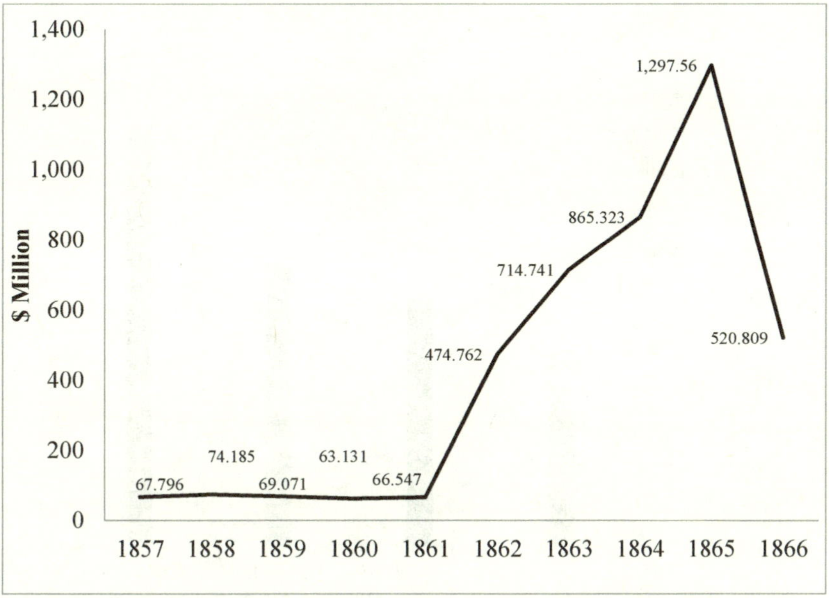

FIG. 4. Federal government spending, 1857–66. *(Source:* HSUS, *Series Ea584–87)*

creation. This last can generate an "inflation tax" or, as I'll discuss later, can also imply deferred taxation. The federal government used each of these methods to pay for the Civil War, and each spawned a new way of doing business that remains with us today.

Taxation

Taxes offered only a meager source of revenue to the federal government during the Civil War, especially at the outset of hostilities. Although the first Morrill tariff kicked in just as Lincoln took office and the second Morrill tariff passed on August 5, these measures simply did not raise much money.[6]

[6]H.R. 338 initiated the process that led to the first Morrill tariff. The House voted to pass the bill on May 10, 1860, but the Senate did not vote until March 1861. President Buchanan signed the measure into law two days before Abraham Lincoln took office. The second Morrill tariff was included in the Revenue Act of 1861, sess. 1, ch. 45, 12 Stat. 292. All taxes raised during the Civil War covered less than one-quarter of the expenses. See, for example, Gordon, "The High Cost of War"; Gary Giroux and Sharon Johns, "Financing the Civil War: The Office of Internal Revenue and the Use of Revenue Stamps," working paper (http://acct.tamu.edu/giroux/financingcivil.htm). Also see http://www.usgovernmentrevenue.com/.

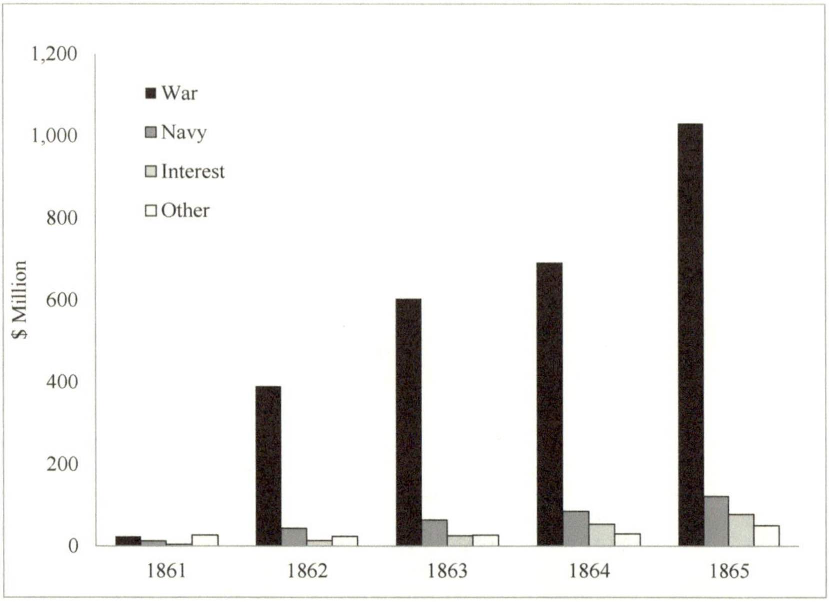

FIG. 5. Federal expenditures by category, 1861–65. *(Source:* HSUS, *Series Ea636–43)*

This was partly because Southern customs officers failed to send revenues to Washington after President James Buchanan took office.[7]

The August act also provided for property and income taxation, although proceeds from these taxes did not roll into federal coffers until various amendments were enacted and Congress perfected a tax collection mechanism.[8] Income taxes raised only $20 million in 1864 and $60 million in 1865.[9]

Despite the yawning gap between tax receipts and federal expenditures, even these relatively low taxes troubled people at the time. The *Times* of London scoffed at the Union's efforts, saying, "If this mosquito cloud of taxation ever should get settled upon the states of the north it will be more effective

[7]Bray Hammond, *Sovereignty and an Empty Purse: Banks and Politics in the Civil War* (Princeton, N.J., 1970), p. 31.

[8]Especially important was the Revenue Act of 1862, sess. 2, ch. 119, 12 Stat. 432, passed July 1. President Lincoln also issued a series of executive orders creating collection districts and appointed assessors and collectors. Cynthia Fox, "Income Tax Records of the Civil War Years," *Prologue* 18 (1986):250–59 (https://www.archives.gov/publications/prologue /1986/winter/civil-war-tax-records.html).

[9]http://www.tax.org/Museum/1861-1865.htm.

than any fugitive slave law in preventing any one, black or white, from crossing the border states."[10]

President Lincoln probably would have liked to use progressive income and property taxes more than he did. As an Illinois state legislator, he had pushed—unsuccessfully—for a graduated property tax on the basis of both equity and political feasibility, observing that the "wealthy few . . . are not sufficiently numerous to carry the elections."[11] But the lack of institutional structure, the controversy surrounding direct taxation and apportionment, and the recalcitrance of Treasury Secretary Chase meant that federal income and property taxes were difficult to impose and collect.[12] So the revenue effect of direct taxes during the Civil War was minimal.

Conventional Borrowing

Borrowing was the Union's primary means of finance, as figure 6 makes clear. Per capita federal debt went from 98 cents in 1857 to $2.06 in 1860 to $76.12 in 1865.[13] The federal government borrowed in two ways: conventional debt and, as discussed in the next section, greenbacks.

Raising revenue using conventional debt was a tricky matter. At the time of the Civil War, the U.S. adhered to a bimetallic monetary standard. The federal government was required to conduct all transactions in specie (gold or silver), and it had to do so via the Independent Treasury, which oversaw a number of subtreasuries scattered throughout the larger cities of the

---

[10] Apr. 23, 1862. Reported in A. Curtis Wilgus, "Some *London Times*' Comments on Secretary Chase's Financial Administration, 1861–1864," *Mississippi Valley Historical Review* 26 (1939):395, 397. The *Times* later reversed itself, saying that Mr. Chase "made exactly the opposite mistake to that made by our Chancellor of the Exchequer in the Crimean War. Mr. Gladstone thought he could do without loans; Mr. Chase thought he could do without taxes" (Wilgus, "*London Times*' Comments," p. 397).

[11] Roy P. Basler, ed. *The Collected Works of Abraham Lincoln*, 9 vols. (Princeton, N.J., 1953–55), 1:148.

[12] The U.S. Constitution requires all direct taxes to be apportioned among the states according to their population (Art. I, sec. 2, cl. 3). People differed as to whether income taxes constituted direct or indirect taxes. The Sixteenth Amendment settled the matter by carving out income taxes from all other forms of taxation. On Chase's attitude, see Hammond, *Banks and Politics in the Civil War*, pp. 40–42.

[13] *HSUS*, ser. Ea650–61. The denominator equals the entire resident population of the United States, including those living in states that seceded.

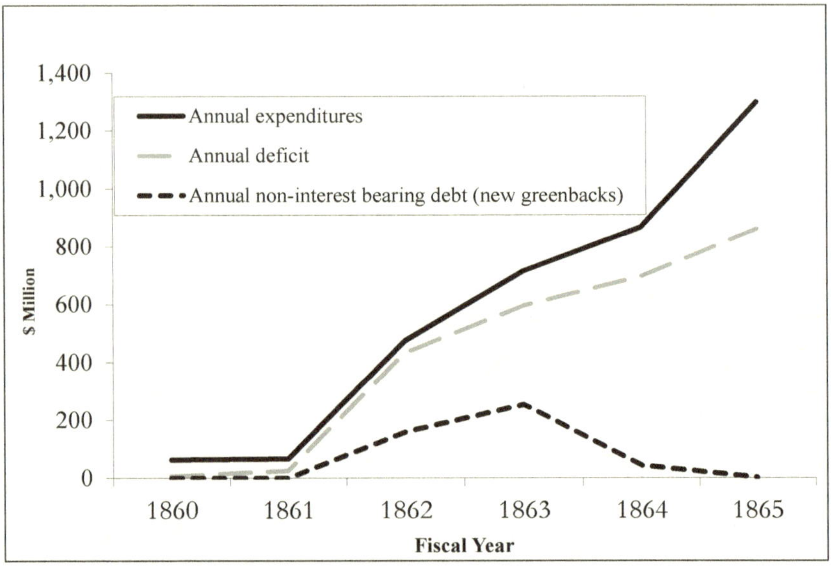

FIG. 6. Federal expenditures, deficits, and greenback issuance, 1860–65. *(Source:* HSUS, *Series Ea650–61)*

nation.[14] When the federal government wanted to borrow funds, the Treasury traditionally had sold bonds to commercial banks. Commercial banks gave up some of their specie reserves to buy these bonds.

But the staggering amount of borrowing needed to finance the war strained the system. Just before the Civil War, commercial banks had enjoyed a recent inflow of specie from abroad—the Crimean War plus European crop failures meant increased food exports from the United States and thus an increased amount of specie coming into the country.[15] But commercial banks still held only $101 million in specie as of June 1861.

How much did the Treasury want to borrow? When Salmon Chase—fresh from a disappointing run for the presidency—took over as secretary of the treasury in March 1861, his predecessors had tried floating a total of $18 million worth of federal bonds in the previous five months, only succeeding

[14]The Independent Treasury Act passed in 1846 (9 Stat. 59–66 §§18, 19). For history and discussion, see David Kinley, *The History, Organization, and Influence of the Independent Treasury of the United States* (New York, 1893).

[15]Hammond, *Banks and Politics in the Civil War*, p. 38.

with part of it.[16] Before Congress convened in July, Chase attempted to sell close to $40 million more in treasury bonds and notes. A special session authorized him to borrow another $250 million, with the act of July 17, 1861, permitting Chase to issue $50 million in treasury notes payable on demand.[17] Several additional tranches of bonds were scheduled for issue later in the fall.[18]

Recall that commercial banks held only $101 million in specie. This would not have been a constraint if the Treasury quickly spent the specie paid by banks for the bonds and people redeposited the specie in banks, or if banks quickly resold treasury obligations to the public for specie. Lincoln provided yet another way to grease the skids: he signed a bill in August 1861 permitting the treasury secretary to deposit borrowed funds into solvent specie-paying banks rather than in the subtreasuries (which tended to lock up the funds for long periods of time).[19]

Unfortunately, despite Lincoln's blessing, Secretary Chase refused to deposit specie into banks. Instead, he chose to accumulate gold in the subtreasuries.[20] Banks had trouble selling bonds as they tried to juggle their reserves. Eventually, financier Jay Cooke stepped in with a plan to market federal bonds directly to the public, and his efforts eventually succeeded.[21] As a consequence, President Lincoln in his first State of the Union address thanked "citizens of the industrial classes" for their "patriotism" and "zeal for their country's deliverance from present peril" for sharing their limited resources by buying government bonds.[22]

---

[16]Howell Cobb asked for $10 million in October 1860 and succeeded in raising only $7 million; John Dix asked for $8 million in February 1861 and obtained $7 million in proceeds. Ibid., p. 43. Dix even suggested trying to retrieve the federal surplus distributed to the states in 1837 (ibid., p. 32).

[17]12 Stat. 259.

[18]Hammond, *Banks and Politics in the Civil War*, p. 86.

[19]Act of Aug. 5, 1861, 12 Stat. 292.

[20]Wesley C. Mitchell, "Greenbacks and the Cost of the Civil War," *Journal of Political Economy* 5 (1897):123. Hammond, *Banks and Politics in the Civil War*, p. 113. For a scathing attack on Chase, see Representative Elbridge Spaulding's letter in the *New York Times*, http://query.nytimes.com/gst/abstract.html?res=9F06E0D9143BE63BBC4F51DFB266838B669FDE.

[21]Jerry Markham, *A Financial History of the United States* (Armonk, N.Y., 2002), p. 212, discusses Cooke's activities, as does Heather Cox Richardson, *The Greatest Nation of the Earth: Republican Economic Policies during the Civil War* (Cambridge, Mass., 1997), pp. 39–40.

[22]Basler, *Complete Works of Abraham Lincoln*, 4:39.

Yet even this was not sufficient to prevent bank reserves from plummeting.[23] On September 30, 1861, the *New York Herald* reported that specie in local banks had dropped from $48 million to $37 million over a span of six weeks, whereas additional gold in the local subtreasury over the same period bulged by an equivalent $11 million.[24] From December 7 to December 28, New York bank gold reserves shrank by another one-third.[25]

Not only were the banks flailing, so were the military and the administration. By the end of 1861, things looked bleak for the North. Although Union troops had enjoyed a few limited successes, they had lost significant battles at Wilson's Creek and Ball's Bluff, not to mention Bull Run.[26] And Abraham Lincoln faced political fallout from the *Trent* affair.[27] On December 28, 1861, New York banks suspended specie redemption; other banks soon followed.

Suspensions had occurred before, most notably in 1837, 1839, and 1857. But this time the country had a war to worry about. Financial chaos was the last thing it needed. Not only that, the halt in specie outflow from banks meant there was no market for federal bonds. Something else had to give—the government couldn't raise tax revenue and couldn't engage in conventional borrowing. The answer? Print money.

Money Creation, the Introduction of National Banking, and the Costs of Inflation

When Lincoln took office in March 1861, he inherited a financial crazy quilt of 1,600 state-chartered banks[28] circulating some 10,000 different types of

---

[23]In part this may have been due to people pulling specie out of banks and using it to buy government obligations, rather than using specie they had on hand outside banks. Specie hoarding by individuals became an even more acute problem later in the war. The percentage of specie held by the public went from about 60 percent in the period June 1861 to December 1862 to 80 percent or more throughout the remainder of the war. *HSUS*, ser. Cj26–41.

[24]Hammond, *Banks and Politics in the Civil War*, p. 116.

[25]Ibid., p. 154; Mitchell, "Greenbacks and the Cost of the Civil War," p. 124.

[26]The Battle of Bull Run occurred July 21, Wilson's Creek was August 10, and Ball's Bluff October 21. For a list of battles, see http://americancivilwar.com/tl/tl1861.html.

[27]On Nov. 8, U.S. Captain Charles Wilkes boarded HMS *Trent* and seized two Confederate officials, John Slidell and James Mason. The British bristled at what they considered a violation of sovereignty. The situation was eventually defused when the United States let the captives go and disavowed the captain's acts. For further discussion, see Allan Nevins, *Ordeal of the Union*, vol. 5: *The War for the Union: The Improvised War, 1861–62* (1959), pp. 384–412.

[28]*HSUS*, ser. Cj149–57.

banknotes.[29] With the urgent need for funds, Lincoln sprang into action. Often working behind the scenes, he used Secretary Chase and various members of Congress[30] to conduct a radical overhaul of the nation's financial system. The federal government issued some $450 million in fiat money (known as greenbacks for the distinctive green ink on the reverse side), and it designated greenbacks and treasury notes as legal tender.[31] Reflecting his desire to increase recognition and further his career, Salmon Chase chose to grace the greenback with his own visage, as figure 7 shows.

The creation of federal currency went hand in hand with the establishment of federally approved (rather than state-chartered) banks. National banks were capitalized with treasury bonds—that is, they could issue national currency if it was backed by treasury securities. So the federal government issued debt, and that debt was monetized via the workings of the new national banking system.[32] To reinforce the power of federal

[29]Richard Sylla, "Reversing Financial Reversals: Government and the Financial System since 1789," in Price Fishback et al., eds., *Government and the American Economy, a New History* (Chicago, 2007), p. 134.

[30]Supportive House members included Justin Morrill (Vt.), chair of the House Ways and Means Committee in 1863; Samuel Hooper (Mass.), a Boston financier; and Elbridge Spaulding (N.Y.). The Senate Finance Committee chair was first William Pitt Fessenden (Maine), then John Sherman (Ohio), who replaced Fessenden in 1864 when he left for Treasury to take over from Salmon Chase, who became chief justice of the U.S. Supreme Court. More details appear in Richardson, *The Greatest Nation of the Earth*, pp. 9–10.

[31]The first Legal Tender Act passed on Feb. 25, 1862, sess. 2, ch. 33, 12 Stat. 345. Gold was still required to pay customs duties and, ironically, interest on government bonds. This act also authorized the issuance of greenbacks, and it clarified that the notes of July 17, 1861, and Feb. 12, 1862, qualified as legal tender. Additional greenbacks were authorized on Jan. 14, 1863, and Mar. 3, 1863. Demand notes and the later-issued U.S. notes look very much the same except for the removal of the words "on demand" and the addition of the Treasury seal. The Treasury even made ungummed stamps printed on both sides to circulate as replacements for small-denomination coins. Wesley Mitchell, "The Circulating Medium during the Civil War," *Journal of Political Economy* 10 (1902):556. See Mitchell generally for information on Civil War currency. Also see Hammond, *Banks and Politics in the Civil War*, pp. 239ff. Legal tender status enabled banks to use paper as reserves, as Kenneth Dam pointed out. Kenneth Dam, "The Legal Tender Cases," *Supreme Court Review* (1981):367, 406.

[32]The National Bank Act, ch. 58, 12 Stat. 665, passed on Feb. 25, 1863, exactly a year after first Legal Tender Act. This law also established the office of the comptroller of the currency. A second National Bank Act passed in 1864 to correct some technical problems. National banks could issue national banknotes backed by a deposit of U.S. treasury securities. The amount of notes depended on the bank's capital and the amount of bonds it deposited with the comptroller, who was its chartering agent. One attractive feature of the treasury bonds was that they paid interest in specie. For background, see Richard Grossman, "U.S. Banking History," http://eh.net/encyclopedia.

FIG. 7. The greenback. *(National Numismatic Collection, National Museum of American History, Smithsonian Institution)*

currency, late in the war the federal government taxed state banknotes out of existence.[33]

Essentially, fiat money means currency backed only by the full faith and credit of the government issuing it. Using greenbacks as legal tender thus meant that the United States had decided to go off the bimetallic standard.

Potential side effects of a departure from "hard" money are inflation and uncertainty. Figure 8 shows what can occur when many more pieces of paper are suddenly added to the economy—people use these pieces of paper to bid up prices. Sadly, victims of price hikes included soldiers and their families. White Union privates received $13 a month in greenbacks for most of the war; African Americans earned only $10 a month, of which $3 went to pay for a clothing allowance.[34] As wages remained stagnant, prices of basic foods and commodities doubled. Sugar and coffee prices quadrupled.[35] Although Confederate data are scarce, substantial anecdotal evidence suggests that conditions were worse in the South.[36]

---

[33]The act of Mar. 3, 1865 imposed a tax of 10 percent on state notes to take effect July 1, 1866. The U.S. Supreme Court upheld the act as complying with the U.S. Constitution in *Veazie Bank v. Fenno*, 75 U.S. 533 (1869).

[34]Pay information is given in Mark Boatner, *Civil War Dictionary* (New York, 1991).

[35]Several price series appear in *HSUS*, for example, ser. Cc113–24. See also Richard Roll, "Interest Rates and Price Expectations during the Civil War," *Journal of Economic History* 32 (1972):476.

[36]See, for example, C. Vann Woodward, ed., *Mary Chesnut's Civil War* (New Haven, Conn., 1981).

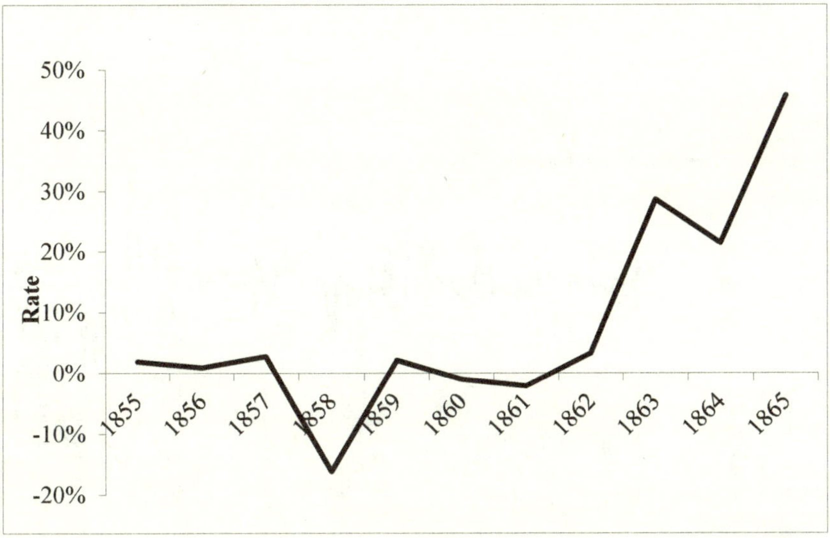

FIG. 8. The price of money creation: inflation rates, 1855–64. *(Source:* HSUS, *Series Cc1–2)*

Figures 9 and 10 link the fortunes on the battlefield to the volatility of exchange rates—and, indirectly, to the trust people placed in the value of greenbacks (and graybacks, as Confederate currency was sometimes termed). Figure 9 depicts the wild swings in currency value around the time of major battles, with even bigger swings for the Confederacy, especially near the end of the war. Figure 10 shows that both currencies bought progressively less gold as the war dragged on, reflecting the eroding effect of inflation on people's purchasing power. In fact, what happened in the Confederacy looks a lot like what happened in Germany after World War I—hyperinflation, in part due to an inability to convince people that the government and the government's finances were stable. The probability that the Confederate government could redeem its currency shrank more and more as Appomattox approached.

Union success gave the greenback a bit more staying power, although many ordinary Northern citizens did suffer from wartime inflation associated with the use of fiat money. But Lincoln and Congress never intended a permanent departure from the bimetallic standard. Greenbacks therefore explicitly counted as part of the federal debt and, like other government borrowing, constituted an implicit form of future taxation. The nation did in fact return to a gold standard in 1873, which gave rise to substantial

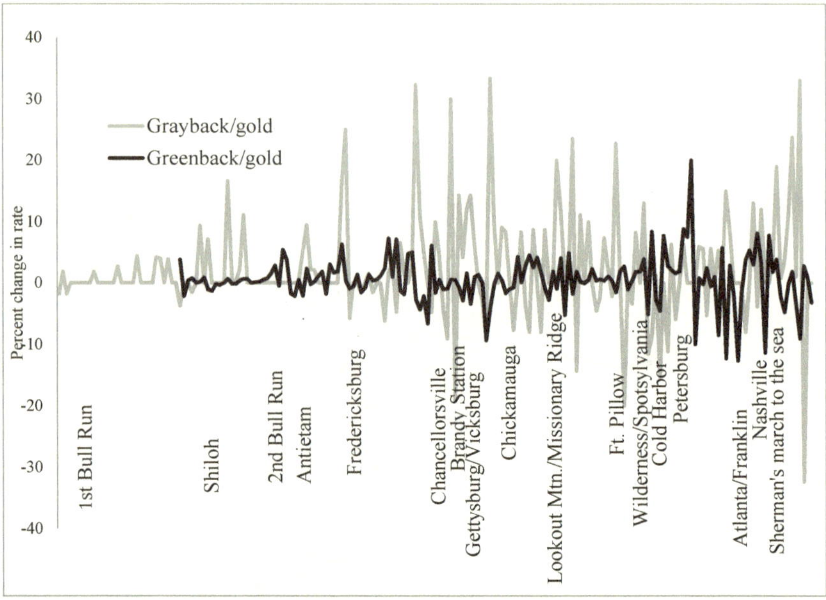

FIG. 9. Percent change in weekly exchange rates. *(Sources: Wesley Mitchell, "The Value of the Greenback during the Civil War,"* Journal of Political Economy *6 [March 1898]:139; Marc Weidenmier, "Turning Points in the US Civil War: Views from the Grayback Market,"* Southern Economic Journal *68 [2002]:875)*

postwar deflation and to William Jennings Bryan's famous Cross of Gold speech in 1896—but that is history for another day.

Legacies of Civil War Finance

Despite the relative unimportance of tax revenue to the war financing effort, tax developments during the Civil War left at least two lasting contributions to federal taxing powers. It smoothed the way for the Sixteenth Amendment, and it instituted the office of the commissioner of internal revenue.[37]

Government borrowing practices during the Civil War had a far more substantial effect on public finance, both at the time and thereafter, than

[37]The Sixteenth Amendment states that "The Congress shall have power to lay and collect taxes on incomes, from whatever source derived, without apportionment among the several States, and without regard to any census or enumeration." The law creating the commissioner's office is 12 Stat. 432, 26 U.S.C. 7802.

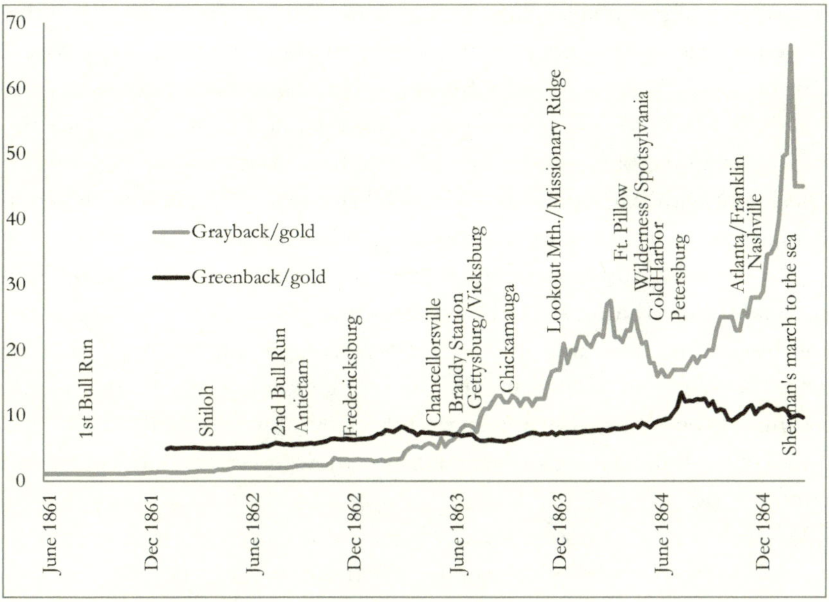

FIG. 10. Weekly exchange rates and the fortunes of war. *(Sources: Wesley Mitchell, "The Value of Greenbacks during the Civil War,"* Journal of Political Economy *6 [March 1898]:139; Marc Weidenmier, "Turning Points in the US Civil War: Views from the Grayback Market,"* Southern Economic Journal *68 [2002]:875)*

tax policy. Jay Cooke's efforts pioneered the way for direct sale of treasury bonds and notes to the public rather than intermediation by commercial banks. Deficit financing became the norm during wartime—and, recently, during peacetime as well.[38] And the United States performed its first large-scale experiment with fiat money.

The experiment had its strange moments. When Secretary Chase dithered about the constitutionality of fiat money, Lincoln reassured him: "I have that sacred instrument [the U.S. Constitution] here at the White House, and I am guarding it with great care."[39] Chase then enthusiastically embraced

[38]Federal expenditures, revenues, and debt are reported in *HSUS*, ser. Ea584–87 and Ea679–82.

[39]Quote appears in Carl Sandburg, *Abraham Lincoln: The War Years*, 4 vols. (New York, 1939), 1:652. The Constitution gives the federal government the power to coin money and says that states cannot coin money or issue bills of credit. But it makes no mention of banks or paper currency. The Tenth Amendment says this: "The powers not delegated to the United States by the Constitution, nor prohibited by it to the States, are reserved to the States respectively, or to the people." Andrew Jackson and others viewed this as requiring

the issuance of greenbacks, imprinting them with his own image. But when Chase ascended to the Supreme Court, he flip-flopped. Writing for four of eight justices, Chase decided in *Hepburn v. Griswold*[40] that Congress actually lacked the power to make paper money legal tender! Despite Salmon's flip-flopping, national banknotes survived, state banknotes disappeared, and the experiment with fiat money as a financial stopgap foreshadowed the country's later permanent departure from the gold standard.[41]

The United States thus emerged from the Civil War with a far different financial system than it had when the conflict began. Perhaps most important, by binding the banks to federal borrowing via mandatory capitalization with treasury obligations, the government bound the bankers to the fortunes of the Union. But it also tied the federal government to the vicissitudes of the financial sector, which, as we know today, can have significant economy-wide effects.

What may be the most enduring legacy wrought by the need to pay for the Union Army, however, is actually something that does not happen. Take a look at any bill in your wallet. Do you ever see a living person's image? No. Why not? Simply recall the last living person depicted on U.S. currency, disappointingly denied his dreams of the presidency: none other than the great flip-flopper himself.[42]

---

the Constitution to state all federal powers explicitly. This interpretation gave Jackson permission to deny a recharter of the Second Bank of the United States. A good discussion of the bank war appears in Robert Remini, *Andrew Jackson*, rev. ed. (New York, 1969), chap. 8. Alexander Hamilton was a leading proponent of an alternative interpretation of the Tenth Amendment—that the Constitution implicitly gives some powers to the federal government even if it does not contain explicit language. Ron Chernow, *Alexander Hamilton* (New York, 2004), provides a comprehensive biography of Hamilton and descriptions of his beliefs.

[40]75 U.S. 603 (1870). A fifth justice concurred in a separate opinion. Robert Spector, "Lincoln and Taney: A Study in Constitutional Polarization," *American Journal of Legal History* 15 (1971):199, suggests that Chase took his reasoning from a manuscript written by his immediate predecessor, Roger Taney, infamous author of the *Dred Scott* opinion.

[41]President Richard Nixon made the dollar nonconvertible to gold on Aug. 15, 1971.

[42]Federal law now prohibits using the image of any living person on U.S. currency (http://www.treasury.gov/resource-center/faqs/Currency/Pages/edu_faq_currency_portraits.aspx). Before this law passed, legend has it that George Washington's refusal to allow his image on U.S. coins set a precedent that no living president's portrait appear on U.S. currency. Supposedly, this was to distance the president from any whisper of royal standing. But perhaps the Civil War experience also left the whiff of jinx. Not only was the disappointed Chase on the $1 greenback, Abraham Lincoln was on the $10. Even more than Chase, Lincoln did not enjoy a good end.

Mischa Honeck

Why We Fight

German American Revolutionists Confront Slavery and Secession

THE AMERICAN CIVIL War goes by many names, and a European student of United States history is immediately struck by the bewildering variety of definitions that have developed over time. During and after the war, pro-Union writers referred to the conflict as the "War of the Rebellion" and disparaged their opponents as rebels and traitors. Bent on rescuing the legitimacy of their cause, Southerners found comfort in phrases such as "War between the States," "War of Southern Independence," or the more extreme "War of Northern (or Yankee) Aggression." Not much historical awareness is required to grasp that these names reflect the political and cultural outlooks of the persons using them. The same holds true for another term that held special resonance for a group of foreign-born agitators who stand at the center of this essay.

Historians Charles Beard and James M. McPherson popularized the notion that the American Civil War was a "Second American Revolution," but they did not invent it. That concept was already ingrained in comments made immediately after the eruption of the sectional conflict. Expecting that the war could only end with the liberation of four million black slaves and "by annihilating that Oligarchy that formed and rules the South," abolitionist Wendell Phillips insisted that the Civil War "is primarily a social revolution." Thaddeus Stevens, the congressional leader of the Radical Republicans, seconded Phillips. The war must be treated "as a radical revolution," Stevens said. It must "revolutionize Southern institutions, habits, and manners . . . or all our blood and treasure have been spent in vain."[1] Assessments of that type were not confined to the American hemisphere. European radicals from Karl Marx to Giuseppe Garibaldi, too, noted the war's revolutionary potential. That much became clear when Garibaldi refused to don the uniform of a major general in the Union Army in July 1861. Purportedly, the Risorgimento leader declined the offer because the U.S. government was reluctant to give in to his demand that the war should be fought for the abolition of slavery.[2] Fritz Anneke, Garibaldi's German-born comrade and a revolutionary in his own right, was less dogmatic. When dispatches announced that the United States had gone to war, Anneke crossed the Atlantic to offer his services in the battle against the Southern rebellion. A former Prussian artillery officer and veteran of the botched European uprisings of 1848–49, Anneke became colonel in Wisconsin's heavily Germanized 34th Infantry. For him and thousands of other immigrant volunteers, the fighting could begin.

The nearly 500,000 foreign-born soldiers, or one-fourth of the Northern army, who followed in Anneke's footsteps to fight and die for the Union provide compelling evidence of the Civil War's international relevance. More than 200,000 of these ethnic Americans came from the German-speaking parts of Europe, making them the largest immigrant contingent to rally around the Stars and Stripes.[3] Over the past century, historians have crafted a plethora of explanations for this striking identification of these newcomers with their adopted homeland. Classic assimilationist surveys such as Wilhelm Kaufmann's *Germans in the American Civil War* tend to showcase German American heroism in the fight against the Southern Confederacy to celebrate the contributions of this group to the rise of a modern American

[1]Charles A. Beard and Mary R. Beard, *The Rise of American Civilization*, 2 vols. (New York, 1927), 2:53–54. James M. McPherson, "The Second American Revolution," in *Abraham Lincoln and the Second American Revolution* (New York, 1991), pp. 3–7.

[2]Frank W. Alduino and David J. Coles, *Sons of Garibaldi in Blue and Gray: Italians in the American Civil War* (New York, 2007), pp. 23–46.

[3]Martin Öfele, *True Sons of the Republic: European Immigrants in the Union Army* (Westport, Conn., 2008). The Confederates also had their share of German-born soldiers. Between 13,000 and 18,000 German immigrants fought for the South, thus serving in numbers only slightly less proportionate (in terms of population) than their Northern kinsmen. Compare to Andrea Mehrländer, "'Gott gebe uns bald bessere Zeiten . . .': Die Deutschen von Charleston, Richmond, und New Orleans im Amerikanischen Bürgerkrieg, 1861–1865," Ph.D. dissertation, Bochum, 1998.

nation-state.[4] This older filiopietist interpretation has been challenged by several studies contending that confrontations between native-born and immigrant soldiers during the war hardened, rather than softened, ethnic identities.[5] Simultaneously, a more nuanced, middle-of-the-road outlook has emerged that, although devoid of nativist or ethnonationalist undertones, still regards assimilation as the dominant issue stimulating foreign-born military engagement.[6]

While both the ethnocultural and neo-assimilationist theses have merit, they fall short of covering the full spectrum of motivations behind the German American war effort. One reason for the impracticality of projecting one model onto an entire populace is the sheer diversity of American immigrant life. Because there was no single German America, responses to the sectional conflict between German Catholics, Protestants, Jews, freethinkers, workers, entrepreneurs, conservatives, liberals and radicals, old and new immigrants, differed widely. Also, as this essay will show, many newcomers were disinclined to view the war in an American framework alone. Many of the highly politicized refugees of the European revolutions of 1848–49, men and women with strong democratic convictions, identified a vibrant transnational discourse that braided together the struggles against hierarchy and privilege on both continents. Although these foreign-born revolutionists represented merely a trickle in the tide of the more than four million discontented Europeans who entered the United States between 1840 and 1860, they used their intellectual prowess and public visibility to present the Civil War as a milestone event in the universal unfolding of liberty: an epic conflict between freedom and tyranny whose outcome would influence developments in other parts of the world. The two explosive issues of slavery and secession are particularly useful to elucidate how these "Forty-Eighters" intervened in the war to further a transatlantic vision of

---

[4]Wilhelm Kaufmann, *The Germans in the American Civil War*, trans. Steven Rowan (Carlisle, Pa., 1999). The German original dates from 1911.

[5]Recent prominent examples of this trend are Wolfgang Helbich, "German-Born Union Soldiers: Motivation, Ethnicity, and 'Americanization,'" in Wolfgang Helbich and Walter D. Kamphoefner, eds., *German-American Immigration and Ethnicity in Comparative Perspective* (Madison, Wis., 2004), pp. 295–325; and Christian B. Keller, *Chancellorsville and the Germans: Nativism, Ethnicity, and Civil War Memory* (New York, 2007), chap. 7 in particular.

[6]See especially William Burton, *Melting Pot Soldiers: The Union's Ethnic Regiments* (New York, 1998), and Öfele, *True Sons of the Republic.*

democracy that could potentially inspire the forging and framing of liberal nations everywhere.

For the standard bearers of Forty-Eighter democracy on American soil, chattel slavery was a moral anachronism, a flagrant contradiction of the founding ideals and democratic promises of their host country. Imbued with a traditional republicanism that held that citizenship was perpetually threatened by corruption, the foreign revolutionists believed that slaveholders and their abettors imperiled freedom for all men. As early as August 1851, a group of recent German arrivals proclaimed opposition "to Slavery in whatever shape it might be seen," demanding universal manhood suffrage for blacks and whites alike, and that the Union refuse to admit any additional slave states. Three years later, Pittsburgh's Forty-Eighter newspapermen jointly proclaimed, "We are enemies of slavery, and consider all extension of it a treason to mankind." This same sentiment also prevailed at the 1855 meeting of the national Turner Confederation, the leading Forty-Eighter association in the United States. The delegates took an open stand against slavery, denouncing the institution as "unworthy of a republic and directly opposed to the principles of freedom." Such declarations warmed the heart of black abolitionist Frederick Douglass, who hailed "the many noble and high-minded men, most of whom, swept over by the tide of the revolution in 1849, have become our active allies in the struggle against oppression and prejudice."[7]

Hostility to slavery, to be sure, featured as one among many interrelated concerns of a more broadly focused group of immigrant radicals, many of whom cared equally about a plethora of other revolutionary goals. Most found their way into one of the principal manifestos of German American radicalism prior to the Civil War. In February 1854, a delegation of about thirty freethinkers and labor activists convened in Louisville, Kentucky, to discuss steps toward establishing a German reform party. Their deliberations resulted in what became known as the "Louisville Platform," which spelled out several key demands from the radical democratic lexicon: next to attacking the clergy, championing the interests of labor, and petitioning for quicker procedures to acquire citizenship, the delegates, more boldly,

---

[7]*New York Daily Tribune*, Aug. 29, Sept. 9, 1851. *Daily Pittsburgh Gazette*, Feb. 20, 1854. "Verhandlungen der Turner-Tagsatzung zu Buffalo, vom 24. bis 27. September 1855," Sozialistischer Turnerbund Papers, New York Public Library. "Adopted Citizens and Slavery," *Douglass' Monthly* (Aug. 1859).

went on to demand the abolition of the presidency and equal rights for women. Slavery, of course, did not escape the drafters' scorn. They termed it "a political and moral cancer, that will by and by undermine all republicanism" and supported its "gradual extermination" by prohibiting its expansion into new territories. Furthermore, the platform condemned the discrimination against free blacks in the North, asserting that "skin color cannot justify a difference of legal status." Because of internal frictions among the drafters, the envisaged party never came to pass. Their declarations, however, held special significance for Forty-Eighter radicals across the country until after the Civil War.[8]

With their humanist aspirations, the authors of the Louisville Platform represented only a small fragment of the recent immigrant generation. Liberal and conservative commentators repudiated the Louisville stipulations as impractical or recklessly irresponsible, fearing that they would enhance, rather than decrease, the nativist menace. The proposal favoring female suffrage met the opposition of outstanding Forty-Eighters as well. If women were given the vote, Christian Esselen and Friedrich Hecker scoffed, social progress "would be retarded by a hundred years." Moreover, though few German Americans defended slavery as a positive good, not that many actively campaigned against it either. The overwhelming majority centered their attention on issues that affected their lives more immediately. Foremost in their list of requests were fair wages, protection from Sabbath and temperance laws, local self-rule, and free homesteads for those seeking their fortune farther west—policies which German immigrants initially tended to entrust to the Democratic Party. Black slavery mattered little in this equation. Cruel as it seemed, it was widely regarded as a sectional and therefore remote problem, with virtually no practical relevance for immigrant self-advancement. Why complain about the Southern way of life when there was plenty of land to be had in the West?[9]

This collective apathy disappeared almost overnight when Illinois Democrat Stephen A. Douglas introduced his Kansas-Nebraska bill in the Senate on January 4, 1854. The measure was much needed. Settlers were already streaming westward into the unorganized region, and plans for a

---

[8]"The Louisville Platform," in Don Heinrich Tolzmann, ed., *The German-American Forty-Eighters, 1848–1998* (Indianapolis, Ind., 1998), pp. 98–105.

[9]Compare to Carl Frederick Wittke, *Refugees of Revolution: The German Forty-Eighters in America* (Philadelphia, 1952), pp. 164–65.

transcontinental railroad were waiting to be realized. For a speedy organization of the Kansas and Nebraska territories, Douglas had to make concessions to Southern senators on whose assent he depended. The bill passed both houses in May but now carried two controversial stipulations: first, the application of popular sovereignty to the problem of slavery, which held that it was the right of each community to choose its own domestic institutions; second, the explicit repeal of the Missouri Compromise of 1820, which banned slavery north of latitude 36°30', in what was then Louisiana Territory. A provision that further aroused passions (but was killed later) was the Clayton Amendment. It would have denied foreign-born residents the right to vote or hold public office anywhere in the new territories.[10]

As foretold by Douglas, the Kansas-Nebraska Act raised "a hell of a storm" in American party politics.[11] Across the North, scores of meetings expressing indignation took place, demanding nothing less than the immediate withdrawal of the Kansas-Nebraska bill. German immigrants conducted formidable anti-Nebraska rallies of their own in New York, Philadelphia, Cleveland, Cincinnati, Indianapolis, Chicago, and other Northern cities. On March 3, 1854, Josef Hartmann, editor of the *New Yorker Demokrat*, and labor leader J. A. Försch presided over one of the largest German anti-Nebraska gatherings at New York's Washington Hall—with a crowd of at least 2,000 in attendance. Resolutions were adopted labeling Senator Douglas's popular sovereignty rhetoric "an insulting untruth, intended to deceive and betray the people," and declared every defender of his bill a friend of "those who would steal away the rights of the free North." Similar motions were carried two weeks later, on March 16, in Chicago, where German Americans had assembled in defiance of the Nebraska measure. As elsewhere, the protesters saw in it "an ominous prophecy of further attacks on Northern liberty" and immigrant rights, and contended that it was "high time to make war" against all ventures aiming "to increase the preponderance of the slaveholding interests in the Union." It was comments like these that made the *Cincinnati Gazette* report "that our German population are almost to a man opposed to the bill," and which

[10]The Clayton Amendment was named after proslavery and nativist Senator John Clayton from Delaware. See also Bruce Levine, *The Spirit of 1848: German Immigrants, Labor Conflict, and the Coming of the Civil War* (Urbana, Ill., 1992), pp. 155–56.

[11]The following account relies heavily on ibid., pp. 149–209. Robert W. Johannson, *Stephen A. Douglas* (Urbana, Ill., 1973), p. 419.

duped Horace Greeley into claiming that the Germans "feel . . . more deeply" about slavery "than the native citizens."[12]

The truth, however, proved far less flattering to the German Americans. Despite a palpable discontent with Douglas's policy, many were hesitant to leave the Democratic fold and try their luck in new and untested coalitions. The most acrimonious split occurred along sectional lines. In 1855, the Charleston, Savannah, Augusta, Mobile, and New Orleans branches of the national Turner Confederation pulled out, as they could no longer identify with the organization's avowed opposition to slavery. Differences of religion and class played a crucial role as well. Whereas urban German workingmen were most likely to wave the anti-Nebraska flag, wealthy entrepreneurs and immigrants living in rural areas, most of them Catholic, largely stayed away from these rallies. For them, the antislavery measures proposed by their revolutionary countrymen bore the stamp of the kind of radical democratic ideology that also ranted against the uneven distribution of property and vilified religion as a tool of oppression. "Maintenance of the Union!—Democracy vs. Abolitionism!" were slogans with which the *New Yorker Staats-Zeitung*, the chief organ of German American conservatism, entered the fray. It thus linked its anti-Nebraska kinsmen to the disunionism and evangelical fanaticism commonly associated with native-born abolitionists, for many older immigrants the harbingers of chaos.[13]

Were such ascriptions justified? A closer look demonstrates that even within the German American antislavery camp motivations could be quite diverse. The broad coalition they made up was divided by important political and ideological differences. Of eighty-eight German-language newspapers in the United States, eighty opposed Douglas's bill, but only a handful of them advocated a sharper response. The most militant protests emerged from the radical plebeian milieu and the intellectuals associated with it. Their speeches and resolutions mocked attempts to pacify the "slave barons" and often declared solidarity with the slaves. A stronger, more mainstream current arose from the ranks of German American liberalism, led mainly by

[12] *New York Daily Times*, Mar. 4, 1854. *Chicago Daily Tribune*, Mar. 18, 20, 1854. *Daily Cincinnati Gazette*, Feb. 24, 1854. *New York Daily Tribune*, Feb. 28, 1854.

[13] Horst Überhorst, *Turner Unterm Sternenbanner: Der Kampf der deutsch-amerikanischen Turner für Einheit Freiheit und Gerechtigkeit* (Munich, 1978), p. 50; and Gottlieb Betz, "Die Deutschen und die Sklaverei," in Karl J. R. Arndt and May E. Olson, eds., *The German Language Press of the Americas* (New York, 1980), p. 575. *New York Daily Tribune*, Feb. 23, 24, 1854.

established middle-class immigrants who objected to the Nebraska bill but also hoped to restore the sectional peace of earlier decades. Reopening the slavery issue, they feared, could ignite the fuse to the powder keg that would blow the country apart. As partisan politics deepened, some returned to the Democratic Party, while others joined the Republicans.[14]

The small but strident group of Forty-Eighter democrats who harbored abolitionist beliefs and subscribed to the Louisville Platform usually framed their opposition to the Kansas-Nebraska Act around a strong enmity toward slavery as such. German left-wingers readily evoked their European past to warn against vacillators who believed in tempering Northern attitudes toward slavery to appease their slaveholding countrymen. If the Southern planters and their allies in the Democratic Party called to mind the European counterrevolution, then Northern compromisers seemed like a reincarnation of Frankfurt's inept liberal majority. Seeing the signs of a gathering storm, as had been the case in 1848, German radicals fought hard to sharpen the nascent Republican Party's antislavery planks. Labor leaders Victor Pelz and Peter Rödel called for completing the work begun in 1776 and 1848, thereby turning this country into "a free democratic republic" where "slaveholders will brandish no whips" and would not break up any more families on the auction block. The Jewish German journalist Ottilie Assing favored total emancipation and considered it a shame "that many Germans here are loyal Democrats who are outspoken in their support of slavery, and that others take a thoroughly passive attitude."[15]

What Assing referred to as "passive" was indeed the customary outlook in the greater portion of the German anti-Nebraska and Republican constituencies. Most voiced their indignation over Douglas's bill not out of a sudden urge to carry freedom southward, but because they wanted to make sure that the West remained free from Southern influence. Like the average Northern protester, they adhered to the notion promulgated by the slaveholder Thomas Jefferson that white yeomen were the mainstay of a healthy republican society. The civic traits they embodied—honesty, industry, independence—dovetailed nicely with the popular idea that America was the

---

[14]See Carl Frederick Wittke, *The German Language Press in America* (Lexington, Ky., 1957), p. 139.

[15]Pelz and Rödel are quoted in Levine, *The Spirit of 1848*, p. 221. Ottilie Assing, "The Presidential Election and Slavery," in Christoph Lohmann, trans. and ed., *Radical Passion: Ottilie Assing's Reports from America and Letters to Frederick Douglass* (New York, 1999), p. 73.

place where every white man could escape permanent dependency by hard work. Slavery belied this free-labor ideal. Equating labor with servitude, it could not possibly coexist with a society that regarded labor as the ticket to the economic autonomy of self-employed craftwork or free farming. The Kansas-Nebraska Act, its critics argued, ignored this basic insight. By theoretically sanctioning the introduction of slave labor into the two territories, it not only insulted the dignity of those toiling for their own improvement—worse, it moved the white laborer outrageously close to his black counterpart and the nightmare of chattel slavery for which he stood.[16]

Hence antislavery, free-soil, and antiblack sentiments conflated rather smoothly in the mass protests against the Nebraska bill. A racist system was fought with racist arguments, and German Americans proved no exception to this rule. More important than the dislike of slavery was the white farmer's fear that by tilling next to black slaves he might ultimately be mistaken for one. Consequently, the bulk of the German American free-soilers found nothing hideous about homestead initiatives welcoming only "free white persons" to vacant public lands. Keeping slavery out of the territories, the *Baltimore Wecker* emphasized, was first and foremost about "white development." What really mattered, the *Wecker* affirmed, was not black emancipation but making sure "that the black race would not be allowed to expand further at the expense of the white race." Doing nothing to stop the influx of "ignorant, savage Africans" from the South, Friedrich Hecker augured, magnified the threat of a slave revolt that could turn out far bloodier than the much-dreaded Haitian Revolution. Horrified by the prospect of racial assimilation, the St. Louis *Mississippi Blätter* warned as late as 1859: "If the system of slavery and the black race with it spread even wider across the continent, then . . . this only works to speed up amalgamation and the demonstrated result of a mongrel race."[17]

---

[16]See also Eric Foner, *Free Soil, Free Labor, Free Men: The Ideology of the Republican Party before the Civil War* (New York, 1971), pp. 1–45; Hartmut Keil, "German Immigrants and African-Americans in Mid-Nineteenth Century America," in Ragnhild Fiebig-von Hase and Ursula Lehmkuhl, eds., *Enemy Images in American History* (Providence, R.I., 1997), pp. 142–43; David Roediger, *Wages of Whiteness: Race and the Making of the American Working Class* (New York, 1999), pp. 80–84; William Gienapp, *The Origins of the Republican Party, 1852–1856* (New York, 1987), pp. 355–59; Sean Wilentz, *The Rise of American Democracy: Jefferson to Lincoln* (New York, 2006), pp. 671–77.

[17]*Baltimore Wecker*, Jan. 19, 1856, quoted in Betz, "Die Deutschen und die Sklaverei," 584–85. *Belleviller Volksblatt*, Aug. 30, 1856. *Mississippi Blätter*, Oct. 9, 1859, in *Germans for a*

Statements like these give an idea of the extent to which antislavery German immigrants had begun appropriating the languages of scientific racism and white supremacy, and how they used them for their own purposes. Rather than simply object to slavery's expansion, most German Americans presented their assessment of the institution in a way calculated to make them acceptable citizens in the eyes of native-born whites. Next to respecting the Fugitive Slave Law, this meant subscribing to the tenets of white free-labor republicanism as well as learning to eschew those who challenged its racial boundaries. "We have nothing in common with the abolitionists," avowed the anti-Nebraska *Philadelphia Demokrat*, "but we stick fervently to Jeffersonian democracy and the Constitution of the United States." Nativist feelings were rampant in antebellum society, and many of the older German Americans ascribed the anti-German protests of the 1850s explicitly to "the arrogance . . . and domineering conduct of the refugees."[18] Ethnic leader Gustav Körner echoed this concern at a Republican rally in Chicago in June 1856, stating that while the "Germans were for free territory," they "were not given to fanaticism of any kind."[19]

Körner's radical kinsmen cared little about the efforts of the older and less activist immigrant population to become part of the dominant Northern discourse on slavery and race. For the recently arrived democrats from overseas, the battles against the aristocracies of the Old World and the Southern "slave barons" were intrinsically connected. The comments of prominent Forty-Eighter radicals on John Brown's raid illustrate this. In their accounts, Brown swung an axe not merely at black slavery; he laid it deeper, striking at the root of the ancient division of mankind into masters and servants. Brown reportedly started out as a religious fanatic, but his death at the hands of a tyrannical state enshrined him in a pantheon of secular revolutionists alongside Robert Blum, Felice Orsini, and other European martyrs of freedom. Hailing Brown's martyrdom, the German American labor leader August Willich exhorted his followers "to whet their sabers and nerve their arms for the day of retribution," when slavery and its supporters "would be crushed

Free Missouri: Translations from the St. Louis Radical Press, 1857–1862, trans. Steven Rowan, intr. and commentary James Neal Primm (Columbia, Mo., 1983), pp. 85–86.

[18]Gustav Körner, *Memoirs of Gustav Körner, 1809–1896* (Cedar Rapids, Iowa, 1909), p. 549.

[19]*Philadelphia Demokrat*, Feb. 4, 1854, quoted in Betz, "Die Deutschen und die Sklaverei," p. 584. *Boston Daily Atlas*, June 19, 1856.

into a common grave."[20] The cycle of insurrection, imprisonment, and execution which the abolitionist endured resembled a ritual of political sacrifice with which Willich and his fellow radicals were perfectly conversant. The enemy was clearly delineated. As a reincarnation of the landed gentries of the Old World, the slaveholder was a perfect model of malice. His despotic rule, Forty-Eighters thought, emboldened conservatives on both sides of the Atlantic and hampered the universal spread of liberty. "Opposition to the politics of slavery in America," mused the exiled German editor Karl Heinzen, "is a battle against reaction in Europe."[21]

The chants of revolution resonating from the quarters of the exiled radicals made them enemies of the state and, in the eyes of their critics, moved them outrageously close to America's homegrown crusaders against slavery, the abolitionists. The Virginian proslavery writer George Fitzhugh belabored this point, prophesying that the "black republicanism" of antislavery Northerners would meld with the "red republicanism" of the Forty-Eighters to inaugurate an age of anarchy.[22] In this, Fitzhugh was not mistaken. Individuals from both camps had indeed begun to reach out to one another. However, except for their shared hatred of slavery, little connected the reformers from New England and elsewhere to the Europeans who had mounted the barricades in 1848. The atheist and anticlerical stance of many freethinking Forty-Eighters, who portrayed the churches as hierarchical institutions that had helped throne and police state crush the revolution, clashed head-on with the evangelical Protestant beliefs of most native-born American reformers. Other controversial causes popular among immigrant radicals such as socialism and anti-temperance tested the patience of Northern abolitionists as well. When, after the election of Abraham Lincoln, Southerners began preparations to lead their states out of the Union, William Lloyd Garrison, Horace Greeley, and their followers refused to shed a single tear. Rather build a new, smaller nation untainted by the curse of slavery, they preached, than continue living under the old leviathan that had proven deaf to pleas for moral improvement.[23]

---

[20] *Cincinnati Republikaner*, Dec. 5, 1859.

[21] Heinzen is quoted in Levine, *The Spirit of 1848*, p. 149.

[22] George Fitzhugh, *Cannibals All! Or, Slaves without Masters* (Richmond, Va., 1857), p. 287.

[23] On disunionism in American abolitionist thought, see Lewis Perry, *Radical Abolitionism: Anarchy and the Government of God in Antislavery Thought* (Ithaca, N.Y., 1973), esp. pp. 129–57; James Brewer Stewart, *Holy Warriors: The Abolitionists and American Slavery* (New

The battle-hardened Forty-Eighters could not but shake their heads as they heard the peace-minded Garrisonians pronounce disunionist sentiments. Unlike many native-born abolitionists, they found the Southern planters guilty on two counts: as slaveholders, they defiled the high ideal of universal freedom; as secessionists, they betrayed the revolutionary principle of national unity.

Surprisingly little attention has been paid to the impact of budding national identities on transatlantic discourses over slavery and abolition. Judged by today's standards, nationalism and abolitionism may seem strange bedfellows, but their affiliation should become clear once we excavate their common roots. Early nineteenth-century nationalism was inherently progressive and democratic. As older forms of authority were eroding under the twin forces of economic and political modernization, the nation emerged as the principal nexus with the ability to bind together an imagined people across a given distance. Not only did it satisfy deep needs of community which traditional systems could no longer fully uphold and modern class conflict threatened to undermine; nations also became the main vessel for peoples' aspirations for freedom and equality. Revolutionaries from Germany to England, from France to the United States, nurtured the tenet reverberating in the key texts of 1776 and 1789 that national sovereignty, individual rights, and civic equality were mutually reinforcing. Sixty years later, on the eve of the American Civil War, the Italian patriot Giuseppe Mazzini echoed this conviction when he asked, "What is a country . . . but the place in which our individual rights are most secure?"[24]

Early nineteenth-century nationalism was also homogenizing. Since liberal reformers and radical agitators believed that modern nations could only be free if they were united, it is easy to imagine the fear the longevity of an institution such as chattel slavery struck into their hearts. In places where benighted forms of dependency lingered on, they reasoned, freedom could not reign supreme. Opposing slavery became more than a moral or economic

York, 1997), and Louis Menand, *The Metapyhsical Club: A Story of Ideas in America* (New York, 2001), pp. 10–22.

[24]Mazzini is quoted in Lynn Hunt, *Inventing Human Rights: A History* (New York, 2007), p. 177. On the cultural foundations of modern nationalism, see Benedict Anderson, *Imagined Communities: Reflections on the Origin and Spread of Nationalism* (London, 1991); and Eric Hobsbawm, *Nations and Nationalism since 1780: Programme, Myth, Reality* (Cambridge, U.K., 1992).

imperative; national unity demanded it. "Liberty and Union," the ringing declaration of Massachusetts Senator Daniel Webster, grew out of this strand, as did Abraham Lincoln's famous observation that a country like his own "cannot endure, permanently half *slave* and half *free*." Nations were seen as elevating and unifying; absolutist rule, whether exercised by a monarch or a plantation master, was seen as oppressive and divisive. Americans and Europeans increasingly accepted this binary, associating freedom, equality, and progress with republican nations, while associating slavery, despotism, and backwardness with aristocracies.[25]

Leading Forty-Eighter intellectuals rejected Southern secession out of an attachment to a romantic nationalism that conflated the concern for universal human rights with the idea that nations reflected the collective soul of an entire people. The German refugee scholar Gustav Struve made this point when he stated that only republics embodied the shared traditions, values, and aspirations of a national community, whereas fragmentation and dissolution were the tools of despotism.[26] Fritz Anneke applauded the "wonderful unity of all parties" in the Northern war effort and condemned the Southern Confederacy on the grounds that it misrepresented the will of the powerful as the will of the people. This "disgraceful rebellion," Anneke wrote, fed on the "monarchical ambitions" of the privileged classes and invoked popular sovereignty with the intention of misleading the ignorant and consolidating slaveholder rule.[27] Similarly, Ottilie Assing saw nothing glorious in the invocation of states rights as long as it was used to defend a social system where "neither life and freedom nor the property of the most peaceful, innocent citizen are safe."[28]

Although many European revolutionaries believed national unity to be the logical outcome of historical development, they desired powerful nation-states because they felt that strong central governments were required to

[25]Daniel Webster, "Second Reply to Hayne," in *Papers of Daniel Webster*, ser. 4: *Speeches and Formal Writings*, 2 vols. (Hanover, N.H., 1974–89), 1:348. Abraham Lincoln, "A House Divided," in *Abraham Lincoln: Speeches and Writings, 1832–1858* (New York, 1989), p. 426. Charles Sumner, "The Crime against Kansas," in *The Works of Charles Sumner*, 15 vols. (Boston, 1870–83), 4:243.

[26]Gustav Struve, *Weltgeschichte*, 9 vols. (New York, 1853–60), 9:784.

[27]Fritz Anneke, *Der Zweite Freiheitskampf der Vereinigten Staaten von Amerika* (Frankfurt, 1861), pp. 196, 243–45.

[28]Ottilie Assing, quoted in Maria Diedrich, *Love across Color Lines: Ottilie Assing and Frederick Douglass* (New York, 1999), p. 239.

protect the achievements of liberty against all enemies, foreign and domestic. Gustav Körner, though not a Forty-Eighter himself, bound these arguments together in an open letter published in several German-language papers in early 1861. Livid over President Buchanan's reluctance to use force, Körner argued that secession was unconstitutional, but also viewed the sectional crisis in a transnational scope. Letting the Southern slaveholders depart would mean "the end of the only free government in the world, which we [are] bound by every consideration of moral and material prosperity to transmit intact to our posterity." Thus "civil war was preferable to the destruction of our Union, and that, should it come, the government should call at once for such a military force as would make resistance impossible." The German Republican was preaching to the choir when he tried to get Abraham Lincoln's attention. But in case further persuasion was required, Körner impressed the president-elect with an example from recent European history. The Swiss, he explained, had managed to coerce seven seceding cantons back into their confederation by raising 100,000 men. Why should a country with superior resources such as the United States not be able to bring the secessionists to terms with a similar display of military might?[29] Little more was needed to bolster Lincoln's resolve.

Back in 1849, the failure to overcome German particularism—the country's division into a multitude of petty principalities—and unify the country had allowed the reactionary powers to regain control. Eleven years later, secession roused painful memories of German disunion and reminded the Forty-Eighters of the vulnerability of the transatlantic project of democracy. Perhaps the most eloquent expression of this imagined correlation can be found in Reinhold Solger's play *The Hon. Anodyne Humdrum; or, The Union Must and Shall Be Preserved.* Written on the eve of Lincoln's election, the drama was a modification of Solger's 1850 German-language play *The Professor in the Parliament: Farce in One Act.* A persecuted and exiled republican who had settled in Boston, Solger explicitly connected the failed creation of a German nation-state to the current struggle to preserve the Union. But unlike the cynical tone of the original, the English version ends with an invitation to activism. The two main characters, the lovers Frank and

[29]Gustave Körner, *Memoirs of Gustav Körner, 1809–1896*, ed. Thomas J. McCormack, 2 vols. (Cedar Rapids, Iowa, 1909), 2:108–9.

Emily, board a train departing north to support the Union, while a fugitive slave, sitting on top of the train, thumbs his nose at his baffled Southern oppressors.[30]

Solger's identification with the antislavery movement points to another important strand in the Forty-Eighter opposition to Southern independence. For many immigrant democrats, secession was not only treasonous but a crime against civilization. Carl Schurz (fig. 1), the rising star of German American republicanism in the West, elaborated this position in a speech he delivered in St. Louis on August 1, 1860. There was much excitement surrounding Schurz's speech. The presidential campaign had just begun, and secessionist feelings were strong in Missouri. With special empathy, Schurz sided with the local Republicans, but he also seized the opportunity to address the slaveholders directly. Americans, Schurz stressed, need not shudder at the prospect of disunion. Rather, he depicted the proslavery faction as hopelessly isolated in a world thrown into flux by the machinery of civilization. "Look around you and see how lonesome you are in this wide world of ours," Schurz exhorted his adversaries. For him, the slaveholders' claims to supremacy were built on sand, because their antiquated regime could never compete with the "great beehive" of free societies where the railroads and telegraphs reached "every village, almost every backwoods cottage, drawn within the immediate reach of progressive civilization." Measured against these accomplishments, Southerners seemed divorced from the spectacle of human progress, violating the ethics of self-advancement and social improvement. Asserting the superiority of free over slave labor, Schurz concluded with this revealing statement:

> This is the world of the nineteenth century. As far as modern civilization throws its rays, what people, what class of society is there like you? . . . There is no human voice to cheer you on in your struggle; there is no human eye that has a tear for your reverses; no link of sympathy between the common cause of the great human brotherhood and you. You hear of emancipation in Russia and wish it to fail. You hear of Italy rising, and fear the spirit of

---

[30]Lorie A. Vanchena, "From Domestic Farce to Abolitionist Satire: Reinhold Solger's Reframing of the Union (1860)," in Lynne Tatlock and Matt Erlin, eds., *German Culture in Nineteenth-Century America: Reception, Adaptation, Transformation* (Rochester, N.Y., 2005), pp. 289–316.

Fig. 1. Carl Schurz. Schurz's denunciation of secession as a crime against civilization was typical of many Old World revolutionaries, who viewed southern slaveholders as the progeny of the European aristocracy. *(Library of Congress, Prints and Photographs Division)*

liberty may become contagious. Where all mankind rejoices, you tremble. Where all mankind loves, you hate.[31]

Clearly, Schurz and his coworkers placed the sectional conflict in a broader historical context, interpreting the Civil War as the latest episode

[31]Carl Schurz, "The Doom of Slavery," in Frederic Bancroft, ed., *Speeches, Correspondence and Political Papers of Carl Schurz*, 6 vols. (New York, 1913), 1:131, 157–58.

in a worldwide struggle against tyranny and ignorance. If Schurz was right to say that the "last remnants of feudalism were fast disappearing," and if even the sultan of Turkey and the czar of Russia had been forced to yield to the irresistible march of progress by abolishing slavery and serfdom, then the days when American slaveholders could defend their customs at the bar of history were surely numbered.

The belief that the United States was reenacting midcentury European upheavals and thus joining the family of democratic revolutions propelled many Forty-Eighters to once again marshal for war. German Americans were among the first to respond to Lincoln's call for volunteers in the spring of 1861. Soldiers and officers trained in Europe knew how to organize regiments and drew heavily on the large number of immigrants who had already joined the paramilitary Turner societies. Across the North, immigrant units, often led by veterans of the 1848 revolutions, formed into columns and paraded the streets with their ethnic uniforms and battle flags (fig. 2). In Cincinnati, when telegraph wires were running hot with the news that Fort Sumter had been shelled, German-born Turners practiced military drill in their Halle and melted into the 9th Ohio Infantry.[32] The New York 7th "Steuben" Infantry proudly fused their European heritage with a devotion to preserving the Union by displaying the black-red-golden flag of German republicanism along with the American national colors. And when witnessing the parade of the New York 20th United Rifles regiment, a unit composed almost entirely of immigrant radicals, a refugee of the Old World revolutions cheered that "the spirit of 1848 has once more awakened."[33]

To ensure German American support for the Northern war effort, the Lincoln administration early on endorsed the formation of ethnic regiments. Over time, twelve German immigrants were promoted to the rank of general officers, among them the Forty-Eighters Franz Sigel, August Willich, Ludwig Blenker, and Carl Schurz, who went on to become the most prominent ethnic politician of his time.

---

[32]Joseph R. Reinhart, *August Willich's Gallant Dutchmen: Civil War Letters from the 32nd Indiana Infantry* (Kent, Ohio, 2006), pp. 3–13.

[33]Taken from Levine, *The Spirit of 1848*, p. 256. See also Martin Öfele, *German-Speaking Officers in the U.S. Colored Troops, 1863–1867* (Gainesville, Fla., 2004), pp. 1–34.

FIG. 2. The Garibaldi Guard filing past Abraham Lincoln and General Winfield Scott, *London Illustrated News*, August 3, 1861. For immigrant soldiers serving in ethnic regiments such as the 39th New York Infantry, the Garibaldi Guard, the outbreak of the Civil War signaled that the United States was joining the transatlantic family of democratic revolutions. *(Library of Congress, Prints and Photographs Division)*

True, immigrant recruits signed up for more mundane reasons as well. Some sought military adventure; others joined the army as a result of peer pressure or vaguely defined notions of civic duty; others, especially the jobless and urban poor, hoped for financial relief. The majority of these men would not have listed the abolition of slavery as a primary war aim. Conservative soldiers dreaded black emancipation altogether. Then again, the democratic idealism of several Forty-Eighter officers did eventually percolate into the lower ranks, because the vocabulary of freedom and equality turned out to be effective for combating nativism and proving oneself a worthy citizen of the republic. Ethnic identity, civic equality, and transnational democracy converged easily in German American narratives of the Civil War. As a German-language newspaper in St. Louis celebrated after the victory of Union forces at Camp Jackson,

> The current revolution of the people is greater and far more momentous than the one of 1776. In its victory rest all hopes of all the free people in America

> and the whole world. . . . Following our victory—and we shall, we must be victorious—the triumphant shout of the liberated European nations will echo over the ocean and greet us as their saviors and brothers. . . . Thus . . . everyone to the sacred fight for the restoration of freedom, of the republic, of humanity's unshakeable rock of hope.[34]

Yet despite the universalism of the rhetoric, the German immigrant perspective was limited in a number of ways. First, Forty-Eighter writers often presented their identification with human rights in glaring ethnonationalist colors. A people as highly cultured as the Germans, they argued, should not lapse into the bigotries and prejudices of other people. In many of their accounts, the idea of the freedom-loving German was traced back to ancient Germanic clans resisting the onslaught of a voracious Roman Empire. Steeped in that kind of ethnonationalist thinking, a group of Forty-Eighter journalists, who haughtily associated Germanness with the abolition of slavery, proclaimed: "A German who becomes a slaveholder betrays his heritage, history, and destination. . . . An American who keeps slaves stains a principle, but a German who keeps slaves stains his character. . . . A German must not keep slaves because doing so violates the creed of his countrymen and dishonors the great movement of black emancipation which is predominantly supported and represented by the German element." Struggling to retain their ethnic identity, German American liberals claimed that their brand of abolitionism was culturally and morally superior because it was unburdened by the causes of temperance and Sabbatarianism that allegedly constricted the worldview of most native-born abolitionists.[35]

On another level, the views of the exiled revolutionists on secession were a lot more convoluted and not always straightforwardly negative. While Europeans and Americans tended to view national independence movements abroad sympathetically, they were also fast to bar from their communities those whom they came to look upon as detrimental to their national identity. The Forty-Eighters were no exception to this rule. When the question was how to best implement civic equality in a bounded national space,

---

[34]Quoted in Martin Öfele, "German Americans and the War Up to Gettysburg," in Christian B. Keller and David L. Valuska, eds., *Damn Dutch: Pennsylvania Germans at Gettysburg* (Mechanicsburg, Pa., 2004), p. 24.

[35]*Pittsburger Courier*, Jan. 25, 1858. See also Allison Clark Efford, "German Immigrants and the Arc of American Citizenship during Reconstruction, 1865–1877," *Bulletin of the German Historical Institute* 46 (2010):70–71.

sovereignty quickly became associated with territory, often at the expense of ethnic minorities in that area. The Magyar freedom fighter Louis Kossuth, for instance, championed the dissolution of the Austrian Empire but had little to say on the freedoms of the Czechs, Poles, or Croats in a new Hungarian nation-state. For Gustav Struve, the only viable way to secure uniformity and equal citizenship was partitioning territory along the lines of imagined communities of common ancestry. Since Poles or Danes would not find comfort in a unitary German republic, they should be encouraged to secede and join their kinsmen to the north and east.[36]

In truth, the democratic ideals of 1848 were always a bit flawed, and the disposition among the Old World revolutionists to measure the significance of the American Civil War in the light of recent European chronicles of oppression made it difficult for them to appreciate the specific roots of the sectional conflict. Entrenched in their Eurocentric worldview, they were all but unable to grasp the peculiarities of the South's "peculiar institution," the racial foundations of which were arguably the most important. This is not to suggest that the Forty-Eighters were not sincere in their statements that egalitarian democracy meant removing all artificial distinctions of rank and skin color. Yet most refugees saw in Southern slavery little more than an offspring of Old World feudalism. To them, overthrowing black bondage was less about fighting racial injustice than furthering a campaign for human liberation born in the upheavals of post-Napoleonic Europe. As the German American historian Friedrich Kapp declared before the outbreak of sectional hostilities, "The slavery issue is not a negro issue. It is the eternal conflict between the privileged few and the non-privileged many, between aristocracy and democracy."[37]

Yet debates over the future of people of African descent on American soil proved difficult to sidestep if one hoped that slavery would eventually vanish. What ignited controversy was whether blacks would one day reach a stage in their evolution that would allow them to stand on equal footing with whites. Julius Fröbel was decidedly negative on this point. Turning against interpretations that cast the Africans out of the family of human beings, the

[36]Struve, *Weltgeschichte*, 9:784, and *Diesseits und Jenseits des Ozeans*, 4 vols. (Coburg, 1864), 4:77–78. See also Thomas Bender, *A Nation among Nations: America's Place in World History* (New York, 2006), pp. 156–57.

[37]Friedrich Kapp, *Die Geschichte der Sklaverei in den Vereinigten Staaten von Amerika* (New York, 1860), p. 517.

German American scholar nonetheless postulated "that the negro race incontrovertibly holds a position below that of the white race."[38] Another major skeptic regarding black development was Gustav Struve. His qualms, though, were not so much scientifically as politically motivated. Troubled by anti-immigrant writers claiming that not all whites were fit for civic participation, Struve replied that they were. Speaking in the racialized language of his opponents, he chided nativists for neglecting the European origins of the republic they sought to sustain. America had always been the project of a common "indocaucasian race," and Struve considered it a dangerous folly to lump the newly arrived immigrant and the ostracized black worker in a universal outsider caste. Immigration, Struve emphasized, was the seminal question of the age; it would decide whether the country preferred "freedom or slavery, progress or stagnation, the Caucasian or the African element." Struve's fear of racial antagonisms elucidates that shared oppression did not automatically generate interracial solidarity. Rather than challenge white supremacist ideas, some émigrés came to reproduce them, conceiving them as an indispensable tool for promoting their interests in an increasingly race-conscious society.[39]

On the other hand, there were also German-born intellectuals whose democratic convictions did translate into sincere egalitarian attitudes. Journalist Christian Esselen regularly discussed in his *Atlantis* theories from the nascent field of ethnology, and more than once he grappled with scientists favoring a biologically fixed hierarchy of races. Even if there were racial differences, for Esselen they were always in flux and remained secondary to the advancement of human rights. Ottilie Assing, Germany's self-anointed "Negro expert," thought likewise. Entering America as a half-Jewish German woman, she soon discovered parallels between her own quest for self-assertion and the survival tactics employed by the Northern free black community. With special empathy, Assing could write about African Americans as a downtrodden but noble people who, despite ongoing maltreatment, had not lost faith in a better tomorrow. "[A]lmost without exception

[38]Julius Fröbel, *Aus Amerika: Erfahrungen, Reisen und Studien*, 2 vols. (Leipzig, 1857–58), 1:124–88. "Die Negersclaverei in den Ver. Staaten als eine Frage der Ethik, Politik, und Kulturgeschichte," *Atlantis* (May 1856):278–87.

[39]*Sociale Republik*, May 1, Sept. 4, 1858; Struve is quoted in Ansgar Reiß, *Radikalismus und Exil: Gustav Struve und die Demokratie in Deutschland und Amerika* (Stuttgart, 2004), pp. 330, 375, 396.

they are endowed with a kind and cheerful disposition, and the least Negro possesses a natural politeness and friendliness that is as far from servility as it is from importunity," she detailed, trying to correct pervasive antiblack stereotypes among whites. Though Assing often resorted to typical nineteenth-century racial idioms in her journalism, her experience of belonging to an ostracized minority in Europe helped her espouse the cause of black Americans, sometimes with more ardor than the native-born abolitionists.

In the long run, however, the interest of the foreign-born revolutionaries in the African American freedom struggle declined steeply once slavery had been abolished and the Confederacy defeated. A new, more momentous conflict erupted on the other side of the Atlantic that fully absorbed German American attention. Reports of victory in the Franco-Prussian War of 1870–71 and the creation of the Second Reich sent America's German immigrant population into paroxysms of joy. At last, age-old dreams of national unity and the establishment of a strong fatherland capable of projecting power and civilization seemed to have come true.[40] Again, many of the old Forty-Eighters were the first to unsheathe their swords and celebrate that Germany, like the United States a few years earlier, had joined the concert of modern nation-states. But something had been lost. The quest for national unity, which once had fused the political quests for self-determination and civic equality, had displaced the emancipatory ideals of previous democratic upheavals. In 1848 and 1861, the revolution had still been fought for unity *and* freedom. The experience of nineteenth-century nation-making, often accompanied by violence and bloodshed, diluted these liberal promises and gave birth to an inflated rhetoric of national belonging that seeded new antagonisms in the Atlantic world and beyond.

[40]For a more detailed discussion of the German American response to German unification, see Hans L. Trefousse, "The German-American Immigrants and the Newly Founded Reich," in Frank Trommler and Joseph McVeigh, eds., *America and the Germans: An Assessment of a Three-Hundred-Year History*, 2 vols. (Philadelphia, 1985), 1:160–75.

L. Diane Barnes

Make Mine an Abolition War

George Luther Stearns, Frederick Douglass, and the Black Soldier

THE OUTBREAK OF war in April 1861 galvanized some opponents of slavery and left others holding their breath, waiting to see what would materialize. Radical abolitionist William Lloyd Garrison abandoned his earlier attacks on the Union and cautiously expressed a new flag-waving brand of patriotism. Garrisonians found themselves caught between hope for an abolition war and their commitment to nonresistance.[1] Wendell Phillips, who had preached his doctrine of disunion even through the secession winter, quickly came to support the Union war effort. In a speech at Boston's Music Hall on April 21, he condemned the South's actions, proclaiming that "[we] welcome the tread of Massachusetts men marshaled for war." Although he and other Garrisonians had long supported separation from the slave South, taking as their motto "no union with slaveholders," Phillips now declared the South's secession illegal and saw the war as a just battle to end slavery.

Others, including Frederick Douglass (fig. 1) and George Luther Stearns, were more reticent. They welcomed the outbreak of hostilities, but feared that Northerners would support a compromise that would reunite the nation but leave slavery intact.[2] Early in the war, Lincoln's actions clearly suggested

[1]Henry Mayer, *All on Fire: William Lloyd Garrison and the Abolition of Slavery* (New York, 1998), pp. 518–20.

[2]Quoted in James Brewer Stewart, *Wendell Phillips: Liberty's Hero* (Baton Rouge, 1986), pp. 220–21; David W. Blight, *Frederick Douglass' Civil War: Keeping Faith in Jubilee* (Baton Rouge, 1989), pp. 81–82.

Fig. 1. Frederick Douglass, photograph by John White Hurn, 1862. *(Prints and Photographs Division, Library of Congress)*

he was not willing to consider abolishing slavery. While the president issued a call for volunteer troops and built up his war machine, he also adopted a conciliatory tone that urged the seceding states to return to the Union with their slaves protected. Determined to preserve the Union, and with concern to keep the Border States loyal, Lincoln appeared to be proceeding more carefully than abolitionists wanted. During the war, however, both Douglass and Stearns came to understand that the Republican Party held the power and the will to abolish slavery through its military policies. Both men became intimately involved in the war effort, and particularly in advocating a role for African American soldiers.

Many of the classic texts on the abolition movement offer a scant chapter or a few pages to the war period and move more quickly to the conflict over the disbanding of the American Anti-Slavery Society and other groups formed in the immediatist years. In *Holy Warriors*, James Brewer Stewart jumps from Lincoln's 1860 election to the war's end in less than fifteen pages. Lawrence Friedman's *Gregarious Saints* accords abolitionist activity during the war years a mere eleven pages. Jane and William Pease's *They Who Would Be Free* ends with the beginning of the war. Benjamin Quarles allotted a scant three pages, ending his masterful *Black Abolitionists* with an observation from Frederick Douglass's monthly newspaper about the peril of the impending war, noting, "The struggle to make men free might entail armed resistance, but he was crisis-oriented from birth." Even recent texts shy away from delving too deeply into the abolitionists' wartime alliances. The final chapter of John Stauffer's award-winning *The Black Hearts of Men* is titled "The Alliance Ends and the War Begins," quickly shifting focus to postwar memories and meanings. And Stacey Robertson's very recent exploration of women abolitionists and their political involvement in the Old Northwest ends with the woman's rights conventions of the 1850s.[3]

A few recent works do emphasize the wartime and postwar-era activities of abolitionists, but these tend to emphasize disorganization among the

---

[3]James Brewer Stewart, *Holy Warriors: The Abolitionists and American Slavery* (1976; rev. ed., New York, 1996); Lawrence J. Friedman, *Gregarious Saints: Self and Community in American Abolitionism, 1830–1870* (Cambridge, U.K., 1982); Jane H. Pease and William H. Pease, *They Who Would Be Free: Blacks' Search for Freedom, 1830–1861* (New York, 1974); Benjamin Quarles, *Black Abolitionists* (New York, 1969), quote on p. 249; John Stauffer, *The Black Hearts of Men: Radical Abolitionists and the Transformation of Race* (Cambridge, Mass., 2001); Stacey M. Robertson, *Hearts Beating for Liberty: Women Abolitionists in the Old Northwest* (Chapel Hill, N.C., 2010).

major abolitionists, who were forced to reconcile their pacifist proclivities and long-held objections to a union with slaveholders. Among the more interesting recent studies on "latter-day" abolitionists is a recent dissertation by A. J. Aiseirithe, which traces the actions of white followers of William Lloyd Garrison through the Civil War up to the disbanding of the American Anti-Slavery Society in 1870.[4] By examining the most prominent white abolitionists, such studies are able to explore the inherent contradiction that pushed abolitionists into alignment with and even support for a federal government they had long disdained, and toward endorsing candidates for national office, when they had previously rejected electoral politics and political participation altogether.

Civil War–era scholarship has also recently shifted its focus to Northern ideology and to reexamining the commitment of citizens and Northern politicians to both the Union and the abolition of slavery. According to Gary Gallagher, the emphasis on racial issues and emancipation has obfuscated the strength of the Northern commitment to preserve the American Union. In *The Union War*, he argues that the moral argument made by a minority of abolitionists "carried less weight than those presenting emancipation as a military measure necessary to defeat the Rebels and restore the Union."[5] Gallagher believes that the majority of Northerners were more concerned with preservation of the Union than with ending slavery, but James Oakes argues that the Republican Party sought to take down slavery from its inception, and that it enacted twin policies of emancipation at the state level and military emancipation as a key core to Northern war strategy from the onset of the conflict.[6] He argues that the political abolitionism of men like Douglass and Stearns played a significant role in "the formulation of Republican antislavery polices and the coming of the Civil War."[7] Although they, too, believed in the importance of maintaining the Union, the connection between Douglass and Stearns gained strength from their faith in the Republican Party's role in the destruction of slavery, and the alliance they formed proved stronger than any forces of cultural division.

---

[4]A. J. Aiseirithe, "Piloting the Car of Human Freedom: Abolitionism, Woman Suffrage, and the Problem of Radical Reform, 1860–1870," Ph.D. dissertation, University of Chicago, 2007.

[5]Gary Gallagher, *The Union War* (Cambridge, Mass., 2011), pp. 2–3.

[6]James Oakes, *Freedom National: The Destruction of Slavery in the United States, 1861–1865* (New York, 2013), pp. xii–xiii.

[7]Ibid., p. xvii.

Scholarly wisdom has held that war caused tension among prominent abolitionists as they tried to determine whether the Civil War and the impending end to slavery in the United States spelled the end to their life's work. It has also been common to see a racial divide among nineteenth-century reformers. While all supported abolition, many white abolitionists gave only lip service to their commitment to full racial equality and strove for black civil rights. Douglass, however, always supported biracial cooperation in the fight against slavery and in the quest for full equality for African Americans. Sometimes he was criticized for placing too much faith in white reformers and mainstream politics, but he understood (and rightly so) that to achieve the momentous goals of abolition and advancing black rights, African Americans could not act alone. The cooperation between Douglass and Stearns during the Civil War demonstrates that momentous things could be achieved across color lines, and that some white reformers did share a desire for full equality.

For many Garrisonians, the anticipation that the Civil War would finally end slavery in America foreshadowed the completion of their life's work. For men like Douglass and Stearns, however, an "abolition war" meant more: in addition to ending slavery, they believed that it was important that African Americans have an active role in the conflict. They shared what David Blight has noted: the conflict had to be understood "not only as a testing of manhood, but as a full, dignified, humane recognition of manhood." Indeed, it was for Stearns and Douglass a time for the "revolutionary reinvention of the rights of man and of republican government."[8] They understood that the Civil War should and could do more than end slavery: they believed it was a moral struggle to determine the economic and political future of blacks in the United States. However, their belief that a biracial war effort would advance the state of race relations within the nation was not shared universally, and the high expectations they placed in the meaning and potential of the conflict left them with a bittersweet sense of accomplishment. Both were elated at the end of slavery, but frustrated at the lack of progress on civil rights at war's end. While the Republican Party and the federal army pushed an agenda of military emancipation, Union support for African

[8]David Blight, "The Meaning or the Fight: Frederick Douglass and the Memory of the Fifty Fourth Massachusetts," *Massachusetts Review* 36 (1995):142.

American civil rights was less forthcoming, leading both Douglass and Stearns to question their role in the conflict.

Frederick Douglass was a familiar figure in antebellum America. Born enslaved on Maryland's Eastern Shore in 1818, he spent most of his youth in the port city of Baltimore. Escaping slavery at age twenty in 1838, he soon became an antislavery lecturer, author, and newspaper editor. His personal account of slavery, *Narrative of the Life of Frederick Douglass*, appearing in 1845, proved to be a lasting testament to the horrors of American slavery, and sold thousands of copies in the United States and Great Britain. A longtime advocate of biracial cooperation in reform circles, Douglass formed close alliances with both white and African American activists. His abolitionist career began in 1841 when he was hired as a lecturer for the Massachusetts Anti-Slavery Society, and he spent the following decade as a close associate of William Lloyd Garrison. In the early 1850s, Douglass also rose to become an important leader among African Americans, regularly attending national and regional conventions aimed at improving the position of blacks in U.S. society. He also broke publicly with the Garrisonians and endorsed political means for ending slavery. By the time of the Civil War he was the most recognizable black man in America, and was moving toward being a loyal adherent of the Republican Party.

George Luther Stearns spent less time in the public eye than Douglass, but was equally committed to the abolition of slavery and to African American civil rights. Most famously, he was one of the "Secret Six" who funded John Brown's raid on the federal arsenal at Harpers Ferry in 1859. Born in Medford, Massachusetts, in 1809, his life story is representative of the "self-made man" ideal popular in the mid-nineteenth century. Beginning as a clerk in a relative's store, he pooled some investors and established a linseed oil manufactory in Medford, and subsequently made his way into the lead pipe business. The oil was used as furniture varnish and for floor coverings. Stearns amassed a considerable fortune and used his wealth and his connections to powerful Massachusetts politicians to advance the antislavery agenda in the 1850s.[9]

---

[9]Charles E. Heller, *Portrait of an Abolitionist: A Biography of George Luther Stearns, 1809–1867* (Westport, Conn., 1996); Edward J. Renehan Jr., *The Secret Six: The True Tale of the Men Who Conspired with John Brown* (Columbia, S.C., 1997), pp. 57–59.

Stearns supported antislavery causes, and especially politicians, helping to fund the election of both Charles Sumner and Henry Wilson to the U.S. Senate, where they represented Massachusetts on the eve of the war. He was part of a small group of Massachusetts political activists known as the "Bird Club," after the group's founder, manufacturer Francis Bird. The group was instrumental in forming the commonwealth's Republican Party. Through the group, Stearns gained the acquaintance of other important men, including John A. Andrew, who would be Massachusetts's wartime governor. In the 1850s he was also chair of the Kansas Committee of Massachusetts, funneling money and Sharps rifles to John Brown in the struggle to make Kansas a free state. He played a similar role in funding Browns raid on Harpers Ferry. Stearns escaped unscathed from the congressional investigation into the events surrounding Harpers Ferry, and as the Civil War erupted in the spring of 1861, he joined ranks with other political abolitionists to demand that emancipation be made a war aim.[10]

Stearns and Douglass shared the belief that to fully wage an abolition war, the Union Army must arm African Americans, but their respective worldviews led them to take different paths toward that end. Early in the war, Stearns was instrumental in forming the Emancipation League of Boston in 1861. In the first six months of the war, the League operated as behind-the-scenes lobbyists for emancipation and African American participation in the war effort. Stearns and other prominent political abolitionists wrote to fellow industrialists and national politicians, urging them to push for emancipation. Initially keeping their individual identities secret, members of the League circulated unsigned letters, many of which were published in Northern newspapers. Unlike the immediatists of the prewar period, who stressed the moral necessity of abolishing slavery, Stearns and other radicals of the Emancipation League demanded abolition on the grounds of justice for African Americans and military necessity.[11] He even wrote to President Lincoln, urging him to understand that blacks needed to be freed specifically to aid the Union war effort. In July 1861, he quietly cheered the Union loss at First Bull Run, fearing that a quick end to the war would reunite the country with slavery intact.

---

[10]Heller, *Portrait of an Abolitionist*, pp. 69–74, 83–92.

[11]Richard H. Abbott, *Cotton and Capital: Boston Businessmen and Antislavery Reform, 1854–1868* (Amherst, Mass., 1991), pp. 77–80.

When the League made a public announcement of its existence in December 1861, more than a hundred prominent men had fixed their name to its declaration. In its constitution, the Emancipation League declared its intention to "urge upon the people and the government emancipation of the slaves as a measure of justice and as a military necessity; it being the shortest, cheapest, and least bloody path to permanent peace."[12] Committed from the outset to both ending slavery and achieving black civil rights, the Emancipation League soon had a sister organization in New York City.

Interestingly, the tactics of the Emancipation League were similar to those of the antebellum works of immediate abolitionists. They held conventions, published tracts and pamphlets emphasizing their cause, and petitioned Congress to address their concerns, but on a grander scale. They sponsored discussion sessions, public lectures, circulated more than 100,000 pamphlets, and had access to the editorial pages of the North's most prominent newspapers. But unlike the immediatists, because many members held prominent public office or commanded wealth, they were able to exert much more influence.

As 1861 came to a close, Douglass reflected on the first months of the war. While Stearns was busy with Emancipation League activities, Douglass had turned his agitator's voice to the war effort, addressing numerous white and black audiences. In January 1862, he delivered a scathing criticism of the government's lack of sensibilities in failing to make abolition a war aim. Addressing a black self-improvement society in Philadelphia with a speech entitled "Fighting the Rebels with One Hand," he argued that African Americans were necessary to a full and effective war strategy. He complained that the federal government aimed to preserve slavery in the South, and that even General Benjamin Butler's actions and the Confiscation Act of 1861 were demeaning because they labeled men and women contraband, a term Douglass believed applied "better to a pistol, than to a person." His plan to subdue the Confederate Army required the full acceptance of black participation in the Union Army. "We are striking the guilty rebels with our soft, white hand, when we should be striking with the iron hand of the black man, which we keep chained behind us."[13]

---

[12]Quoted in *Liberator*, Dec. 13, 1861.

[13]John Blassingame et al., eds., *Frederick Douglass Papers*, ser. 1: *Speeches, Debates, and Interviews*, 5 vols. (New Haven, Conn., 1979–92), 3:478, 483.

In the second year of the war, Douglass threw the full force of his energy into agitation through multiple editorials in each issue of *Douglass' Monthly*, speeches, letters, and private conversations. His assessment of the Union Army's dismal performance eased a bit with General Ulysses S. Grant's successful capture of Fort Henry on the Tennessee River and Fort Donelson on the Cumberland River in early February 1862, and Grant's demand for "unconditional surrender" by the Confederates. Nevertheless, Douglass continued to condemn Northern politicians and public sentiment as too lenient on the rebels. In March, he editorialized, "the North has been angry with the South only as a child is angry with a pet, and that anger soon passes away when the pet has been well kicked. We are now ready to make up and hug the darling slaveholders with a fondness as ardent as ever." To Douglass's mind it was clear that the Confederate forces were making full use of the labor of enslaved Southerners and that the North should go even further to make the ultimate policy one that would both free the slaves and arm them once emancipated. Following the Union victory at the Battle of Antietam in September 1862, he would learn that Lincoln was indeed beginning to see just such a necessity.[14]

As the Emancipation League lobbied for action in 1862, Stearns became the organization's treasurer, and his disgust with the president's war effort continued to parallel Douglass's. The Emancipation League circulated the speeches of Charles Sumner and essays of abolitionist Elizur Wright among Washington's important lawmakers, but Stearns was frustrated. In early 1862 he wrote to Sumner that he believed he "could hope for nothing good from the imbecility in Washington." Emancipation had to become the war's aim, he proclaimed, because it was the "shortest, cheapest, and least bloody path to permanent peace, and the only method of maintaining the integrity of the nation."[15]

In February 1862, Douglass delivered an important address titled "The Future of the Negro People of the Slave States" before a meeting of the Emancipation League at Boston's Tremont Temple. It is not clear whether this was the first meeting of Stearns and Douglass, as the two were certainly familiar with each other from Douglass's public persona, and through their

---

[14]"The Situation of the War," *Douglass' Monthly* (Mar. 1862); Frederick Douglass, *Life and Times of Frederick Douglass* (1892; repr. New York, 1962), pp. 335–37.

[15]Quoted in Heller, *Portrait of an Abolitionist*, p. 139.

common friendship with John Brown. Douglass celebrated the formation of the League, and then lectured at length about the place of African Americans in the United States: "My friends, the destiny of the colored American, however this mighty war shall terminate, is the destiny of America."[16]

Douglass's appearance before the Boston activists of the League was the beginning of a collaboration that would last through the last year of the war. Following the Tremont Temple meeting, Douglass embarked on a two-week lecture tour on the League's behalf, spreading the message of emancipation along a journey that covered a thousand miles.[17] Of this new era of cooperation between opponents of slavery, Douglass wrote: "We form a common league against slavery, and whatever political or personal differences, which have in other days decided and distracted us, a common object and a common emergency makes us for the time at least, forget those differences, and strike at the common foe—and to give victory to the common cause."[18] In the process he formed a lasting friendship with Stearns and other League members, including Massachusetts Senator Charles Sumner.

The Emancipation Proclamation was the game-changing event that allowed Douglass and Stearns to push beyond agitation and lobbying and into action. Although it applied only to enslaved men and women in areas of the Confederacy then under rebellion, for abolitionists it spelled the end to slavery and made the Civil War an abolition war at last. It also firmly asserted and reinforced military emancipation, and paved the way for the enlistment of African American soldiers.[19] Upon learning that Lincoln's proclamation meant that slaves in areas under rebellion would be free on January 1, 1863, Douglass rejoiced: "We shout for joy that we live to record this righteous decree." He charged fellow abolitionists to get to work ensuring that Northern sentiment favored the implementation of the policy. Douglass sprang to action: "We are ready for this service or any other, in this, we trust, the last struggle with the monster slavery."[20] Over the next year, his efforts would focus on the recruitment and service of African American troops in the Union Army.

---

[16]"The Future of the Negro People," *Douglass'* Monthly (Mar. 1862).

[17]John Stauffer, *Giants: The Parallel Lives of Frederick Douglass and Abraham Lincoln* (New York, 2008), pp. 239–40.

[18]"The Popular Heart," *Douglass' Monthly* (Feb. 1862).

[19]Oakes, *Freedom National*, pp. 342–43.

[20]"Emancipation," *Douglass' Monthly* (Oct. 1862).

Even before the preliminary Emancipation Proclamation was issued in September, the Second Confiscation Act and the Militia Act, both passed in July 1862, paved the way for African American military participation. The Second Confiscation Act freed those slaves captured in the course of the war, and the Militia Act empowered the army to put African Americans to work at menial labor or "any military or naval service for which they may be found competent."[21] Under the supervision of General Benjamin F. Butler, who commanded military occupation activities in and around New Orleans, in the late summer regiments of black troops were mustered into service in Louisiana, with units soon following in South Carolina and Kansas. As many as 4,000 African American troops had been raised in areas of the South by the time of the issuance of the final Emancipation Proclamation on January 1, 1863. At that point Stearns's and Douglass's urgent desires for black participation in the war effort came together.

While Douglass agitated on the public stage, Stearns lobbied behind the scenes. In an interview on the subject, he noted, "Slavery is dead; that is the first thing."[22] His Emancipation League formed a committee to press Lincoln on the issue of black troops and civil rights. In January 1863, Stearns and the committee met with Lincoln, urging the president to do three things: they sought the appointment of John C. Frémont as military governor of the areas of North Carolina under Union control; the speedy enrollment of black regiments in the North; and the full and complete abolition of slavery. Among their concerns, only the enlistment of African American units gained the president's favor. To convince more politicians and the Northern public to support African American troops, the League gathered data from field commanders and others, who testified to the bravery and usefulness of the "contrabands" and other blacks seeking to aid the Union war effort. Publishing the data at their own expense, Emancipation League members distributed the pamphlet among influential Washingtonians.[23]

Emancipation League member and Massachusetts Governor John A. Andrew was among the first Northern governors to request permission to raise a regiment of black volunteers. Lincoln granted permission to raise the

---

[21]*The War of the Rebellion: A Compilation of the Official Records of the Union and Confederate Armies* (Washington, D.C., 1880–1901), ser. 3, vol. 2, p. 281 (hereafter *O.R.*).

[22]Ira Berlin et al., eds., *Freedom: A Documentary History of Emancipation, 1861–1867*, ser. 2: *The Black Military Experience* (Cambridge, U.K., 1985–93), p. 415

[23]*Facts Concerning the Freedmen: Their Capacity and Destiny* (Boston, 1863).

first Northern regiment, the 54th Massachusetts, and Douglass and Stearns were intimately involved. Andrew put the task of recruiting in Stearns's hands. Stearns turned to Douglass and other prominent African Americans to do the recruiting. Here began their "abolition war." Stearns regularly assured potential recruits: "When you have rifles in your hands, your freedom will be secure."[24]

Headed by white company officers and commanded by Colonel Robert Gould Shaw, the 54th Massachusetts recruited black men from beyond the commonwealth's borders, as Massachusetts had fewer than 2,000 African American men of military age in 1863. Douglass recruited in upstate New York, and fellow abolitionists Henry Highland Garnet, John Mercer Langston, and Martin R. Delany sought to fill the volunteer ranks from among the citizens of New York City, Ohio, and Chicago. Blacks across the Northeast were so eager to join in the fight that ranks were quickly filled in the 54th, and a second black unit, the 55th Massachusetts, had to be formed. Among the early volunteers were two of Douglass's sons, Charles and Lewis. Lewis, the eldest, became the regiment's first sergeant major, while his younger brother served as a private. They were mustered first at Boston and then in more permanent barracks at Readville, and on May 18 Governor Andrew himself came to present the unit with their regimental colors. Among the celebrants were William Lloyd Garrison and Wendell Phillips, fully shed of their pacifism, and a throng of the city's black residents. On May 28, the men of the 54th Massachusetts arrived in Boston in preparation for transport to South Carolina. There they marched to the statehouse, where Governor Andrew accompanied their procession across Boston Common. Douglass was reportedly so proud of his sons' service that when the regiment sailed from Boston harbor, he rented a boat to wave the men off from the bay, although Charles had fallen ill and was not among those departing.[25]

In addition to helping advance the war effort in the face of waning white enlistment, both Douglass and Stearns believed that service in the Union Army would elevate the standing of blacks in U.S. society and that their brave service would be rewarded with equal treatment and move the cause

---

[24]Stearns, quoted in Heller, *Portrait of an Abolitionist*, p. 148.

[25]Edwin S. Redkey, "Brave Black Volunteers: A Profile of the Fifty-Fourth Massachusetts Regiment," in Martin H. Blatt, Thomas J. Brown, and Donald Yacavone, eds., *Hope and Glory: Essays on the Legacy of the 54th Massachusetts Regiment* (Amherst, Mass., 2001), pp. 22–23; William S. McFeely, *Frederick Douglass* (New York, 1991), pp. 217–25.

of civil rights forward considerably. Although African American troops initially received lower pay, poor assignments, and little opportunity for advancement, Stearns particularly believed that within six months' time, as black soldiers demonstrated their worth to the nation, equality, including officers' commissions, would come their way.

Stearns proved to be such a successful recruiter that he was soon called upon to assist in recruiting black troops at the federal level. Following a meeting with Secretary of War Edwin Stanton, Stearns accepted a major's commission June 1863.[26] He set up recruiting in Philadelphia and soon looked to Douglass for assistance.

The spring's recruiting efforts left Douglass tired but pleased that he had made a significant contribution. At the age of forty-five, he knew that his talent as an orator and agitator was better suited for a nonmilitary role in the conflict, and he never seriously considered enlisting in the Union Army. When his old friend Stearns called him back into the recruiting field, Douglass prepared to go to Philadelphia. Douglass felt duty-bound to continue his recruiting efforts, writing to his friend Gerrit Smith, "The work is not to my taste—and I had enough of it while recruiting for Massachusetts: Nevertheless as this is not a time to be governed by one's taste—I shall probably go soon into the work again."[27] Understanding that his influence could be of assistance in filling out the ranks of black regiments, he rejoined Stearns's efforts.

While encouraging Douglass to continue in the recruiting field, Stearns was experiencing considerable frustration of his own. Even as he assured black recruits of their valuable contribution and promised a future where their rights and freedoms would be recognized, he struggled to place black troops into field assignments even as the number of white soldiers in arms dwindled perilously. In his recruiting duties, Stearns experienced the full force of racial prejudice among Union officers and white troops. In the weeks before the Battle of Gettysburg and the New York draft riots, he tried to send African American troops to fill the ranks of several units under the command of Major General Darius Couch, who headed the Department of the Susquehanna. Couch refused to accept the recruits, thinly disguising

[26]*Senate Executive Journal*, Jan. 7, 1864, p. 356.

[27]Douglass to Gerrit Smith, June 19, 1863, Gerrit Smith Papers, George Arents Research Library, Syracuse University, Syracuse, N.Y.

his racism by claiming he was unauthorized to accept them because colored troops were not committed to a three-year enlistment. Stearns reported the incident to Secretary of War Stanton, but despite the secretary's dispatch advising Couch to accept the troops regardless of color, the recruits were returned. In his reply to Stearns, the secretary acquiesced, noting, "if there is likely to be any dispute about the matter, it will be better to send no more," and advising, "it is well to avoid all controversy in the present juncture."[28] Clearly, the secretary was not willing to endure the ire of a valued department head to uphold the rights of African American troops regardless of their value and bravery.

The summer of 1863 proved to be the major turning point in the war, but it did not bring about full abolition or real movement on racial equality. The frustration of Stearns and Douglass was exacerbated as racial tensions flared in the North. While recruiting in Philadelphia in mid-July, Douglass and Stearns learned of the violent anti-draft riots that erupted in New York City and other parts of the North as a result of Congress's conscription policy. The exclusion of African Americans from the conscription lottery served to exacerbate tensions between African Americans and working-class white men, especially in Northern cities, where competition for limited jobs and economic opportunities had raged even before the onset of the Civil War. As a result of whites' anger and fear over the potential effects of the Emancipation Proclamation, which made ending slavery a goal of the Union war effort, blacks found themselves targeted by frustrated workers and immigrants in Northern cities.

Dismayed by violent attacks and the lynching of eleven men during the riots in New York City in particular, Douglass's elation over emancipation and an expanding role for African Americans in the war effort quickly began to wane.[29] The possibility of personal loss also struck home when he received a letter from Lewis describing the engagement of the 54th Massachusetts at Fort Wagner in South Carolina (fig. 2). Volunteering for a recklessly dangerous attack on the fort across an open beach, the black regiment suffered 281 casualties, including their commander, Colonel Shaw, who was mortally wounded. Lewis's description made his father's blood run cold: "I had my sword sheath blown away while on the parapet of the Fort. The

[28] *O.R.*, ser. 1, vol. 27, part 3, p. 203.

[29] "The Mob in New York," *New York Times*, July 14, 1863.

FIG. 2. "The Gallant Charge of the Fifty-Fourth Massachusetts (Colored) Regiment: On the Rebel Works at Fort Wagner, Morris Island, Near Charleston, July 18th, 1863, and Death of Colonel Robt. G. Shaw," engraving by Currier and Ives, September 11, 1863. *(Prints and Photographs Division, Library of Congress)*

grape and canister, shell and minnies [*sic*] swept us down like chaff, still our men went on and on, and if we had been properly supported we would have held the Fort, but the white troops could not be made to come up."[30] The 54th had been sent into great peril and likely suffered extreme casualties partly because inept leaders failed to send to their support their white fellow soldiers. In the month following the debacle, Douglass published Lewis's letter in his monthly, along with several others upholding the bravery of Colonel Shaw, but his heart was heavy.[31] Coupled with the realization that participation in the Union Army did little to dispel racial inequality, and the antiblack violence of the draft riots, the report of events in South Carolina served to push Douglass into a state of despair. He lost faith with Lincoln's slow steps forward in abolishing slavery and issues of racial justice.

All of Douglass's agitation for a larger role for blacks in the war effort left him bitter and frustrated at the reality of mistreatment and unequal policies emanating from the War Department, and seemingly from President

[30]"The 54th Massachusetts at Fort Wagner," *Douglass' Monthly* (Aug. 1863).

[31]*Douglass' Monthly* (July 1863).

Lincoln. Military emancipation brought nothing but freedom as African American soldiers continued to be given inferior assignments, and were ineligible for commissioned officer posts. Set to manual labor in miserable and hot conditions across the South, or sent into dangerous situations such as at Fort Wagner, African American soldiers were clearly not valued on an equal footing with whites.

When the Confederate Congress responded to the Union enlistment of black troops with a proclamation in May 1863 that any captured African Americans would be liable to death or sale into slavery, the president offered no assurances that they would be protected from such a fate. Instead, in June the War Department formalized an unequal pay policy by which white privates were paid thirteen dollars per month, while black privates were allowed ten dollars, from which another three dollars was deducted for clothing and equipment. Denied the ability to advance, African American sergeants, including Lewis Douglass, soon learned that white privates earned more than they did each month. Originally enthusiastic recruiters, Douglass and Stearns began to question the prudence of encouraging men to commit to such a situation. Enlistment began to concentrate in the Border States and the Deep South, where even impoverished blacks began to protest loudly against the policy.

The War Department's policy thwarted Douglass's double battle against slavery and racism, as David Blight has noted, and strained his ability to promise black recruits that freedom and equality would be possible at war's end.[32] With potential new recruits in the Northeast drying up, on August 1, Douglass wrote to Stearns declining further recruiting responsibilities. "I owe it to my long abused people, and especially those of them already in the army to expose their wrongs and plead their case. When I plead for recruits, I want to do it with all my heart, without qualification. I cannot do that now," he told Stearns.[33]

As Douglass penned these words to his old friend, he was unaware that Lincoln had acted in the wake of the debacle at Fort Wagner, after which a number of captured black enlisted men were forced into slavery. In his monthly newspaper he lashed out at Lincoln's seeming failure to insist

[32]Blight, *Frederick Douglass' Civil War*, pp. 160–63.

[33]James M. McPherson, *The Negro's Civil War* (New York, 1965), pp. 173–75; Douglass to G. L. Stearns, *Douglass' Monthly* (Aug. 1863).

that black prisoners be exchanged and his failure to retaliate for the atrocities black soldiers had faced at Charleston. He demanded justice: "For every black prisoner slain in cold blood, Mr. Jefferson Davis should be made to understand that one rebel officer shall suffer death, and for every colored soldier sold into slavery, a rebel shall be held as a hostage. For our Government to do less than this, is to deserve the indignation and the execration of mankind."[34] Although not exactly the eye-for-an-eye retribution Douglass sought, the president did issue a retaliatory order on July 30 demanding that one Confederate soldier be put to hard labor for each Union soldier remanded to slavery.[35] Douglass still published his critical letter to Stearns in his monthly, but he followed it with a disclaimer noting that protections were being offered to black soldiers. He believed it to be a small concession that black troops had purchased "dearly," noting that "it really seems that nothing of justice, liberty or humanity can come to us except through tears and blood."[36] He determined to agitate more fiercely for black soldiers, and to do so he needed to communicate directly with the one man who had the ability to level the playing field. At the urging of Stearns, Douglass traveled to Washington to plead the case for black troops and their grievances directly to President Lincoln.

Using his connections to a Kansas senator to gain access at the highest levels, Douglass met first with Secretary of War Stanton, and then with President Lincoln. He outlined his demands that African American troops be granted both equal protection and equal pay. He was surprised to learn that Stanton was receptive to the issue of pay equity, and that protections had already been stepped up for U.S. Colored Troops in the field. He went away rejuvenated and with faith restored in the importance of his recruiting mission. During his August 1863 meetings in Washington, Douglass was promised an officer's commission to travel south to the Mississippi Valley to recruit for the U.S. Colored Troops with Lorenzo Thomas, but that never came to pass.[37] With eastern recruits thinning, in the late summer of 1863 Stearns was ordered to the West, recruiting in Nashville, Tennessee, but also clashing loudly with Andrew Johnson, Tennessee's military governor. There

---

[34]"The Commander-in-Chief and His Black Soldiers," *Douglass' Monthly* (Aug. 1863).

[35]Blight, *Frederick Douglass' Civil War*, p. 166.

[36]Douglass to G. L. Stearns, *Douglass' Monthly* (Aug. 1863).

[37]L. Diane Barnes, *Frederick Douglass: Reformer and Statesman* (New York, 2012), pp. 94–95.

he witnessed the poor treatment of black troops as they were pressed into hard labor repairing railroads and other war-torn structures in the region.[38]

Douglass left the recruiting field altogether and returned to agitation. His lectures shifted message; instead of merely calling for an abolition war, he called for an abolition peace. He began to look beyond the war toward a Reconstruction that would include full equality for his race. His speeches called for an all-out attack on and conquest of the South and full emancipation throughout the region. This message was hammered home again and again in a speech titled "The Mission of the War," which he delivered on numerous occasions in Rochester, Philadelphia, Boston, and other cities across the North. His most famous speech occurred on January 13, 1864, at the request of the Woman's Loyal League, which was actively working in favor of a constitutional amendment banning slavery. Delivered before a large crowd at New York's Cooper Institute, the speech outlined four main principles all loyal Americans needed to embrace. First, he told his audience they were compelled to recognize that the war "shall be, and of right ought to be, an Abolition war." By the same token, no peace but an "Abolition peace" could be considered a satisfactory outcome. This meant that the nation must recognize the contributions of African Americans to the war and to society as a whole, and to extend to blacks full rights and opportunities. Finally, he insisted that such full equality would only be achieved when the nation invested "the black man everywhere with the right to vote and to be voted for, and remove all discriminations against his rights on account of this color, whether as a citizen or as a soldier."[39] That same month, Stearns's frustration reached its pinnacle, and he resigned his commission. He returned to his business activities in Massachusetts, feeling he had not accomplished what he set out to do in 1863.

As 1864 wore on and the prospects for an end to the war grew dimmer with repeated military blunders and extended campaigns, both Douglass and Stearns became increasingly aggravated with the president's lack of action on civil rights. They watched and listened carefully to the words and actions of the Republican Party, and they grew skeptical of Lincoln and his ability to wage their brand of abolition war or to effect any type of peace.

---

[38]Heller, *Portrait of an Abolitionist*, p. 160.

[39]Blassingame, *Frederick Douglass Papers*, 4:3, 11–12.

Efforts to resolve the equal pay controversy lasted well into the summer's election season, and the Republicans made no move to extend suffrage to blacks in the areas of the Border States under Union control. In May, Douglass stood among a group of abolitionists and Radical Republicans calling for a convention to meet at Cleveland to choose an alternative presidential ticket headed by John C. Frémont. In a letter appearing in the *New York Times*, Douglass explained that if the proposed alternative convention supported black equality and suffrage rights, "I cheerfully give my name as one of the signers of the call."[40] The actual convention managed to attract around 400 disaffected Republicans, but Douglass was not among their number. Although he was enamored of Frémont's actions on behalf of African Americans, particularly with his emancipation policy early in the war, in the end Douglass's practicality once again prevented him from fully committing to an unlikely candidacy in such a troubled time.

Stearns went even further in considering an alternative to Lincoln's candidacy, inviting Frémont to a meeting in August of several prominent members of the Emancipation League, but eventually came to reject both Lincoln and Frémont as candidates. Instead, he drafted a letter to Frémont, signed by himself and other activists, angry with the both Frémont's and Lincoln's lack of leadership on the race question. Stearns asked Frémont to step aside if Lincoln would agree to do the same, so that a new convention and new candidates could be named. The letter asserted the aim to "unite the thorough and earnest friends of a rigorous prosecution of the war in a new convention, which shall represent the patriotism of all parties."[41] In the end, though, Stearns also turned to practicality, giving Lincoln his lukewarm support.

For both Douglass and Stearns, the Civil War was an imperfect struggle to keep the American nation together, but also an imperfect struggle for the racial equality they both so desired. Although both rejoiced in December 1865 at the ratification of the Thirteenth Amendment, they had both hoped to achieve so much more. They fought bitterly for their own brand of "abolition war" and were in the end deeply disappointed. Douglass went on to fight another round for racial equality and black civil rights, but Stearns

[40]Douglass to E. Gilbert, May 23, 1864, in Philip Foner, ed., *The Life and Writings of Frederick Douglass*, 4 vols. (New York, 1952), 3:403.

[41]Stearns et al. to Frémont, Aug. 21, 1864, quoted in *Atlantic Monthly* 41 (Mar. 1878):370.

did not. At the close of the war he helped found the weekly *Nation* magazine, but soon withdrew support because his partners opposed suffrage and civil rights for African Americans. He died in New York City in 1867, exactly two years after Lee's surrender at Appomattox Courthouse brought the long war to a close.

Ten years following Stearns's death, Frederick Douglass was appointed to a minor federal office by President Rutherford B. Hayes. Among the dozens of congratulatory notes he received upon confirmation of his appointment was one he surely cherished above many others. It was from Mary Stearns, the wife of his coadjutor in the cause of black equality. She wrote, "It is not twenty years since John Brown was hung for a practical application of the Golden Rule to your suffering race and today as its representative you are Marshal of the District of Columbia! Very dear seems the spirit of my noble husband in this sublime triumph of reason and virtue. For this he gave his life and fortune."[42] Although Douglass surely knew that the struggle for racial equality was far from over, he also knew that cooperation across the color line continued to be the only means to move the struggle forward.

[42]Mary E. Stearns to Douglass, Mar. 26, 1877, Frederick Douglass Papers, Library of Congress.

Chandra Manning

Military Emancipation before the Emancipation Proclamation

Overcoming Structural Obstacles

I FIRST BEGAN THIS essay in 2012, coincidentally in the very same week that I needed to find my then-toddler's social security number. The search for that little blue card that signals national belonging in a practical sense led me to reflect on how the membership (and the membership benefits) of any national community change over time. As I revisit this essay in 2017, we find ourselves in a very different climate, when inclusion within the national community appears to be shrinking rather than growing. Our moment of contraction is not the first or only one in U.S. history, and it serves as an important reminder that national belonging has *always* been in flux, sometimes expanding and sometimes contracting, and always with the potential to go either way. The dynamic nature of national belonging—its constant state of change—makes it all the more important to understand moments of both expansion and contraction in the past. The Civil War and its aftermath marked a dramatic, though imperfect, episode of expansion, during which more than four million enslaved people excluded from the national community in 1860 gained entrance to that community, and with it a direct, claims-making relationship with the national government.

The transition from exclusion to inclusion did not happen all at once (or, for that matter, once and for all), but one early, important step was military emancipation, which began even before the Emancipation Proclamation as a not entirely planned collaboration between the army, the executive and legislative branches of the U.S. government, and men, women, and children fleeing bondage. By 1862 military emancipation determined that once a formerly enslaved person made contact with the Union Army, that person was (under most circumstances) no longer a slave. But the year 1862 made equally clear that military emancipation could only do so much. While military emancipation could determine who a person was *not* (a slave owned by another person), it could not by itself determine who that person *was* instead. More specifically, military emancipation *by itself* could not provide full inclusion within the national community. For that reason, military emancipation can seem like an incomplete and disappointing development, and from the perspective of the formerly enslaved, it undoubtedly was, so we tend to skip over it in our recounting of the slavery-to-freedom story. But we need to slow down the action to understand more fully exactly how this step happened, because military emancipation was not automatic. Major obstacles had to be overcome first, not just the orneriness of certain commanders or individual racism among Northern soldiers or civilians, but bona fide structural obstacles that had seemed unyielding on the immediate eve of the war. One of the most important, and most overlooked, was a conviction held very firmly in the nineteenth century but not as firmly now: the conviction that civil authority must supersede military authority. The purpose of this essay is to better understand military emancipation before the Emancipation Proclamation by explicating the structural obstacles it faced, including principles relating to the relationship between civil and military authority, examining how the interactions of former slaves, the army, the executive branch, and Congress began to breach those obstacles, and highlighting the questions around national belonging that military emancipation could not answer, but did place prominently on the national agenda, where they would be addressed in the latter half and in the aftermath of the war.

Military emancipation was not unheard of in world history in 1862, but it was no foregone conclusion in the U.S. Civil War. World history provides plenty of examples of armies manumitting enemy combatants' slaves as a war measure—the British had done so in the American Revolution and War of 1812—and numerous Republicans (such as Joshua Giddings) made the case for Union forces doing likewise even before hostilities broke out.[1] But

[1]See James Oakes, *The Scorpion's Sting: Anti-Slavery and the Coming of the Civil War* (New York, 2014).

the official position of the federal government, despite prominent dissent from that position, held such emancipation to be illegitimate. After the War of 1812, Secretary of State John Quincy Adams, who personally hated slavery, plainly stated in his official capacity that "the emancipation of enemy's slaves is not among the acts of legitimate war," no more permissible than "the right of putting to death all prisoners in cold blood . . . or the right to use poisoned weapons, or to assassinate." Newspaper readers in 1862 knew that position well, because Northern newspapers reprinted Adams's position in the summer and fall of 1862 as they waged a debate over the legitimacy of wartime emancipation.[2] The point is not that all Northerners opposed emancipation—plainly they did not—but rather that the question of the legality of *military* emancipation was a hotly contested topic in 1862.

The reason for the fevered battle over military emancipation in 1862 was that it faced hulking impediments in the United States, impediments that had seemed insurmountable before the war began. Opposition to American slavery was older than the republic, with resistance to bondage arising from the very beginning among the enslaved themselves, and with growing numbers of free black Americans and white Northerners calling for its abolition as the nineteenth century progressed. Still, the institution of slavery withstood all of that resistance, not because the resistance was half-hearted, but because powerful obstacles prevented it from achieving its goal. Many of those obstacles were structural forces beyond the power of any individual humans to control. In addition to the economic, demographic, and political structural forces that shored up slavery, certain prevailing ideas and assumptions were so strong and pervasive that they operated with all the power of structural forces, hindering action as much as congressional representation, the power of the dollar, or other obvious structural forces.[3]

---

[2]John Quincy Adams, Dispatches to U.S. Minister to Russia Middleton, and letter to Benjamin Rush, July 1820, reprinted in "Views of John Quincy Adams" (Washington, D.C.), *Daily National Intelligencer*, Sept. 2, 1862, which itself was reprinting an exchange among New York papers from earlier that summer. For evidence that this view was an official administration view that Adams's role as a member of the federal government required him to take, and not his own personal view (which diverged widely), see John Quincy Adams's Diary, Jan. 1, 1819–Mar. 20, 1821, Adams Family Papers, Massachusetts Historical Society.

[3]William Sewell Jr. has influentially defined "structures" as "sets of mutually sustaining schemas and resources that empower and constrain social action and that tend to be reproduced by that social action." See "A Theory of Structure: Duality, Agency, and Transformation," *American Journal of Sociology* 98 (1992):1–29, especially p. 19. See also

At the beginning of the Civil War, two ideas in particular (besides the obvious widespread racism, which did not completely disappear even with the abolition of slavery) operated as structural forces inhibiting the abolition of slavery. One was that slavery was a civil institution governed by civil authority. The other was that a positive, direct relationship existed between the national government and white property owners, but no positive, direct relationship existed between the U.S. government and enslaved people. These widespread ideas challenged the likelihood of abolition in general, but more specifically, they *especially* militated against military emancipation because collectively they suggested that the Union Army ought to have nothing to do with slaves or slavery.

But the army *did* free slaves, and it started doing so remarkably quickly—so quickly that it is easy to lose sight of the dramatic nature of such freeing, unless we stop to recall that prior to the war, the army (both the U.S. Army and state militias) acted quite differently. President James Buchanan called out U.S. forces on behalf of the proslavery side during the Kansas troubles of the 1850s, and state militias did things such as putting down slave rebellions and helping return fugitive slaves to their owners.[4] In the period after secession but before war broke out, four slaves presented themselves to Lieutenant A. J. Slemmer, commanding officer of the First Artillery (U.S.) at Fort Pickens, in Pensacola, Florida, "entertaining," as Slemmer put it, "the idea that we were placed here to protect them and grant them their freedom." To "teach them the contrary," Slemmer took the freedom-seeking slaves to city marshals, who returned them to their owners.[5] Slemmer's actions underscored two important points—one about the relationship between civil and military authority, and one about the relationship between the United States government and white and black people—at the start of the war. First, neither Slemmer nor a subordinate returned slaves to

---

Elizabeth S. Clemens, "Toward a Historicized Sociology: Theorizing Events, Processes, and Emergence," *American Review of Sociology* 33 (2007):528.

[4]Michael D. Doubler, *Civilian in Peace, Soldier in War: The Army National Guard, 1636–2000* (Lawrence, Kans., 2003); John K. Mahon, *History of the Militia and the National Guard* (New York, 1983).

[5]Lieutenant A. J. Slemmer, First Artillery, Fort Pickens, Florida, Mar. 18, 1861, to Lieutenant Colonel L. Thomas, Assistant Adjutant-General, U.S. Army, in *The War of the Rebellion: A Compilation of the Official Records of the Union and Confederate Armies* (hereafter *O.R.*), ser. 2, vol. 1, p. 750 (http://ebooks.library.cornell.edu/cgi/t/text/pageviewer-idx?c=moawar;cc=moawar;idno=waro0114;node=waro0114%3A3;view=image;seq=764;size=100;page=root). All subsequent references to the *O.R.* also accessed via ebooks.library.cornell.edu.

their owners personally, but rather took them to "the city marshal," a civil rather than military official, to do so, because slavery was the product of civil law, and civil authority therefore governed it. Second, the correspondence in which Slemmer described how he disabused the enslaved men of their misplaced notions began with the sentence, "I have the honor to report that since my last report nothing has happened to disturb the peaceable relations existing between the U.S. forces and those opposing us," a sentence that clearly testifies to the assumption shared by the army, the U.S. government, and white Americans alike at the start of the war: "relations" existed between the "U.S." and white people, such as the slaves owners and the city marshal. The notion that "relations" might exist between the U.S. and black people struck Slemmer as so incongruous that it was nothing more than an "idea" that misguided slaves could "entertain."

War made the prospect of allying with the U.S. government in opposition to slaveholders something more than mere entertainment to enslaved people, who knew an opportunity when they saw one. Two months later, three enslaved men ran to Fort Monroe, Virginia, and presented themselves to Union pickets. By that time, war had broken out, which created space for military rather than civil authority to play a role in determining what to do with the fugitives. But even then, wartime did not automatically predict a course of action. Wartime manuals of conduct did not exist. The most applicable existing treatises, such as Francis Lieber's *Manual of Political Ethics* (1838–39) and Henry W. Halleck's *International Law* (1861), offered no clear guidance. Halleck's was the most thorough volume, and it included sections on guerrillas, prisoners, enemy soldiers, enemy noncombatants, neutrals, and one's own deserters and fugitives found among the enemy, but it did not even mention slaves, let alone recommend what to do with any slaves who fled to an army in wartime.[6]

The officer in charge at Fort Monroe, General Benjamin Butler, crafted an innovative response to the circumstances, but even his bold solution

[6]Arthur Nussbaum's classic *Concise History of the Law of Nations* (New York, 1858) confirms the absence of any formal precedents for dealing with noncombatants of any kind until the 1860s, with Henri Dunant, the International Committee of the Red Cross (1863), and the First Geneva Convention (1864), while Richard Baxter's seminal article "Human Rights in War," *Bulletin of the American Academy of Arts and Sciences* 31 (Nov. 1977):4–13, makes quick mention of Dunant, the Red Cross, and Geneva as a quick warm-up before the bulk of the article, which clearly treats the whole notion of noncombatants' wartime existence, let alone rights and proper procedures concerning them, as twentieth-century phenomena.

remained within preexisting structures because it presumed a direct relationship between the U.S. government and white masters, but not black slaves. General Butler met with the black men on the morning of May 24, and once he ascertained that the Confederate Army was using their labor in its efforts to wage war against the United States, he "determined for the present and until better advised, as these men were very serviceable and I had great need of labor in my Quartermaster's Department, to avail myself of their services. I determined also that I would send a receipt to Col. Mallory that I had so taken them." An incensed Colonel Charles Mallory sent his agent, Major M. B. Carey, straight back to remind Butler of his "constitutional obligations to deliver up fugitives under the Fugitive Slave Act." Butler reminded Carey that Virginia claimed to be out of the Union, and therefore the Fugitive Slave Act was inapplicable. If Virginia was a loyal state, like Maryland, then Mallory would have a right to reclaim the men. Even if Virginia seceded but Mallory "would come to the Fortress and take the oath of allegiance to the constitution of the United States," Butler would "deliver up" the men if Mallory insisted, or better yet, continue to use them in the Quartermaster Department and pay Mallory for their services in a very common practice known as "hiring out."[7] But since none of these conditions were met, Butler was entitled to confiscate the three men as "contraband of war." Determination as to what to do about the men, in other words, was a function of their owner, Colonel Mallory's, loyalty and his intentions for their use; it was with the white owner that the U.S. government had a direct relationship, and therefore the attitude and inclination of the owner would determine what to do about the three enslaved men. As for the men themselves, Butler's approach focused on the labor they could provide rather than their status as individuals, and thus avoided any consideration of a relationship between the U.S. government and the men as individuals. The technicalities meant little to the parties most directly involved. For the enslaved men, the operative factor was that they were not returned to their owners, and word to that effect immediately spread in slave communities. The slave owner wanted no part of a relationship with the U.S. government, but he did want his slaves back,

[7] *Private and Official Correspondence of Gen. Benjamin F. Butler during the Period of the Civil War in Five Volumes*, 5 vols. (Norwood, Mass., 1917), 1:105–7 (hereafter *Private and Official Correspondence*). For a discussion of the practice of hiring out, see Jonathan Martin, *Divided Mastery: Slave Hiring in the American South* (Cambridge, Mass., 2004).

which he was not going to get, so Major Carey huffed off. The Civil War "contraband" phenomenon was born.

It was immediately obvious that something important had happened, even if nobody was quite sure what that "something" was. Before Carey arrived, either Butler himself or possibly a clerk had been dutifully writing out a report detailing staffing, supply levels, and other mundane matters in meticulous penmanship. Carey's visit forced Butler to stop abruptly, and when Butler afterward picked up his pen, it was to scrawl, "I had written thus far when I was called away to meeting Major Carey" in galloping, disorderly cursive, as though the words simply could not keep up with what had just happened. Butler told the whole story to the War Department, underscoring the "questions which have arisen of very considerable importance both in a military and political aspect," and then asked for further "direction."[8]

It was not long before that direction was needed, because more slaves started coming to the fort, not all of them men of prime laboring age. Just two days later, Butler wrote once again to General Scott to tell him that slave escapes from their masters had now become "very numerous," and included "women and children." It was one thing to receive "able-bodied men and women who might come within my lines," thanks to international law's provision for confiscation of the "contraband of war" an enemy used against you, as Butler noted.[9] But what about people who could not work because they were too young, old, sick, ill-suited, or occupied with childcare? Did they count as "contraband," too?

At first, Butler tried to fit newcomers into the logic he had used so far, since most of the women and children entering his lines were related to men whose labor Butler was expropriating from the enemy and channeling toward the Union cause. On May 28 he ordered that rations be served to the family members of men working in Union "trenches and on the works."[10] To Butler, it made practical sense to put black laborers to work building

[8]*Private and Official Correspondence*, 1:105–7. For the original handwritten copy, see Benjamin F. Butler, May 24, 1861, Benjamin F. Butler Papers, Manuscript Division, Library of Congress.

[9]*Private and Official Correspondence*, 1:112–14. Edward L. Pierce, a private in the 3rd Massachusetts Infantry who was detailed to oversee fugitive slaves housed at Fort Monroe, similarly pointed to international law, the "law of nations," and "Common Law" to justify the seizure "as lawful prize" of "contraband goods, which are directly auxiliary to military operations." See Pierce, "The Contrabands at Fortress Monroe," *Atlantic Monthly* 8 (Nov. 1861):626–40.

[10]Major General Butler, HQ Dept of VA, May 28, 1861:

Union earthworks rather than Confederate ones, and it also made sense in "the humanitarian aspect," because "as a question of humanity, can I receive the services of the father and mother and not take the children?" But eventually, more people were going to come, and they might not all have been building Confederate fortifications, so in the long run, Butler admitted that he was "in the utmost doubt what to do."[11]

Secretary of War Simon Cameron got into the action on May 30, when he sent a letter "approv[ing]" Butler's "action in respect to the negroes who came within your lines from the service of the rebels," while also taking care not to disturb preexisting structures concerning civil authority or direct relationships between government and individuals. "Persons held to service under the laws of any state" were still held to service under those laws if the state was loyal, and the Fugitive Slave Act was still the law of the land, Cameron wrote. Where things differed from normal was that "armed combinations" in Virginia outside the perimeter of Fort Monroe had temporarily set aside civil authority. With the usual relationship between civil and military authority thus disrupted, Butler needed to take extraordinary measures, but he was not (yet) to completely disregard preexisting structures. What he should do, Cameron instructed, was keep strict "account of the labor by [fugitive slaves] performed, the value of it, and the expense of their maintenance," so that the "question of their final disposition" could be worked out later with the owners, once the unnatural state of rebellion was no longer disrupting the ordinary relations that existed between the United States government and white slave owners.[12]

Col. Phelps

ALL able-bodied negroes within your lines will be taken and set to work in the trenches and on the works. Rations will be served to them and their families. An accurate record of the time when they came, and of their services, as well as of the rations supplied to them, will be kept. Their names, descriptions, and the names of their owners will also be correctly kept for further use.

By order of B. F. BUTLER, *Maj. Genl. Comdg*

Private and Official Correspondence, 1:114.

[11]Ibid., 1:113. In "The Contrabands at Fortress Monroe," Pierce agreed that the fugitive slaves presented "a new question, and a grave one, on which the Government had as yet developed no policy."

[12]Secretary of War Simon Cameron to Benjamin Butler, May 30, 1861, in Ira Berlin et al., eds., *Freedom: A Documentary History of Emancipation* (Cambridge, U.K., 1985), ser. 1, vol. 1, p. 72.

FIG. 1. "Stampede of Slaves from Hampton to Fortress Monroe," in *Harper's Weekly*, August 17, 1861, depicted slaves fleeing by night to Union Army lines. Note the presence of Union soldiers protecting the fugitives. *(Prints and Photographs Division, Library of Congress)*

It is important to emphasize that neither Cameron nor Butler resisted the idea of freeing slaves; Cameron in particular was quite keen to do exactly that, and if left to his own devices would happily have wiped the institution out, but he was not left to his own devices, because of the powerful structural forces supporting slavery in the mid-nineteenth century. Neither Cameron nor Butler was yet prepared to overturn presumptions of civil over military authority, nor of the U.S. government's direct relationship to white property owners rather than to black men, women, and children held as slaves.

The actions of slave men, women, and children who poured into Fort Monroe continued to increase the strain on the structures propping up slavery. By the end of July 1861, "nine hundred negroes," roughly two-thirds of whom consisted of women, children, or sick and elderly men incapable of labor, had found their way to Fort Monroe and the adjoining city of Hampton, where they enjoyed army protection "from marauding parties of rebels" (fig. 1).[13] As 1862 drew to a close, that number exceeded 10,000, including

[13]Butler to Secretary Cameron, July 30, 1861, *Private and Official Correspondence*, 1:185–88; Pierce, "The Contrabands at Fortress Monroe."

FIG. 2. An 1862 photograph, attributed to James F. Gibson, of a "group of contrabands" at Pamunkey Run, Virginia, was described as "one of the common and characteristic scenes in the Union army." *(Civil War Photographs Collection, Prints and Photographs Division, Library of Congress)*

families that had made their way from as far away as Richmond or even North Carolina.[14]

In fact, men, women, and children kept up that pressure on preexisting structures wherever the Union Army went, for fugitive slaves began to arrive at Union lines whenever and wherever those lines appeared (fig. 2). To take just three of many other locales in 1861, pickets at Fort McHenry in Baltimore turned away three runaways from Anne Arundel County in Maryland in the very same week that a robust group of "contrabands in the shape of negroes" helped build Union fortifications at Cape Girardeau, Missouri, while later that same year, a war correspondent for *The Liberator*

[14]Testimony of Captain C. B. Wilder to the American Freedmen's Inquiry Commission, 1864, Records of the American Freedmen's Inquiry Commission, File 2, pp. 7, 11, Record Group 94, Letters Received by the Office of the Adjutant General (Main Series), 1861–1870, 1863-328-0, microfilm 619, reel 200, frames 142 and 146, National Archives and Records Administration (hereafter NARA).

reported over eighty slave refugees making their way to Union lines in the Sea Islands off the coast of South Carolina in a single typical day.[15]

The actions of these men, women, and children, undertaken in time of war rather than peace, put military emancipation squarely on the table, not just at Fort Monroe, but wherever Union troops went, and because we know that the army did emancipate, it is easy to presume that turning to military emancipation was obvious, inevitable, even unavoidable. Such a presumption is false, but for far more intricate reasons than facile assumptions about Northern racism, or "a war about Union, not about slavery." That Northern racism existed, and that some members of both the army and the Congress opposed emancipation, are both obvious. When George McClellan assured residents of western Virginia on May 26, 1861, that "[N]ot only will we abstain from all such interference" with "your slaves," but Union forces would also "with an iron hand, crush any attempt at insurrection on their part," he did so largely because *he* did not want anything to do with emancipation.[16] Similarly, a Democratic congressman from Illinois, John A. McClernand, unabashedly announced, "I am for prosecuting this war for the purpose of vindicating the Federal authority and putting down rebellion and not for the purpose of subjugating the seceding States and holding them as conquered provinces; nor for the purpose of abolishing slavery," and for similar reasons.[17] It should surprise nobody that such personal opposition existed among some individuals.

But the turn toward military emancipation had to overcome more than just the personal feelings of individuals; it also had to breach major structural obstacles, and it is worth looking closely at *how* those obstacles operated in order to appreciate what was involved in breaching them. A close look at one of the most notorious orders barring fugitive slaves from Union Army camps—General Henry Halleck's General Orders No. 3, issued on November 20, 1861, for the Department of the Missouri—is instructive. That order directed that fugitive slaves not "be hereafter permitted to enter the

---

[15]Major General John A. Dix to General George B. McClellan, Baltimore, Md., Aug. 25, 1862, *O.R.*, ser. 2, vol. 1, p. 766; Brigadier General U. S. Grant to Captain J. C. Kelton, Cape Girardeau, Mo., Aug. 30, 1862, *O.R.*, ser. 2, vol. 1, p. 766; "Doings in South Carolina," *Liberator*, Nov. 29, 1861, accessed via American Periodicals Series Online.

[16]Stephen W. Sears, ed., *The Civil War Papers of George B. McClellan* (New York, 1992), p. 26. Also available in *O.R.*, ser. 2, vol. 1, p. 753.

[17]*Congressional Globe*, July 11, 1861, 37th Cong., 1st sess., p. 77.

lines of any camp or of any forces on the march and that any now within such lines be immediately excluded therefrom."[18]

General Halleck consistently explained that the purpose General Orders No. 3 was neither to free nor to reenslave fugitives, but rather to retain civil rather than military authority over slavery. In December 1861, Halleck criticized General Alexander Asboth when a soldier under his command returned a slave to his father-in-law, who claimed to be the owner, writing, "The relation between the slave and his master is not a matter to be determined by military officers . . . [but] must be decided by the civil authorities."[19] Less than two weeks later, Halleck chastised another officer when the enlisted men of an infantry unit refused to deliver a fugitive up to his master. The two reprimands look completely contradictory—one for returning a slave to an owner and one for refusing to do so—but Halleck's explanation the second time was almost identical. "I do not consider it any part of the duty of the military to decide upon the rights of master and slave," he repeated in the second instance. "It is our duty to leave that question for the action of the loyal civil authorities of the State. This is accomplished by keeping all such fugitives out of our camps."[20] If no slaves were in camp, then civil courts, not military ones, would resolve conflicts between fugitives and their alleged masters, Halleck reasoned. There is no way Halleck's logic would be compelling to the men, women, and children who risked all to get to a Union camp, nor is the logic compelling to us today. Yet the consistency with which Halleck applied the logic shows just how tenacious the conviction that civil rather than military authority should govern slavery really was.

In fact, strong convictions about the proper relationship between civil and military authority went back to the very founding of the American republic. Those convictions waned in the twentieth-century United States, which can make it easy to underestimate their force in the Civil War era, but in the 1860s they were very strong and very widespread, even among Republicans who supported the Lincoln Administration and favored emancipation. George B. Loring, a doctor who would later chair the Massachusetts State Republican Committee, worried in the summer of 1861 about how to take

---

[18]General Orders No. 3, *O.R.*, ser. 2, vol. 1, p. 778.

[19]Halleck to Asboth, Dec. 26, 1861, St. Louis, Mo., *O.R.*, ser. 2, vol. 1, p. 796.

[20]Halleck to Colonel Carlin, Commanding Ironton, Jan. 9, 1862, St. Louis, Mo., *O.R.*, ser. 2, vol. 1, p. 799.

the bold actions needed in time of war, while still maintaining the "republic . . . on the same old principle [rather than] base it on military power."[21]

Francis Lieber, an antislavery thinker, jurist, veteran, exile from Europe's Napoleonic Wars, and friend and confidant to some of the most fervently abolitionist Republicans in Washington, longed for the destruction of slavery, but he was terrified of the ascent of military over civil power. If Congress could magically "declare that all negroes coming into our lines are free," he would be all for it, but he knew that lawmakers sitting in the Capitol building were limited in their ability to unshackle the chains of real, live slaves, even as he feared that empowering the army on the ground to do so could have long-term consequences for the survival of the rule of law.[22] "Nothing is more dangerous to modern civil liberty than a large democratic army," Lieber worried, because such an army had both the force of public opinion and the force of arms on its side.[23]

Lieber's worries were not just theoretical, as Union General David Hunter's General Orders No. 11 proclaiming martial law and emancipation in South Carolina, Georgia, and Florida in May 1862 made clear. Hunter issued his proclamation as President Lincoln and Congress were urging state governments to take legislative action, and to both Lincoln and Lieber, the proclamation dangerously threatened to reverse the subordination of military to civil authority. As Lincoln pointed out, "large majorities in both branches of Congress" had adopted a resolution pledging federal assistance to states abolishing slavery by civil authority. Because that resolution had been passed by elected representatives, it stood as "an authentic, definite, and solemn proposal of the nation to the States." The proposal carried the weight of civil authority, and action like Hunter's could seem to undermine it. In contrast, "neither General Hunter nor any other commander or person has been authorized by the Government of the United States to make proclamations declaring the slaves of Any State free," and therefore the president declared Hunter's proclamation "altogether void."[24]

---

[21]George B. Loring to Benjamin Butler, Aug. 6, 1861, Salem, Mass., *Private and Official Correspondence*, 1:192.

[22]Lieber to Sumner, Nov. 29, 1861, New York, Francis Lieber Papers, box 42, Henry E. Huntington Library, San Marino, Calif.

[23]Francis Lieber to A. D. Bache, Dec. 14, 1861, Francis Lieber Papers, box 23, Henry E. Huntington Library.

[24]Hunter's proclamation (General Orders No. 11, Headquarters of the Department of the South, Hilton Head, S.C., May 9, 1862) and Lincoln's proclamation countermanding

Lieber, who often criticized Lincoln for slowness on the slavery question, agreed in this case "that the President could not act otherwise than he did regarding Gen. Hunter's proclamation. A subordinate general has no right to issue a Proclamation of such vast import on his own account," because "if every general commanding a department were to issue his own legislative manifest," then civil government would be in danger and dictatorship would become a genuine threat.[25]

To the men, women, and children seeking a way out of bondage in the area that would have been affected by Hunter's proclamation, chances are that arguments about civil and military authority would have been beside the point, but even there, some evidence suggests that worries about slippery slopes to military dictatorship were not entirely unfounded. When General Hunter followed his proclamation just three days later with quasi-impressment of black men into not-yet-authorized military companies, he did not just affront Washington lawmakers; he also alienated a black woman named Susan, who had come into Union lines searching for freedom and lost her last two sons to Hunter's dragnet. To Susan and many like her, May 12, 1862, was remembered not as a day of liberation but as a "black day" of loss and mourning.[26]

To take stock for a moment: Military emancipation carried out solely by the military could not work because of deep-seated convictions about keeping military authority in proper relation to civil authority. Yet military emancipation *did* happen, even before the Emancipation Proclamation. So the question is: How? The answer is through interactions between former slaves, the army, and both the executive and legislative branches of the government. Again and again, men, women, and children left slavery, made their way to Union lines, and where they could, contributed labor and local intelligence

---

it both appear in *O.R.*, ser. 2, vol. 1, pp. 818–19.

[25]Lieber to Bates, June 8, 1862, New York, plus enclosures, Francis Lieber Papers, box 23, Henry E. Huntington Library. Objections from Lieber, Lincoln, and others to General John C. Frémont's proclamation of August 1861—which resulted in Frémont's removal from command—were very similar, but in that case there was the additional factor of Frémont's losing battle record. Hunter's case allows for clearer analysis of the military–civil authority factor, because Hunter's cause does not introduce the extra variable of ineffectiveness as a commanding officer, as Frémont's does.

[26]Harriet Ware, May 13, 1862, St. Helena, S.C., in Elizabeth B. Pearson, ed., *Letters from Port Royal, 1862–1868* (New York, 1969), p. 43; Laura Towne Diary, May 12, 1862, St. Helena, S.C., in Rupert S. Holland, *Letters and Diary of Laura M. Towne* (New York, 1969), p. 41.

to the Union war effort. Individuals varied in their responses to the new arrivals, though by and large soldiers were fairly quick to recognize the benefits they offered to the Union cause. Like Butler, commanders everywhere sought guidance.[27]

They got it. In August, Congress passed and Lincoln signed the First Confiscation Act, section 4 of which mandated that any slave owner who "employed" a slave "in any military or naval service whatsoever, against the Government and lawful authority of the United States . . . shall forfeit his claim" to the slave so employed.[28]

On August 8 the War Department issued instructions to Union Army commanders on how to implement the First Confiscation Act. Since the legal question of whether slaves were or were not being used in the Confederate war effort was a matter for courts and not for military personnel to decide, the August 8 instructions advised that Union officers should not try to determine which fugitive slaves had and which had not been used in the Confederate war effort. Rather, they should accept all fugitive slaves within Union lines, employ them where possible, and keep careful records of the names of slaves and their owners so that after the war, loyal owners could be compensated for their property loss minus the cost of food and other maintenance provided to slaves in camp. At the same time, Union forces were not to actively entice slaves away from owners. In short, soldiers should not give slaves back, but neither should they be the ones making legal determinations of slaves' status, because "the substitution of military for judicial measures . . . must be attended by great inconveniences, embarrassments and injuries," and should be avoided.[29] The First Confiscation Act and instructions for its implementation, in sum, liberated certain slaves from certain owners, while still recognizing the primacy of civil over military authority.

The First Confiscation Act and the War Department instructions for its implementation also upheld a second structural belief, namely that a direct relationship existed between the U.S. government and white people rather than black people. The First Confiscation Act predicated the emancipation

[27]For a lengthy discussion of this theme, see Chandra Manning, *Troubled Refuge: Struggling for Freedom in the Civil War* (New York, 2016).

[28]12 Stat. 319 (1863).

[29]Secretary of War Simon Cameron to General Benjamin Butler, Aug. 8, 1861, *O.R.*, ser. 2, vol. 1, pp. 761–62. Copies of the same letter went out to Union commanding officers throughout the field of war. Special thanks to James Oakes for drawing my attention to these instructions.

of individuals on assumptions of what those individuals' *owners* did (support the Confederacy), and it avoided explanation of what if any relationship existed between the U.S. government and the emancipated individuals themselves. Leading antislavery Congressman Thaddeus Stevens pointed out as much when he noted that confiscation applied only to slaves "belonging to a rebel, recollect; I confine it to them."[30] The War Department instructions took precautions to respect "the substantial rights of loyal masters" by instructing army personnel to keep careful note of "the circumstances of each case" so that "after tranquility shall have been restored . . . the just rights of all [could] be fully reconciled and harmonized."[31] The side-stepping is not evidence of a reluctance to emancipate—Stevens was anything but reluctant—rather, it emphasizes how powerful the structural forces militating against emancipation were, which in turn helps us better understand why it happened in the sometimes surprising, sometimes disappointing ways that it did.

The progress of the war and the determination of former slaves who entered Union lines in ever-growing numbers continued to place pressure on preexisting structures, and Washington continued to respond. In March 1862, Congress passed a law prohibiting Union soldiers from recapturing fugitive slaves. The more sweeping Second Confiscation Act of July 1862 expanded the category of masters who forfeited their rights to slaves from those slave owners who directly used slaves in support of the Confederate war effort, to those slave owners who gave their allegiance to the Confederacy, whether or not they actively employed their slaves in the Confederate war effort. According to the Second Confiscation Act, all slaves owned by Confederates, and all slaves making their way to Union lines, "shall be forever free of their servitude, and not again held as slaves."[32]

In theory, these two acts answered quite conclusively who black people entering Union lines were *not*: they were not slaves. For many, theory translated into lived experience. Lucinda Walker belonged to a man named Berry Prince who lived in Washington County, Mississippi, when she decided to run with her eight-year-old daughter, Alice, and twelve-year-old daughter,

---

[30]12 Stat. 319 (1863); for Stevens, see *Congressional Globe*, Aug. 2, 1861, 37th Cong., 1st sess., p. 415.

[31]Secretary of War Simon Cameron, Aug. 8, 1861, *O.R.*, ser. 2, vol. 1, pp. 761–62.

[32]12 Stat. 354 (1863) for the March 1862 law, and 12 Stat. 589 (1863) for the Second Confiscation Act.

Winnie. The family made it all the way to St. Louis, where they procured from a Union Army general official papers emancipating them "under the provisions of the Act of Congress of 17th July 1862."[33] To families like the Walkers, and to thousands of others who escaped slavery via military emancipation even before the Emancipation Proclamation, military emancipation was real.

At the same time, for many others military emancipation fell very short, partly because implementing it on the ground was invariably more complicated than it seemed it should have been from the vantage points of Congress or the War Department. But it also fell short because of the persistence of structural assumptions.

Military emancipation could upset the presumption of civil over military authority only in areas where the U.S. government and state governments refused to recognize each other's legitimacy, which is to say, in seceded states and in wartime. It could not so straightforwardly set aside civil authority in states that remained in the Union, nor was it certain that military emancipation could survive the resumption of peacetime after the war. These shortcomings were most apparent during wartime in Missouri, Kentucky, Maryland, and to a lesser extent Delaware, all slave states that stayed in the Union. In August 1862 in Missouri, Colonel Dan Huston Jr., with the blessing of General Odon Guitar, issued orders to "turn out every slave male or female [from Union camps] unless they have been regularly hired from their legitimate owners." Colonel John Edwards of the 18th Iowa Infantry civilly, but with barely disguised impatience, explained that his men could not possibly comply with such an impracticable order.[34] General Guitar had run-ins with other officers as well: for example, as long as Lieutenant Colonel Arnold Krekel remained in charge of a Missouri militia unit near O'Fallon, Missouri, he and his men found ways to defy Guitar's orders to turn fugitives in camp back to their owners, but as soon as Krekel's battalion was mustered out in December 1862, Guitar saw to it "that both Union men and Rebels got their negroes again."[35] Military

[33]Emancipation Deeds of Lucinda, Alice, and Winnie Walker, Oct. 26, 1863, St. Louis, Missouri, Walker Family Papers, Missouri Historical Society.

[34]See J. L. Chandler, By Order of Col. Dan Huston Jr., Aug. 27, 1862, Sedalia, Mo., and Colonel John Edwards, 18th Iowa, to Colonel Dan Huston Jr., Aug. 28, 1862, Sedalia, Mo., Department of the Missouri, box 9, RG 393, part 1, entry 2593, NARA.

[35]Captain Reeves Leonard, 9th Missouri Cavalry, to his father, Jan. 4, 1863, Rolla, Mo., Abiel Leonard Family Papers, folder 461, Western Historical Manuscripts Collection,

emancipation in a border slave state, in other words, resulted in confusion rather than clarity.

Moreover, military emancipation could not by itself unseat the structural assumption that white people but not black people belonged within a national community that could make claims on the U.S. government, and without the ability to make claims on the government to protect them, former slaves' emancipation remained tenuous. Soldiers who sought guidance in remedying day-to-day conflicts with slave owners often got negative language telling them what *not* to do, but offering no clear directions for what *to* do. For example, when Colonel Robert J. Rombauer consulted with his provost marshal on what to do about a local man demanding the return of his alleged slaves, the provost marshal restricted his response to what Rombauer and his men should *not* do, answering that "the U.S. forces will leave negroes and their owners to settle their affairs by civil process and will not engage in the restoration of fugitives nor will they take negroes from their masters."[36]

Such responses provided no clear directives about what soldiers should do, or about the deeper underlying question of who fleeing former slaves now were, if not slaves. Responding to reports from the field, Congress found itself facing those questions more and more in 1862. Senator Ira Harris of New York, for example, stood up in the Senate to ask, "Who are the children of the slaves; who is the wife of the slave?"[37] Similarly, prompted by a clash between two Union officers about how to respond to Louisiana slaveholders who claimed to be loyal to the Union, Senator John Henderson of Missouri and Senator Timothy Howe of Wisconsin debated the "rights" and "protection" of "mother, wife . . . children . . . man . . . or boy of African

Columbia, Mo. Leonard himself was a proslavery Unionist who generally supported Guitar, including in this case, although he had a slight preference for returning slaves to Unionists only and not to Confederates. Other members of the Union Army did not get along so well with Guitar. Major J. R. Murphy of the 28th Iowa managed to get himself imprisoned and then expelled from Missouri by General Guitar for defying orders like the one issued by Colonel Huston. See Testimony of J. R. Murphy, 28th Iowa, to the American Freedmen's Inquiry Commission, Records of the American Freedmen's Inquiry Commission, file 7, RG 94, Letters Received by the Office of the Adjutant General (Main Series), 1861–1870, 1863-328-0, microfilm 619, reel 201, frames 122–23, NARA.

[36]Provost Marshal General Bernard G. Farrar to Colonel Robert J. Rombauer, Apr. 2, 1862, St. Louis, Mo., *O.R.*, ser. 2, vol. 1, p. 814.

[37]Senator Ira Harris, July 15, 1862, *Congressional Globe*, 37th Cong., 2d sess., p. 3341.

descent" compared to "the rights of the loyal white man."[38] Henderson is an interesting case, for he was one of the Border State lawmakers willing to work with Lincoln to encourage Border States to emancipate, and in fact would be one of the lawmakers who helped to draft the Thirteenth Amendment abolishing slavery. His remarks in this case help underscore that both Congress and the army in 1862 found themselves questioning preexisting assumptions about the existence of a direct relationship between the government and white property owners and the absence of such a relationship between the government and black people, but did not yet have satisfactory answers to their questions.

Fleeing slaves and Union Army soldiers would have to work out the answers to those questions themselves, on the fly and embedded in complex and shifting local circumstances. They did not come to the same answer everywhere, and nowhere did they come to a definitive answer all at once; but in facing those questions, questions brought to the fore by military emancipation and its shortcomings, they would initiate the reinvention of the relationship between black men, women, and children and the U.S. government; they would, in fact, begin to redefine national belonging and to reinvent citizenship.[39]

Military emancipation before the Emancipation Proclamation, then, is a story more about beginnings and potential for change than about transformation achieved, but it is important enough to merit close inspection, because no story can reach completion without first beginning. Contact between slaves and the Union Army rendered long-standing structural assumptions—one governing civil and military authority and one governing relationships between individuals and the U.S. government—vulnerable. That vulnerability helped make military emancipation possible. But military emancipation by itself could not unseat those structural assumptions permanently. In 1862, the work of reinventing the national community had begun, but it was nowhere near completion. Then, as now, it remained a work in progress.

---

[38]See Senate debate of July 15, 1862, *Congressional Globe*, 37th Cong., 2d sess., p. 3340–43. The stark contrast between the rights of black women and children and the rights of property-owning white men was made by Senator John B. Henderson of Missouri on p. 3342.

[39]For an extended discussion of this theme, see Manning, *Troubled Refuge*.

Nikki M. Taylor

Negotiating Black Manhood Citizenship through Civil War Volunteerism and Patriotism

Cincinnati's Black Brigade

ABOLITIONIST WILLIAM WELLS Brown recounted a scene on a Cincinnati street on September 2, 1862, one day after martial law had been declared there. The mayor had called every man "who lives under the protection of our laws" to help defend the city from a Confederate invasion. To get clarification on whether they should also report for service, an African American man approached a police officer and asked, "Does the mayor desire colored men to report for service in the city's defence [*sic*]?" The officer replied, "You know damned well he doesn't mean you. Niggers ain't citizens." The African American man added, "But he calls on all, citizens and aliens. If he does not mean all, he should not say so." Annoyed by then, the officer retorted that all the mayor wanted is "for you niggers to keep quiet." These jarring words illuminate a blunt reality for African American men and volunteerism in Cincinnati during the Civil War: the freedom and dignity of volunteerism would be denied to them even in a time of great necessity.[1]

The Civil War laid bare a contest over the parameters and qualifications of citizenship in the Queen City and the state of Ohio. African Americans had been denied citizenship at Ohio's inception in 1803. In fact, noncitizenship had been codified in the foundational documents of the state.

[1]William Wells Brown, *The Negro in the American Rebellion: His Heroism and His Fidelity* (1867 reprint ed., Athens, Ohio, 2003), p. 57.

Although the state constitution prohibited slavery and protected their physical freedom, it also laid the legal foundation that denied African Americans the privileges of citizenship throughout the antebellum era. They were denied access to public education and the rights to vote, to testify in court, and to serve on juries or in the state militia. Legislators soon denied them even the right to settle in the state, with the passage of the Black Laws in 1804 and 1807. In sum, African Americans were denied the most essential aspects of citizenship in the state. Ohio legislators went a step beyond simply relegating them to second-class status; they ensured that African Americans would be noncitizens in perpetuity. Unfortunately, African Americans fared no better at the federal level: as a group, they did not enjoy the rights of citizens until the Civil Rights Act of 1866 and the Fourteenth and Fifteenth amendments, ratified in 1868 and 1870, respectively.[2]

Although they were not considered citizens by either state or federal government, African Americans considered themselves citizens. Ohio's African Americans entered the war era practicing state and national allegiance and patriotism, and possessing a sense of civic duty. The Civil War did not awaken these values; they had been ingrained into their consciousness since the American Revolution. But the Civil War empowered African Americans to act on these values in ways that they had not done since the War of 1812.

Historian Chandra Manning contends that for black men who served in the military during the Civil War, race and nationalism were intertwined. According to her, African American men had a dual mandate: they struggled not only to end slavery, but for the "manhood of the race," which encompasses the masculinity of black men, as well as their vision of a nation that included them as equals.[3] I complicate this construct a bit by invoking a concept I call "manhood citizenship." This chapter explores that concept and demonstrates how the public performance of manhood citizenship in wartime Cincinnati—through drilling and preparation, volunteerism, and demonstrated acts of bravery—allowed African American men to assert their manhood publicly and earn respect from the local community. The

---

[2]Melinda Chateauvert, "Introduction: Discourses on Race, Sex, and African American Citizenship," in *Journal of African American History* 93 (Spring 2008):149.

[3]Chandra Manning, "Wartime Nationalism and Race: Comparing the Visions of Confederate, Black Union, and White Union Soldiers," in William J. Cooper Jr. and John M. McCardell Jr., eds., *In the Cause of Liberty: How the Civil War Redefined American Ideals* (Baton Rouge, 2009), pp. 88, 96–97.

history of Cincinnati's Black Brigade provides a lens to examine the expression and contestation of black manhood citizenship during the Civil War.

The struggle over black manhood citizenship was not a new contest in Cincinnati, but the war brought it to a head: wartime needs on the home front facilitated a public negotiation of who qualified as a man and citizen—the two were inextricably linked—and who had the right to publicly express those ideas through volunteerism, patriotism, and civic duty. Black manhood citizenship was almost as fiercely contested in Ohio as the war itself. On one side were African American men who thought, lived, and asserted themselves as men and citizens. For them, manhood citizenship was not something conferred onto them formally by the state or law; it was a feeling of manly patriotism, nationalism, and duty that compelled them toward volunteerism and other patriotic efforts. In short, they were men and citizens because they believed themselves to *be* so (although they understood they did not have the rights of citizens). The state, city, local whites, and military officials strongly resisted black volunteerism, because, as William Wells Brown concluded, the "permission to volunteer would imply some freedom, some dignity, some independent manhood."[4] Officials violently repressed their public assertions of manhood citizenship and tried, instead, to assign noncitizenship status to them. In the end, African Americans won the contest. Through volunteerism, patriotism, and courage, they negotiated the very meaning of these values, ultimately forcing the state and federal governments to informally acknowledge them as men and citizens.

The History of Black Military Volunteerism in Cincinnati

Because African Americans were prohibited from joining Ohio's militia, they began forming their own a decade before the Civil War. The 1852 Convention of Colored Freemen of Ohio resolved to form independent military companies so that they "may acquire a finished military education, for the purpose of rendering efficient aid to this state or the United States in case of a foreign invasion." Three resolutions at the 1857 state convention encouraged the formation of military companies in which men over the age of

[4]Brown, *Negro in the American Rebellion*, p. 57.

eighteen could study military tactics and become proficient in the use of arms. By then, a company already existed in Cincinnati under the name of the Attucks Blues and waited for the opportunity to "be of service to our State, our people, and our country."[5] These military companies, at their core, allowed African American men to be manly: nineteenth-century gender conventions defined a man as a protector, someone willing to defend his home and nation.[6] African Americans created their own militia groups whereby they would—acting as men—prepare to defend state and nation should the need arise. These militia groups prepared for the day when they might offer their patriotic services to defend home and state, while proving themselves citizens in the process.

That day finally came shortly after the fall of Fort Sumter. Free blacks throughout the North organized themselves into companies, practiced drills, and offered their services to their state militaries.[7] In Cleveland and Albany, Ohio, African Americans vowed to serve the same way they had in the American Revolution and the War of 1812 and promptly organized themselves to do just that.[8]

Call for Local Defense

John Hunt Morgan's Confederate cavalry literally tore its way through Kentucky for two weeks in July 1862 (fig. 1). Cincinnati's location on the edge of the South made it extremely vulnerable. Ohioans reasoned that Morgan would continue onward to try to take Cincinnati—which would be a crown jewel because of its economic strength. As Morgan inched closer to Cincinnati, Ohioans were moved to near hysteria—especially with newspaper headlines like "The Enemy Approaching," and "Eight Brigades Marching on Cincinnati," and reports indicating his forces were "1,500 strong," and

---

[5]*Proceedings of the Convention of the Colored Freemen of Ohio in Cincinnati, January 14–18, 1852* (Cincinnati, 1852), p. 6; *Proceedings of the State Convention of the Colored Men of the State of Ohio, Held in the City of Columbus*, p. 320.

[6]Jim Cullen, "I's a Man Now: Gender and African American Men," in Darlene Clark Hine and Earnestine Jenkins, eds., *A Question of Manhood: A Reader in U.S. Black Men's History and Masculinity* (Bloomington, Ind., 1999), p. 491; Joseph Glatthaar, *Forged in Battle: The Civil War Alliance of Black Soldiers and White Officers* (New York, 1990), p. 72.

[7]Benjamin Quarles, *The Negro in the Civil War* (New York, 1953), p. 27.

[8]Ibid., p. 28.

Fig. 1. The threat of Confederate John Hunt Morgan's raiders on Cincinnati prompted the creation of the Black Brigade. This image of outrages by Morgan's raiders in Kentucky was published the previous year in *Harper's Weekly*, August 30, 1862 (https://babel.hathitrust.org/cgi/pt?id=mdp.39015021016210;view=1up;seq=1). *(Courtesy HathiTrust)*

that "Rebels are howling at our doors," and that no woman would be spared from rape.[9] David Tod, Ohio's governor, hastily sounded the alarm with a broadside: "Rebels determined to Burn Cincinnati! 10,000 Armed Men are wanted from Franklin County to proceed immediately to the defense of that city. Come in armed, organized, and provided with Blankets and two days cooked rations."[10] Governor Tod encouraged citizens to begin forming "Home Guards" in defense of Cincinnati and indicated in a proclamation that "all such bodies of men who are armed, will be received." Ohioans answered the governor's call and began raising companies. In Cincinnati, African American men organized their own company of Home Guards. Probably like other units being organized, they set up a recruiting station with an American flag above the door, and began drilling.[11]

[9] *Cincinnati Daily Times*, July 14, Sept. 2, 9, 1862.

[10] Civil War broadside held at the Ohio Historical Society; *Cincinnati Daily Enquirer*, Sept. 3, 1862.

[11] Peter H. Clark, *The Black Brigade of Cincinnati* (New York, 1969), p. 4; *Cincinnati Daily Enquirer*, Sept. 3, 1862.

It is clear from their very public efforts to recruit, and from the flag that hung outside their meeting place, that they considered themselves patriots and men with an obligation to protect their homes and city. Whites were offended by this bold and public assertion of black manhood citizenship. Cincinnati officials tried at every turn to persuade the black Home Guards to disband. They resisted. Police reportedly seized the keys to their meetinghouse, forced them to take down the American flag and told them, "We want you damned niggers to keep out of this; this is a white man's war." City officials and the local press repeatedly warned them that "serious danger impended" should they continue their drilling and recruitment exercises.[12]

In a city with a long history of mob violence directed at the black community for any presumed violation of the color line, the black Home Guards agreed to issue a public disclaimer and disband—thus ending the black voluntary effort to contribute to the city's military effort, at least for the present.[13] For the time being, they had to forgo their desire to prove their manhood citizenship.

On September 1, 1862, Cincinnati was placed under martial law under the command of General Lew Wallace. The following day, Cincinnati Mayor George Hatch issued a public notice requesting all citizens to organize in defense of the city: "Every man, of every age, be he citizen or alien, who lives under the protection of our laws, is expected to take part in the organization." The call also commanded citizens to report at their regular places of voting.[14] Thousands answered the call. They were matched by another 15,000 from other parts of the state.

African Americans did not answer this call. Three main obstacles related to the state's refusal to recognize them as citizens prevented them from answering the call for volunteers. First, volunteers were asked to report to "regular places of voting." Because African Americans were not allowed to vote in 1862, they *had* no regular places of voting, so it is easy to see why they assumed that an order to organize for duty and meet at their polling stations did not include them.[15] Second, the order was directed at "citizens." Ohio had racialized and gendered citizenship because its constitution

---

[12]Clark, *Black Brigade of Cincinnati*, p. 5; *Colored Citizen*, Nov. 7, 1863.

[13]Clark, *Black Brigade of Cincinnati*, p. 5.

[14]Cincinnati City Council, *Minutes of the Cincinnati City Council*, Sept. 11, 1862; *Cincinnati Commercial*, Sept. 2, 1862; *Cincinnati Daily Times*, Sept. 2, 1862.

[15]Clark, *Black Brigade of Cincinnati*, pp. 5–6.

limited it to white men of voting age. Regardless of the legal definition of citizenship, most people generally understood that the definition did not include African Americans, as the officer stated. In his official account of events, General Wallace noted that "it was well understood that this order was not intended to, and did not, include colored citizens." Although African Americans considered *themselves* citizens, they knew that when officials uttered the word publicly, it did not include them.[16] Finally, with the suppression of their volunteer units still fresh in their minds, they assumed their services were unwanted.

In spite of these factors, a small number of African Americans did "offer themselves for any service in which they might be useful."[17] But their offer was ignored . . . again. Instead of acknowledging and accepting their volunteerism, officials seemed more offended that masses of other black men had failed to report for duty. Their failure to appear was such an affront to the establishment that Cincinnati's mayor established a special military police to round up African American men from around the city. These "police" forced themselves into black homes and businesses and seized every able-bodied male inhabitant without any just cause. According to an eyewitness, "closets, cellars and garrets were searched; bayonets were thrust into beds and bedding; old and young, sick and well, were dragged out, and amidst shouts and jeers, marched like felons to the pen on Plum Street."[18] The same men who previously had eagerly volunteered to defend the city were now being hunted down like criminals and herded like animals by a self-styled police force.

Certainly the unexplained seizures, followed by the disappearance of African American men from the streets of Cincinnati without any warning, was traumatic to the men and their families. African American women found the methods of "recruitment" and detainment wholly objectionable, but they felt helpless. While the men were still in the mule pen, hundreds of these women and their families had surrounded it and tried to make sure their husbands and sons were being treated not as mules, but as men. They

---

[16]William M. Dickson, *Enrollment and Report of the "Black Brigade" of Cincinnati* (n.p., [1864]), p. 1; *Cincinnati Daily Times*, Sept. 3, 1862.

[17]Dickson, *Enrollment and Report of the "Black Brigade,"* p. 1.

[18]Clark, *Black Brigade of Cincinnati*, p. 7; *Cincinnati Daily Enquirer*, Sept. 5, 1862; *Cincinnati Commercial*, Sept. 22, 1862.

brought them blankets and overcoats to make sure they were comfortable—as comfortable as someone can be in a mule pen.

After all the captives had been rounded up, they were marched across the river to Fort Mitchell, Kentucky, without any explanation of what was happening to them. There they were forced to build fortifications and dig trenches. Cincinnati officials may have justified the use of African Americans laborers with the Second Confiscation Act, which had been passed in July. That legislation allowed President Abraham Lincoln to "employ as many persons of African descent as he may deem necessary and proper." The impressed men were treated like prisoners of war, or worse, slaves. One captain forced them to squat and threatened to shoot the first one who rose. These men labored incessantly and without sleep for thirty-six hours straight, and received only half-rations of food. Bands of whites roamed their camp hurling racial epithets and insults. Whites would march selected men back to their camps under bayonet, where they forced them to act as servants or cooks. One witness aptly observed that white soldiers treated them as "abandoned property—to be seized and appropriated by the first finder." Many of these men had been born free, so forced labor was something they were not accustomed to and certainly did not appreciate. As if these indignities were not enough, the impressed men worried that they might be kidnapped yet again—this time by approaching Confederate forces—and sold into slavery further south.[19]

Sympathetic Cincinnatians found the whole series of events cruel, and joined the chorus of condemnation. After considerable public outrage in the press about their "recruitment," William M. Dickson took charge of the impressed men and offered them a chance to *volunteer* for a "Black Brigade" he was forming. Ambivalent at first, the men made it clear they had no problem with serving, as long as they could be protected from kidnapping and would receive "the same treatment as white men." This condition suggests that manhood citizenship included being treated with dignity and equality. Although they were allowed to return home for the evening, the men worried that they would be seized again by the "special" police roaming the city. Although Dickson assured them they had nothing to fear, he was wrong. As soon as these men reemerged on Cincinnati streets, they again were

---

[19]Dickson, *Enrollment and Report of the "Black Brigade,"* pp. 2, 3.

seized with "blows and imprecations, [and] dragged to the nearest cells."[20] Apparently, the special police continued to arrest black men on sight. Dickson eventually secured an order to stay all arrests.

Despite such harrowing and ongoing trauma and abuse, not only did the 400 men return voluntarily the next morning, but 300 additional men came with them—eager to serve in the Black Brigade.[21] Hence, the bona fide recruitment efforts worked, while the impressment proved disastrous and marred with brutality and racism. This time, the men—as volunteers—were organized into companies, captains were selected from among them, and they were named the "Black Brigade of Cincinnati." Given how their manhood citizenship rights had been shamefully denied with the initial seizure, detainment, and impressment, this group bore the semblance of a regular military unit for these men. They were brought into service with military formality, including a parade, patriotic speeches, symbols, and rhetoric. "Patriotic ladies" waved them on with handkerchiefs as they reported to duty. The brigade was given a U.S. flag inscribed with "Black Brigade" and encouraged to "Rally around it! Assert your manhood, be loyal to duty." Who would not imagine they were citizens, with their own flag and patriotic ladies waving them on? Never before had black Cincinnatians been conferred even this ceremonial or symbolic version of citizenship. In a city with a violent history of denying this very thing, it was a small measure of progress. Moreover, Dickson deliberately enforced the idea that they were men and that their manhood was linked to military service: "Assert your manhood," and "he is no *man* who now, in defence [*sic*] of home and fireside shirks duty."[22]

The men of the Black Brigade mobilized their hearts and bodies to serve the local Union war effort. They performed the menial drudgery of military service: digging ditches, building fortifications, chopping trees, and clearing roads. Certainly this degrading, heavy, dirty work was a far cry from the service they had been willing to render earlier as home guards—as men. They received neither uniform nor arms, although they did receive two weeks' pay, of $1 a day for one week and $1.50 a day for the

[20]Ibid., p. 3.

[21]Ibid.; Clark, *Black Brigade of Cincinnati*, p. 15. One thousand black men served in some capacity during the siege of Cincinnati; however, only 700 served in the Black Brigade. The total black population in 1860 was roughly 3,700.

[22]Clark, *Black Brigade of Cincinnati*, p. 9; Brown, *Negro in the American Rebellion*, p. 59.

second week.[23] The local press and brigade commanders reframed their work as patriotic. The *Cincinnati Gazette* tried to cast it as noble work, insisting that defense "depends quite as much on digging as fighting," and labeling the work as a "strategy."[24] The public praise the men of the Black Brigade received from their commanders, the parades, the ceremony, and the thanks for the fortifications they built, which prevented an invasion, amplified their manhood citizenship. When the danger ended, the brigade was disbanded, having served only seventeen days. Still, when these men were released from service on September 20, 1862, their white commanders extolled their virtue, courage, and patriotism. That day, the Black Brigade, in a ceremonious procession as men, marched through the streets of Covington, Kentucky, and across a bridge into Cincinnati, with banners flying and music playing.[25]

Despite the ceremony, we must remember that the Black Brigade was not a real brigade: it was not part of any military or state militia. Unlike other black regiments raised in the Civil War era before the formation of the United States Colored Troops (USCT), the Black Brigade was never intended to advance Union war efforts or to demonstrate the soldiering abilities of black soldiers. It was simply a fatigue unit created to meet a local crisis on a temporary basis. Unlike Louisiana's Native Guards, which *were* part of the state militia, or the First South Carolina Volunteers, which were mustered in officially once the USCT was organized, the Black Brigade lasted only three weeks. It had no grander future ahead.

Some of the men joined the more than 900 black Ohioans who hoped to serve in the USCT. Because Ohio was slow to organize its own regiments, they traveled to Massachusetts to be mustered into the 54th Massachusetts. Ohio sent 155 men to the 54th—the third highest number among the states that sent volunteers.[26] Other former Black Brigade members joined the 127th Ohio Volunteer Infantry, which was organized in August 1863 at Camp Delaware, outside Columbus. Ohio did not begin organizing its own black regiments until November 1863, several months after the federal

---

[23]Clark, *Black Brigade of Cincinnati*, pp. 13, 20; *Cincinnati Commercial*, Sept. 22, 1862.

[24]*Cincinnati Gazette*, Sept. 9, 1862.

[25]Ibid.

[26]Pennsylvania sent 294, New York 183, Ohio 155, and Massachusetts 133. Edwin S. Redkey, "Brave Black Volunteers: A Profile of the Fifty-Fourth Massachusetts Regiment," in Martin H. Blatt, Thomas J. Brown, and Donald Yacovone, eds., *Hope and Glory: Essays on the Legacy of the Fifty-Fourth Massachusetts Regiment* (Boston, 2001), p. 22.

government authorized the enlistment of African American men.[27] Many of the men of the Black Brigade went on to serve in the 5th USCT (Ohio). One of the original members of the Black Brigade, Powhatan Beaty (fig. 2), went on to receive a Congressional Medal of Honor for his service in the 5th USCT. In sum, the brigade is more significant for what it symbolizes than for what it accomplished.

The story of the Black Brigade teaches us a great deal about the plight of those who lived/live without the protections, advantages, and security of citizenship. It underscores the fragility of freedom for those without the rights of citizenship and its accompanying protections. African American men in Civil War–era Cincinnati used manhood citizenship to gain respect as men and citizens. The fact that officials acknowledged their service with ceremony and symbolic military gestures is a more concrete extension of citizenship than African Americans had ever enjoyed before in Cincinnati. In sum, the Black Brigade—as a band of African American irregulars fashioned into a quasi-military regiment—profoundly expanded Ohio's definitions of manhood citizenship and manhood to include African Americans.

[27]David Gerber, *Black Ohio and the Color Line 1860–1915* (Urbana, Ill., 1976), p. 34.

FIG. 2. First Sergeant Powhatan Beaty of the 5th United States Colored Infantry Regiment was awarded the Medal of Honor for taking command of his company when all of its officers had been killed or wounded in the Battle of Chaffin's Farm (September 29, 1864). Beaty had previously served in the Black Brigade and the 54th Massachusetts. *(Prints and Photographs Division, Library of Congress)*

Contributors

L. Diane Barnes is professor of history at Youngstown State University and editor in chief of the Western Antislavery Papers Project. She has worked as an editor or consulting editor of the Frederick Douglass Papers since 1998, and as editor of *Ohio History* (2008–16). She is the author of two books on Douglass: *Frederick Douglass: Reformer and Statesman* (Routledge, 2012) and *Frederick Douglass, A Life in Documents* (University Press of Virginia, 2013).

Fergus M. Bordewich is the author of several books on American history, including *Bound for Canaan: The Underground Railroad and the War for the Soul of America* (Amistad/HarperCollins, 2005), *Washington: The Making of the American Capital* (Amistad/HarperCollins, 2008), *America's Great Debate: Henry Clay, Stephen A. Douglas, and the Compromise That Preserved the Union* (Simon and Schuster, 2012), and *The First Congress: How James Madison, George Washington, and a Group of Extraordinary Men Invented the Government* (Simon and Schuster, 2016).

Jenny Bourne is the Raymond Plank Professor of Incentive Economics at Carleton College in Northfield, Minnesota. She previously held positions at St. Olaf College, George Mason University, and the U.S. Treasury Department. She is the author of *The Bondsman's Burden: An Economic Analysis of the Common Law of Southern Slavery* (Cambridge University Press, 1998); her current research includes a study of the financial legacies left by the Thirty-Seventh Congress and a book manuscript on the Granger movement.

Jonathan Earle is the Roger Hadfield Ogden Dean, LSU Honors College, and associate professor at Louisiana State University. He previously taught in the History Department at the University of Kansas, where he also served as director of the University Honors Program and as associate director of the Robert J. Dole Institute of Politics. Among his publications are *Jacksonian Antislavery and the Politics of Free Soil* (University of North Carolina Press, 2004), *John Brown's Raid: A Brief History with Documents* (Bedford/St. Martin's Press, 2008), and *Bleeding Kansas, Bleeding Missouri: The Long Civil War on the Border* (University of Kansas Press, 2013). He is currently working on a book on the election of 1860 for Oxford University Press.

Paul Finkelman is the President of Gratz College in Melrose Park, Pennsylvania. He has been a senior fellow at the Program on Democracy, Citizenship, and Constitutionalism at the University of Pennsylvania and a scholar-in-residence at the National Constitution Center. In 2016 he held the Ariel F. Sallows Chair in Human Rights at the University of Saskatchewan College of Law. He is also the President William McKinley Distinguished Professor of Law Emeritus at Albany Law School. He is the author of more than fifty books and two hundred scholarly articles.

Lesley J. Gordon is the Charles G. Summersell Chair of Southern History at the University of Alabama. Her publications include *General George E. Pickett in Life and Legend* (University of North Carolina Press, 1998), *Inside the Confederate Nation: Essays in Honor of Emory M. Thomas* (Louisiana State University Press, 2005), and *A Broken Regiment: The 16th Connecticut's Civil War* (Louisiana State University Press, 2014). She is presently at work on a book manuscript entitled *Battlefield Cowardice: Violence and Memory in the American Civil War.*

Mischa Honeck is a research fellow at the German Historical Institute in Washington, D.C. He earned a doctorate in history from the University of Heidelberg in 2008. His main research interests are the histories of race, ethnicity, gender, and youth in the United States and the transatlantic world. He is the author of *We Are the Revolutionists: German-Speaking Immigrants and American Abolitionists after 1848* (University of Georgia Press, 2011) and the coeditor of *Germany and the Black Diaspora: Points of Contact, 1250–1914* (Berghahn Books, 2013). He has two forthcoming works: *More Than Victims: War and Childhood in the Age of the World Wars* (Cambridge University Press, coedited with James Marten) and *Our Frontier Is the World: An Imperial History of the Boy Scouts of America* (Cornell University Press).

Chandra Manning serves as special advisor to the dean of the Radcliffe Institute for Advanced Study at Harvard University. She previously taught at Georgetown University and Pacific Lutheran University. Her first book, *What This Cruel War Was Over: Soldiers, Slavery, and the Civil War* (Knopf, 2007), won the Avery O. Craven Award given by the Organization of American Historians for the best book on any aspect of antebellum, Civil War, or Reconstruction history. Her most recent publication is *Troubled Refuge: Struggling for Freedom in the Civil War* (Knopf, 2016).

Nikki M. Taylor is professor and chair of the Department of History at Howard University. Her books include *Frontiers of Freedom: Cincinnati's Black Community,*

1802–1868 (Ohio University Press, 2005), *America's First Black Socialist: The Radical Life of Peter H. Clark* (University Press of Kentucky, 2013), and *Driven toward Madness: The Fugitive Slave Margaret Garner and Tragedy on the Ohio* (Ohio University Press, 2016).

Eric Walther is professor of history at the University of Houston, where he has taught since 1991. He is the author of three books: *The Fire-Eaters* (Louisiana State University Press, 1992), *Shattering of the Union: America in the 1850s* (Scholarly Resources, 2003), and *William Lowndes Yancey and the Coming of the Civil War* (University of North Carolina Press, 2006). He is currently working on a book and articles concerning LGBT politics in Houston during the 1970s and 1980s and has begun research for *Harvey Milk: The Public Face of Gay Rights Politics* for Routledge Press.

Index